UNSTOPPABLE
PASSION

The Captivating Story of
ALBERTO
MOTTESI

The mission of Editorial Vida is to be the leader in Christian communications meeting the needs of people with resources that glorify Jesus Christ and promote biblical principles.

UNSTOPPABLE PASSION
Published in English by
Editorial Vida – 2012
Miami, Florida

Translation: *Full Well Venture*
Edited: *Tamara Rice and E.M.Garcia*
Interior design: *Grupo del Sur*

ISBN: 978-0-8297-6205-1

CATEGORY: Biography / Autobiography

PRINTED IN THE UNITED STATES OF AMERICA

12 13 14 15 ❖ 6 5 4 3 2 1

Contents

Dedication

To Noemi, the extraordinary woman with whom I have shared my life for more than 50 years.

To our sons, Marcelo and Martin, whom I love and deeply admire and to their wives, Lisa and Lela, two exceptional women who are truly daughters to us.

And to the five champions: Gabriela, Nicolas, Daniel, Isabella, and Sofia, our dear grandchildren.

Acknowledgments

Thanks to our beloved Lord, for the amazing privilege of being his children and for the great honor of being able to serve Him. Everything, absolutely everything is by His grace. To Him be all the glory.

Thanks to my family for their love and support. Thanks to those who have sustained our ministry financially: great will be their reward in the Kingdom of Heaven. And thanks to all our team members, men and women of God of various nationalities without whom the stories told in this book would not have been possible.

Thanks to Paul Garduño Silva, who helped me with the writing of my first autobiography. A special word of gratitude to Gisela Sawin, whom I have known for many years. She took the first autobiography that was published in 1992, and extracted portions of that material, adding the rest of the story from that time to the present. Many thanks for her hard work. Thanks also to Marilys Garcia, a longtime friend of our family, for editing the English version of this book.

Finally, thanks to those who still dare to dream, to those who have not bowed down before the god of materialism, who were stirred to dream about changed lives, homes restored and a world transformed by the Glory of God.

"And He died for all, that those who live should no longer live for themselves but for Him who died for them and was raised again" (2 Corinthians 5:15).

Preface

It was March of 2011. We were wrapping up a crusade at the General Santander Stadium in Cucuta, Colombia, one of the largest football stadiums in the country. Later on we dubbed it "Rivers of Salvation" because there we experienced showers of divine glory and reaped a gigantic harvest of lives for Christ.

On the following Sunday, I had the honor of ministering in the pulpit of José Satirio Do Santos, a pastor who had been a leader in organizing the crusade. When I arrived to present the message, what a surprise! This pillar of the Church in Latin America, along with his entire congregation, sang to me:

> *God is faithful to fulfill*
> *Every Word said to you.*
> *God is faithful to fulfill*
> *Every promise made to you.*
> *You will not die until God*
> *Fulfills in you all the dreams*
> *That He himself has dreamed for you.*

Wow! Those words took on an extraordinary meaning for us, heard as we approached our anniversary "100 Golden Years", meaning a combination of 50 years as an ordained minister, 35 years with the Evangelistic Association, 10 years with the School of Evangelists, plus the next five years of Glory, bringing us to the exact publication date of this book.

On milestones like these, people often pause to celebrate the past and to crown the career of that servant of God, lauding the things that person did in the past.

Ladies and gentlemen, that is a mistake.

Certainly, this ministry is experiencing the fullness of God's blessings. We feel more energized than ever in our lives and we continue moving forward, reaching for everything that He has promised. We are just now launching some of the biggest projects of our ministry.

With deepest devotion, we as a family, along with the entire Evangelistic Association, once again consecrate our all to our beloved Savior, whom we honor, for whom we live, and to whom we dedicate once again our entire existence.

Because in Him and by Him and through Him are all things. To Him be all the glory.

Alberto H. Mottesi

Introduction

How quickly the years have flown by! I began life as a sincerely religious man who obligingly fulfilled the requirements of my church. But what changed the course of my life forever was a personal encounter with my beloved Savior, the Lord Jesus Christ. The discovery that the key of life was not to be found in an accumulation of ceremonies and rituals, not even in a personal commitment to living a moral life, but only in a personal relationship with God through Christ was the fuse, the ignition, the starting point of an exuberant and transforming experience that marked me forever.

To understand that God loved me just as I was, and that He had a purpose for my life, was the most captivating symphony that I could have heard on this earth. That was my real beginning in God.

At the time of my ordination into the ministry, I never could have imagined where the Lord would take me as I labored in His work. However, I would not change my story for anything in the world. The love and the care of God have been so precious.

The fire that was ignited in my youth and compelled me to preach to the lost -in the streets, in the plazas, in the parks, in the churches, and in any place where God allowed- continues to blaze. Today the flame seems even more powerful, more ablaze with the passing of time. It is a passion that devours me, and I wish that my days were 48 hours long and my years had 700 days.

I cannot count the number of times I have traveled throughout Latin America. Over and over again, from city to city, from town to town, I have journeyed sharing the message of the Crucified One, Jesus of Nazareth. For this reason I want to fall on my face and bow before God who has been so good to me. If it had not been for His powerful presence, I never would have gone around the corner from the house where I lived.

Millions of people from all latitudes of our beloved Latin America have heard through radio, on television, and in personal encounters, the Good News of redemption. On many occasions I have lamented my complete inability to divide myself into a thousand pieces so that I could preach in every region, province, and in each tiny village, the blessed Gospel of the Kingdom of God.

I know. It is not possible. I am perfectly conscious that the work is not the effort of one person alone, but of the entire Body of Christ. Even so, I would not want to miss a moment, not even one any opportunity that may present itself to bring souls into the knowledge of Christ.

This is the number one priority of my life. This is my calling. May the Lord sustain me so that I can continue to fulfill his commission until I breathe my last, until my heart stops beating.

CHAPTER 1
THE WORLD WHEN I WAS BORN

It was 1942, a year that consumed the world in war. The Axis countries—Germany, Italy, and Japan—were at the apex of their power as marauders. Hitler had conquered France and most of Western Europe, and his eager eyes were now fixed on Russia. Mussolini had also risen, supporting Rommel in North Africa, as he made his way to Egypt. Hirohito, with his surprise attack on Pearl Harbor in December of 1941, had made the United States' participation in the war unavoidable, and several ruthless battles had already been fought for strategic islands in the Pacific Ocean. These temporary triumphs of the Axis powers encouraged its members to dream of world dominance, and it seemed likely at that point that they would achieve their goal.

On yet another continent, Argentina was experiencing strong political tensions of its own. Being openly sympathetic to Nazism, Argentina allowed the United States' appeal to break off relations with the Axis to go unheeded. The Argentine resistance to joining the Allies at that time unleashed strong economic pressures from North America that eventually forced a rift, just two years later.

Domestically, our then President Ramón S. Castillo openly manipulated elections to maximize the conservative party power in what came to be known as Argentina's "infamous decade," but Castillo's time was coming to a close. Corruption, bribery, and use of force had become his regime's *modus operandi*. The Argentine people, having lost faith in the democratic process and unhappy with the government, were a fertile ground for a coup d'état, a revolution.

Amid this political unrest, in the chaos of 1942, in a quiet house at 1553 Gascón Street in the city of Palermo, a suburb of Buenos Aires, in the region of Río de la Plata, a baby born April 19th wailed for the first time.

I was the second son of the Mottesi-Rondani union, arriving five years after my only sibling Osvaldo Luis. He had arrived five years after our parents' union. My parents, Jose and Esther, had exchanged marriage vows in 1932. Both came from Italian immigrant families, and had not experienced ease in life. My father left school at the tender age of nine to work and help with the financial support of his family. He told us, his children, that he had said farewell to his teacher in a sea of tears. His heart ached at having to leave his studies so prematurely, but the financial need was pressing. He had to do it. From that point on, he'd get up at five o'clock in the morning to haul meat at a freezer-storage facility in the city.

Eventually, Jose's dedication produced a better standard of living. Later he learned cabinetmaking, which improved the family's financial situation even more. Eventually, Jose and his father, Orlando, began their own business of painting and remodeling houses. They prospered. After several years had passed, José, upon his father's retirement, was left in control of the construction business. He had an innate ability to make friends, and he counted some of the cream of society in Buenos Aires in his own inner circle.

Even though economic hardship in his childhood had made it difficult for José to attend school, his desire for knowledge had never been quenched. He continually bought books, which he devoured, making of himself a magnificent cultural resource. He was self-taught in the best sense of the word, eventually amassing a stupendous personal library.

Argentina is truly a melting pot of cultures. About 95 percent of Argentines consider themselves white Caucasians, and are the descendants of Europeans, mostly Italians and Spaniards. A liberal immigration policy at the end of the nineteenth century allowed massive passage into the country. Until 1930, there were several waves of immigrants arriving to populate the immense territory that is Argentina, the eighth largest country in the world in terms of land mass, but with one of the lowest rates of population density. The two world wars and the Great Depression that occurred between them brought more huge waves of immigrants from a variety of European countries, including Italy, Spain, England, Germany, Poland, Denmark, and Switzerland—immigrants who came to build new lives for themselves in the southern hemisphere. This gave rise to the popular description of Argentines as Italians who speak Spanish but would rather be French and yet think of themselves as Englishmen. It is also said that, practically speaking, there is no Argentine family that does not have at least one Italian in its ancestry.

It is certainly true that the Mottesi-Rondani family had a lot of Italian heritage at its heart. On Thursdays and Sundays our pasta dinners were not to be missed, and the ravioli and spaghetti noodles my grandmother Maria made were "finger-licking" good.

The government of our home was strongly influenced by the ancestors who arrived from the City of the Seven Hills. Everything was done in a paternalistic way, through and through. A father was the axis around which all the family's activities turned. He was the "commendatore," the commander of the family, who dictated and enforced every decision. His authority was sometimes exaggerated to such extremes that would make us laugh today- in these modern times, but that's how things were then.

I grew up in a very circumspect home. Any outings from the house, which occurred only sporadically, were mostly business-related. My parents were unaccustomed to entertaining, and the gatherings that we hosted were often nothing more than endless conversations about football and politics. At that time my father already had the entire business on his shoulders. However, being at the helm of a respected construction business allowed for a comfortable life at home.

Our lifestyle was not wasteful, but neither was it wanting. Our social environment included people from the most prominent families. It has never ceased to amaze me that a man with so little schooling, completely lacking a formal education, could in time come to count within his social circle some of the most distinguished citizens of Argentina. My father made many friends among them, including Mr. Julio Giveli. Every Sunday, Giveli, in his latest-model automobile, would come by our house to go with us to the River Plate Stadium. My father was one of the founders of the River Plate team, and because he was a lifetime member, he provided us with a privileged place in the stands, where we were able to watch the team making some of its best goals.

As a small child I loved sports. Swimming, basketball and football, were my favorites to practice. However, from deep inside me, another passion bloomed, inherited from my father: the love of reading.

CHAPTER 2
MY LOVE FOR BOOKS

What an enormous pleasure it was to feel the pages of a book, to begin reading and then finish a book—no cartoon drawings, just pure letters! I was surrounded by a carefully selected and exclusive collection of books, and it was easy for me to simply reach out and grasp any volume that caught my interest.

Reading awakened my imagination. You could say that I became—at a very young age—an intellectual tourist. Through books, I was able to imagine the savage jungles, the searing deserts, the romantic countryside, and the great dramas of humanity that accompanied my earliest consciousness of the world.

I read some of the enduring classics, devouring even the longest manuscripts. When I was not attending class, or when I had two or three days off from school, I would not put a book down until I had finished it. Lying down or seated, standing, walking—I think that I tried every reading position imaginable, and even invented some, to avoid putting down the book of the moment.

One night during a family gathering, while my parents and some aunts and uncles were drinking *mate* and enjoying *empanadas*, I overheard the following conversation about myself. Adolfo, one of my uncles on my father's side, spoke first: "It is unbelievable that little Alberto reads so much. I talked to my wife, Cecilia, about this, and I told her that I think he may be ill. You should be more careful with him. It would be unfortunate if he were to have some sort of brain disorder. You know, so many stories are told …."

"Don't worry," my mother answered in a calm and friendly tone. "Alberto has always liked to read books. Here in the house, instead of decorations, we have books everywhere. It is only natural to me that Alberto, surrounded by so many books, would pick up a book instead of a toy. José and I have watched him. He definitely loves to read."

"But that's not natural," said Guillermo, another uncle whose face seemed too long to me. "I think it's bad for such a young boy to have so strong a desire to read. You know, books contain an unspeakable variety of themes. Who can say that little Alberto is not reading something dirty? His unusual interest could be motivated by adult readings."

"No, Guillermo," my father said emphatically. "What you're saying is absurd. First of all, the books Alberto reads are what he finds in this house, and I have not purchased books that go against our moral values. And secondly, even though you may not believe this, Esther and I are aware of what books our son is reading. I have often checked to see what he is reading. Excuse us, Guillermo and Adolfo, but Alberto is not sick, nor is he reading things that are inappropriate. The only thing we can tell you is that he was born with a desire to read, and he is surrounded by books. What more can we say?"

I went to my bedroom smiling. At least I had learned that my interest in books was obvious to them.

Years later, I would become aware of the importance of my early reading. My love for reading has been one of those rare pleasures in life that I would not trade for anything. What's more, books were my true friends. I rarely went outside to play with the children in the neighborhood. The children from the houses nearby had their cliques, but I never participated in them.

I was a solitary child. Five years older, my brother Osvaldo had different interests at his age, so our moments of playing together were as few and as far between as our arguments.

Because there were no other children in the house, I often took refuge in the first book that came to hand. I would get so absorbed in reading my books that the thought of playing games with the children in the neighborhood seemed ludicrous.

My childhood was marked by an unusual seriousness about life. In fact, the books themselves began to shape me into a somewhat taciturn character, prone to quietness. I always sought the most isolated places in our home to avoid interruptions. I had a favorite old chair for my reading pleasure and I'd sit there, engrossed in books for hours and hours.

From the time I became aware of my own taste and preferences, I was rebellious about certain impositions. For example, the trend at that time for boys was to have one's hair slicked back like Elvis Presley. My mother would put an entire layer of gel on my hair to make sure my hair would look well combed. As if that weren't humiliation enough, short pants were our daily attire. Oh, how I hated the way things were then!

When my mother and my Aunt Pititi took me shopping—which was almost a daily chore—one way I had of trying to make them understand I did not like to go was to sit motionless on the curb of the sidewalk and wait. However, my mother and my aunt always won that battle.

Other opportunities to demonstrate my non-conformity came whenever they bought me new shoes. I didn't like white shoes, so whenever I had to wear white shoes, I would walk along the street kicking at anything along the way to scuff them and make them immediately unsuitable for wearing.

My actions implied an internal opposition to impositions. There was some rigidity in the demands of my parents, and I, in whatever way I could, made my rebellion known. I was silently shouting that they were suffocating me with all of their annoying impositions.

My studies began at the elementary school on Pringles Street, located approximately eight blocks from my house. I walked there and back each day, and the years of schooling simply passed by. I was an ordinary student. My efforts did not go beyond what was necessary to satisfy my teachers and my family. School seemed like a normal activity to me. If all the other children went to that school, then, why would I not go there as well?

Directly across the street from my house, there was a very old building that served as a neighborhood library and recreational center. Naturally, what attracted me to that place were the books. I loved to thumb through the library's card catalog searching for an interesting title. After finding one and asking for the book, I would go sit at the table and chair in the farthest corner of the building. The librarians knew me well. I became so engrossed in the readings that it often pained them to take a book away from me at closing time. Thus, they often allowed me to borrow books and finish reading them at home. Of course, I always returned the books. That same library had a game room that I sometimes used with some acquaintances, where we enjoyed playing indoor games.

There were also moments of sheer joy during my childhood, such as when I played the role of "chaperone.'" A young man named Paco was courting Aunt Angelica, my father's sister. As an excuse to spend some time alone together, they would ask my parents for permission to take me to the merry-go-round. On one side of the carousel there was a clasp placed in such a way that we could reach out and try to hook it while the carousel was spinning us around. If we succeeded we would get a free ride on the merry-go-round. We went once a week in the evening, and it was always a highlight for me. Also each week, Uncle Paco, a car enthusiast, would take me to the stadium of the West Train Club, to see the races featuring those small and fast competition cars, something that I always enjoyed.

Even so, my personality was developing certain pessimistic traits. Some of it due to the traumas suffered at the hands of the "supreme paternal authority," plus the age difference with my brother Osvaldo, the demanding selfishness of my Aunt Pititi, and the experience with Uncle Anselmo, all of them were factors that put an indelible mark in my long-term future.

CHAPTER 3
THE UNANSWERED QUESTION

Anselmo, an uncle on my mother's side, lived just around the corner from the row of houses where we lived. He was so close that it was not unusual to see him almost every day. As a child I went often to his house, whether to deliver something that my mother was sending or to attend family gatherings or simply to say hello.

His house was not large, but neither was it small. It was made of large bricks and had long, vertical windows. The wooden front door opened directly onto a patio featuring a small fountain in the middle. Around the courtyard walls, as at my own house, there was no shortage of birdcages. Uncle Anselmo's rooms seemed cold to me, perhaps because there were no children. Uncle Anselmo had never married.

He was already getting on in years by the time I knew him. His appearance had typical European features, but what really got my attention was his personality. You could say that he was a good man. He had impeccable manners, a strange yet proper way of speaking, and exemplary behavior. People spoke openly of his generosity. His gestures were kind. A smile was frequently on his lips. I never heard a bad word from him, never any deviation that might have led to an argument or even resentment. He was a commendable man.

When I was about seven years old, we did not have the light of the Gospel, neither my relatives nor my own family. We were Catholics, but in name only.

At some point, we became aware that Uncle Anselmo was ill, so ill that there could be no recovery. The doctor went daily to check on him. Finally, the time came when the doctor spent an entire day tending him, and would not leave. The fear of death was palpable in every room of the house. Sad and worried, we waited expectantly for the unavoidable conclusion. But, at an opportune moment, when there were no people waiting around my uncle's bed, I snuck into the room. I wanted to see him.

The room was darkened. The curtains were closed except for one opening that allowed a feeble stream of afternoon light to penetrate the darkness. The objects that stood near my uncle's bed seemed lifeless, as if stifling any breath. Framed portraits stared down from the wall, as if to sternly warn me to walk on tiptoe because any noise from me would be a sacrilege in that place where life was so fragile.

I noticed that my uncle's bed was carefully made. The copper metal frame was shining. The mattress, the blankets and the sheets were perfectly in order, almost as if no one was lying in the bed. His eyes observed me entering the room, and I could see they were glassy, almost opaque. We both remained silent for several moments. Then I noticed on his face an expression of great anguish that, suddenly, sent a strange chill running through my body.

He was emaciated; the yellowish hue of his skin was frightening. His appearance was disheveled, his grey hair hanging down his face partly shadowed a bit of beard after a few days without shaving. All of these things gave the room a somber, almost sullen air.

A smell emanating from the medicine bottles lined up on a small desk beside the bed, permeated the room. An ancient lamp stood nearby, ready to dissipate the darkness with its light at a moment's notice.

When I got close to my uncle, not knowing what to say, he reached forward and grabbed me forcefully by the shoulders. I was seized by great fear.

"Alberto, Alberto!" His voice was thunderous and filled with such grief that I started to tremble from head to toe, reacting with amazement at this unusual exclamation. I observed his white nightshirt and checkered pajamas. His eyes had suddenly recovered their shine, conveying a powerful sense of anxiety such as I had never experienced before. The suffering reflected on his face filled me with an indescribable fear, a dread originating from deep inside this being who was holding me with a strong grip.

"Alberto! Alberto, what will become of my life?" His question left me perplexed. I could never have imagined that someone like him, who had never hurt anyone, who was a good man, would now, in this very moment, ask me such a question.

I was stunned. My brain was just indelibly recording those crucial moments. I felt disconcerted, completely taken by surprise. How can a seven-year-old boy answer such an unusual question?

Once again, the voice of my uncle resounded in my ears.

"Alberto! What will become of my life in eternity? What will become of my life?"

Faced with my mute silence and the rigidity of my trembling body, and not finding an answer to his infinite restlessness, my uncle released me. He fell back on the pillows and closed his eyes as if terribly exhausted, more from the perplexity of uncertainty than from any physical exertion. He seemed to me like someone surrendering to a dream to which he had no desire to return.

Gradually, I walked backward, step by step, until reaching the door. I opened and closed it rapidly, wanting to show the utmost respect. I feared that I had stumbled upon a moment I would never forget for the rest of my life, and I was right. That restless anxiety about the eternal destiny of my uncle would never leave me. As a child, I was powerless; however, the impact of his passing and those sacred moments with him would have a profound influence on the course of my life.

As I was leaving the room, I saw the doctor returning to examine his patient. I was attempting to make myself comfortable in a chair, trying to recover my composure, when the doctor suddenly emerged from the room, his appearance marked by sudden sadness. It was then he announced to everyone present that Uncle Anselmo had died.

His announcement hit me hard. Only two or three minutes earlier I had been with my uncle. Were the words he spoke in my ear his last words on this earth?

Why me, Uncle Anselmo?

Why me?

CHAPTER 4
THE NIGHT OF THE PUNCH

Even now, I'm flooded with memories from my childhood. Some were pleasant, like my encounter with a boxing champion. To extend my arm and shake his outstretched hand in mine was a shining moment for me. However, it did cause problems with my mother afterward because I refused to wash my right hand for several days. I wanted to preserve that feeling.

There were also the times I crossed paths with a venerable old woman, Mrs. Curcio. I usually didn't understand her words, but they always left me thinking. "Alberto, God loves you very much and has a plan for your life." Why did she speak to me this way?

And then there is the memory of the punch. I think that what happened that night, the night of the punch, prepared me to confront greater challengers that would come later.

"Alberto!" I heard my mother's voice calling me from the kitchen. I was in my bedroom with a book in my hands. I left the book face down on my bed, with the pages opened to the exact place where I stopped, fully intending to continue my reading once I learned what my mother wanted. I went to the kitchen.

"Yes, Mother."

"Go to the store and pick up the cheese I ordered. Dinner is ready but I forgot to bring it home."

My mother knew my weakness for cheese. Gladly I took the money that she handed me and left for the store.

It was about 8 o'clock at night. The weather was pleasant. A little breeze blowing from the river, the Río de la Plata, made it a splendid night. Perhaps for that reason I noticed a lot of activity on the street. The lights in the houses were on and windows were wide open. People arriving home from their workplaces chatted, smiling. The tram with its clattering sound seemed to me almost musical. The loud strains of a tango by Carlos Gardel could be heard resounding throughout the neighborhood.

Passing by the barbershop I saw Mr. Juancito, the barber, working on the head of one of his clients with whom he was engaged in pleasant conversation. Others waited their turn, reading the newspaper or the magazines that only adults were allowed to read. At the corner of the streets' intersection, a group of more than forty children, which included almost every child in the neighborhood, was standing around Carlitos.

He was the son of Mr. Juancito, the barber. From a very young age Carlitos had loved sports to such a degree that he was developing a very muscular build. The boys of our age group saw him as someone out of the ordinary, and this reputation was well deserved. He worked hard, exercising all the time. The young boys admired his sturdy build, touching his muscles as if he were from another planet. Obviously, Carlitos derived some benefits from all of this. He was the rough one, the "*tough man*" of the neighborhood.

Carlitos was confident of his strength and of his discipline in sports. Not long after that time he would become an Olympic champion representing our country in the Tokyo Olympics, as well as embarking in a respectable career as an opera singer. I think that he enjoyed then being the "Tarzan" of the neighborhood, the "Superman" everyone respected.

I never got involved with him or with the other boys. Because I almost never went outside on the street, few were the occasions that we had ever seen each other face to face. However, on that night, I was there among them.

As I walked by them nothing was said. Only one boy moved his head and smiled at me. I reached the grocery store run by Mr. Jacinto and asked for my cheese. While he was getting it out of the refrigerator, cutting and weighing it, the storekeeper continued his conversation with another customer.

"I tell you, the fact that the Congress has conferred on Perón the title of 'Liberator of the Republic,' and named Evita, 'spiritual head of the nation,' seems to me an exaggeration."

"But why?" asked the customer wearing a grey coat that seemed too long for a man of his stature. "Has Perón not provided us with a new way of life? The individual guarantees that we have now, their concern that the people, especially the poor, enjoy greater prosperity—do these things not deserve titles as a small sign of gratitude?"

"I respect your opinion," said the storekeeper, who already had a reputation as the philosopher of the neighborhood, "but the truth has already been said. The great thinkers of the past have made it clear that when we speak of true liberty, it is something that is born in the consciousness of the individual and then projected onto society, without false interests. What I see now in the Congress is a host of interested parties who are seeking the favor and sympathy of the one in control. No sir. This is completely self-serving. Tell me if I am wrong, but this matter of Congress being required to stand up one hundred times in a single session to honor the 'chiefs,' does it not seem absurd to you?"

He did not wait for an answer, but turned and said to me.

"That will be forty-five cents, boy."

I paid and exited the store, leaving those two men immersed in their conversation.

About a half a block ahead, I could see the group of boys following behind Carlitos. It was then that I sensed something was going to happen. I began to hear loud voices mocking me. There was the sound of laughter and childish giggling at these obvious insults.

I would have expected anything except that. However, I didn't stop. I continued walking forward until I reached them. There was no way for me to avoid walking past them. There was only one way home, and they stood precisely in that way.

27

The insults became increasingly hateful now coming from Carlitos himself. He definitely wanted to parade his stuff at my expense and in front of the entire flock of boys at his side. And I, being a very introverted child with a lot of issues, became fearful. I endured it all while hiding my fear. I viewed Carlitos and his insults as a giant blocking my path. I saw all the boys from my neighborhood laughing and mocking me, and it hurt my pride.

Perhaps if Carlitos had confronted me in some solitary place, without onlookers, I would not have felt quite so ashamed of myself, and my story would be different. But, no, this was how the stage was set. Forty children with great fanfare standing around us, fully expecting to see blood flowing in demonstration of the strength of those muscles they so admired.

Carlitos and I were standing there in the middle of the street when, suddenly, without dropping the cheese, I placed a tremendous punch right in my enemy's face. He fell backwards onto the pavement and stayed there, dazed, with his hand to his face, stunned to see the blood flowing from his mouth and nose.

The sight of his own blood probably frightened him. He swiftly stood up and ran away. Looking back, I can't really take credit for my punch, much less my own strength. Where did so much strength and courage come from? I don't know.

The mob of boys fell silent for a few moments, stunned because they had expected to see me thrown to the ground and crying for mercy. Then they rushed at me in a show of sympathy, praising my "valor." They practically carried me to the front door of my house. They thought they'd found a new hero, and I didn't mind. It was such a nice feeling of satisfaction to defeat a Goliath, I let myself get carried away by the euphoria of the boys' enthusiasm, and I enjoyed the moment of victory. Then I entered my house and my mother scolded me for taking so long.

I didn't tell her anything. I didn't want to say anything. I just handed over what I'd been sent for. My mind was going round and round in circles thinking about what had happened, and I was experiencing a delightful sensation that I didn't want to lose any time soon.

I think, looking back, that I never again enjoyed cheese quite as much as I did the night of the punch.

CHAPTER 5

WHAT A PRIZE I WON!

I profoundly believe in God's eternal purpose for each individual human life. I find it impossible to accept life as something being guided by chance or determined by blind destiny. No! It does not violate my conscience to believe that God exists and that in His eternal decrees He has provided a process for a definite outcome, without demotion of personal freedom.

The year was 1951, and I was barely nine years old. My life as a child, in the most general terms, was happy. My father, who managed a business for repainting and remodeling, provided us with a comfortable economic situation. We had enough of everything. My mother kept the house in order, assisted by my Aunt Matilde, the one we lovingly called Aunt Pititi.

There was always enough time to clean every one of the birdcages, and there was never any shortage of food for those wild avian singers who cheered the house with their trilling. The doves, with their incessant clamor, added a sense of constant activity to the home of my parents.

Because I attended school in the afternoons, I often had extra time in the mornings, after breakfast and after completing any homework remaining from the previous day. This gave me a chance to go outside to play marbles or some other game with the boys in the neighborhood.

Truly, I was never one to have a lot of friends. Most of my time was spent alone, not because I was anti-social, but because I felt a certain pleasure in playing solitary games. My personality was very introverted, you could say, and perhaps I did have certain insecurities, which I believe may be attributed to my Aunt Pititi's maniacal way of pursuing me with a huge spoon of food at every turn. I strongly rejected her presumptions. She believed that a healthy child should be fat, even if by force, and this explains the persecution I experienced. Other than running around the house with my aunt always following in hot pursuit, I was like any other boy. I played games, behaved mischievously, and received plenty of the scoldings that pervade daily living for most young males.

One morning, sitting at one side of the door to our house, I was entertained watching the automobiles driving down the street. An electric tram, inseparable from its steel-plated rails, was passing nearby, enveloped in a clatter of harsh metallic clanking sounds, and I was absorbed in the sight when, unexpectedly, I felt the heat of a hand resting on my head. I turned and saw a pair of old-fashioned brown shoes and a robe the same color. I followed the trail of brown upward, lifting my eyes until they arrived at the face of an unknown woman, the one who dared to summon my attention with her hand on my head. It was a nun.

"What are you doing?" she asked, her sweet-sounding voice emanating from a small mouth framed by an oval face of white complexion, so fresh and youthful against the dull brown cloth of her habit. Her warm, shining eyes stirred in me a sense of trust.

"Nothing," I replied with a certain air of indifference. Then I bowed my head, unconsciously believing this response would bring the conversation to a speedy conclusion.

"Good. If you are not doing anything, then I would like to invite you to meet with some other children, so that we can play games together, organize some outings, and host little parties where we will be serving sweets. I'm inviting you to a place where you can enjoy yourself. You would have to talk it over with your mother. And of course I would first ask her myself for permission to let you go. I should also tell you that the meeting place is not far from here. Are you familiar with the chapel of the Santa Lucia Church?"

"Yes. It's two blocks from here."

"Excellent! As you can see, it isn't far away. Do you want me to ask your mother?"

I remained silent for a few seconds. Then I looked at her eyes, at the expression on her face, as if, by examining these clues, I might discern any hidden motives. However, I noticed nothing but frank honesty and sincerity in this nun, who patiently awaited my reply.

"That's fine. My mother's name is Esther. Let's go see her," I said.

We entered the house, and I shouted to my mother that someone was looking for her. In a few moments she appeared with a duster in hand, surprised to see a nun standing there at the entrance to her home.

Sister Graciela, with her trust-inducing charm immediately put my mom at ease, and the necessary permission was obtained from my mother, who promised that next Saturday she herself would take me to the Chapel. Sister Graciela said her farewells. I accompanied her to the door where we said goodbye, agreeing that on the following Saturday morning we would meet again. Thus began one of the loveliest experiences of my childhood. There were the games, the outings to the river or the zoo, the parties with balloons and Jell-O treats and above all, there were talks filled with warmth and enthusiasm, in which Sister Graciela shared with us about Her Heavenly Father.

For the first time in my life, through this woman, I began to know God. I was a Catholic but I rarely attended a church.

I was a "nominal" Catholic, and I'd been inside a parish church on just a handful of occasions. My knowledge of the church was next to nothing. After all, my family and I were indifferent to religion.

But this devout sister possessed the gift of teaching, of instructing with grace, and all of us who met with her there had great respect for her. Her kindness was experienced by all of us in equal measure. Her concern was constant and never failing. Her happiness set a distinctive tone that marked everything we did in such a way that all of the children in the group were fascinated by her. There was no meeting at which she did not talk to us about God. She was tenacious in presenting and demonstrating the religious truths she'd been taught. Honest and open and, above all, enthusiastic about what she believed, an unfettered love seemed to emanate from her being.

I began to know and to take very seriously this God that Sister Graciela shared with us. A strong interest in religious matters, unknown until then, awakened inside me. A tiny light of divine revelation flooded my small heart. It was like the planting of a seed that in its time would produce much fruit.

During those almost three years with Sister Graciela, I learned many, many things about religion. I never missed those meetings at the chapel, or in the adjacent room, or in the garden. I was hungry to know more about God; hungry to such a degree that it didn't matter to me that my family never attended church. On my own initiative, I began to volunteer for duties and work projects needed at the chapel. I became a sincere practitioner.

On several occasions, I expressed my newfound religious enthusiasm during family gatherings held at our house. I would tell them I wanted to become a Pope. Some of them were surprised at these revelations, others hesitated, and others laughed incredulously at my shocking statements. Nevertheless, such a desire was born in me that it seemed, with my unbridled ambition, would be satisfied with nothing less than the podium of the Pope himself. I imagined that achieving that place and level of honor was the ultimate success, a place where the soul would finally be full and desirous of nothing more. What's more, this goal budding in my soul, kept me interested in and prone to devour any knowledge, ritual, or labor that might bring me closer to my aspirations.

I was eleven years old when it was announced that there would be a contest among the faithful, mostly among the children and young people. The subjects that we would have to learn were diverse: theology, religion, doctrine, etc., and I did not lose any time. On my own, in my excitement over religious things, I understood that this competition could give me a head start on my plan. I made the effort. I worked. I studied arduously and began winning in the preliminary stages.

In fact, I wasn't caught off-guard the day when I had to compare my knowledge with that of young seminary students during the final event—what a feeling!

The church was filled from front to back. The contestants were many, and among them I was the youngest. The event began with simple questions first, and continued with increasingly more difficult ones. When the winner's name was announced, I experienced a great feeling of satisfaction. I, Alberto Mottesi, was the champion of the contest.

But how was this possible? The others were boys older than me, some were seminary students who had devoted themselves wholly to religious studies, yet I had won!

Later there was a party to celebrate. My family, Sister Graciela and my fellow students from the Saturday morning group could not contain their joy at my success. Ah, but the prize. There was more than just a trophy a bronze statue whose hand held a garland. I am still not sure how the priests managed it, but just a few days later they delivered into my trembling hands a prize that I was not expecting: A gold medal along with a letter handwritten by the Pope himself, Pope Pius XII!

I received it in stunned silence and elation. I never could have imagined such an accomplishment. This opened in me, conclusively, a very strong appetite for the things of God.

CHAPTER 6

PROTESTANTISM

How strange are the ways of God. Following my triumph in the contest, I was elated for several days but, as with all things in this world, there came a moment when the emotions receded.

I began to pursue with greater zeal opportunities to achieve the goal I'd set for myself of becoming the Pope. However, I no longer talked openly about my desire, because I knew that it would only invite negative comments about my religious devotion. I decided it was better to keep it to myself. I was sure of what I wanted, and that was enough for me.

Meanwhile, my life at school was normal, and my accomplishments were those of a regular student. My true enthusiasm was now reserved only for the church. I observed each and every detail of the liturgies that were carried out there. Each of the duties carried out by the priests were of special interest to me. I asked what I needed to do to become a priest, and they explained all of the details. I came to the conclusion that becoming an altar boy would be the first step—it would be how I'd learn all of the liturgical details and practice to become a good priest.

That's how I became a sincere and devout practitioner of Roman Catholicism, until the time when a momentous event, happened in my life.

My brother Osvaldo had become very friendly with the Curcio family. He began to attend an evangelical church, the same church the Curcio family regularly attended. The pastor there had several sons and daughters, and the youngest, Beatriz, was the apple of my brother's eye. He fell in love with her.

Osvaldo began to visit the Curcio family home and their church located in the "Once" district, not far from where we lived. A little while later he told us, with enthusiasm, that he'd accepted Jesus as his Savior at this Baptist church. This news seemed scandalous to me, but not to my parents. In their earlier days they had attended an outstation of the Salvation Army and had heard the preaching of the Gospel, which they liked. Now that Osvaldo had brought this news, they became interested in going there as well, so they attended the Baptist church of the "Once" and eventually they also made a profession of faith.

I abstained from going with them, feeling that attending a Protestant church would be a betrayal of my own Roman Catholic beliefs. I thought evangelicals were people who worked in partnership with the devil; and I didn't want to smell like sulfur, nor did I want to sprout horns and a tail. For almost a year I adamantly refused to accept the repeated invitations of my family to attend services with them.

There were moments when I felt sad about this religious rift in our household, thinking that my family had abandoned me and that they were more concerned about their evangelical church than the feelings of a young child left at home.

Even so, I put on a strong front. "If they want to go to their church," I thought," let them. "I will continue fervently devoted to mine."

I redoubled my efforts at the chapel and fulfilled all of the church's orders. I let the priest know that I wanted to be an altar boy. Of course, practically speaking, I was already fulfilling many of the duties of an altar boy. I just wanted to make the matter official.

So, they told me that I would need to have a suit of clothes made according to their requirements. Without wasting any time, I immediately went to have my measurements taken— I wanted to be an altar boy as soon as possible. However, on Sunday of that very week, after my measurements were already taken, my family's continued insistence that I accompany them to church finally got to me. I agreed to go with them.

What happened on that fateful day? Why, without any explanation and without any specific thing having impressed me was I able to change the direction of my faith?

For me it is still a mystery that I cannot fully explain. But that is how it was.

The entire Mottesi family, all dressed up, was sitting there on a wooden bench at the church of the Once. I was feeling strange, completely removed from my familiar surroundings. I experienced a certain type of fear, as if I were expecting the devil to jump out from some corner of the room and swallow me.

But that didn't happen.

I noticed there were no statues or images anywhere in the room, only a sort of altar on which was a pulpit with flowers in vases on each side. The congregation read Bible verses aloud and sang some songs that seemed familiar, because my family members sometimes had whistled or hummed them at home. Now I was realizing where these tunes had come from.

Pastor Pluis, whose name was announced when the time came for him to speak, was a very formal man. His personality and his Dutch features made him stand out from everyone else. He made some announcements and welcomed the people who were there for the first time, I among them. I noticed that my presence produced delight to the congregation, as if they had been waiting for me. It gave me an immediate sense of security and acceptance.

A little while later we were sent to different rooms outside the main auditorium for Sunday School, a time for Bible lessons appropriate to the various age groups. I was sent to a room with children of my own age. After the teacher finished giving the lesson, we returned to the main church auditorium.

While all of the attendants sat in absolute silence, listening with rapt attention to the preaching of the pastor, inside of me a strong conviction was formed: *I would not return to the Catholic Church.*

And so it was. For almost a year I regularly attended the Baptist Church of the "Once". I liked the way things were done there. I found it interesting that the preaching was not in Latin, but rather in pure Spanish that I could easily understand. There was an interaction among the people that I had never seen before. There were smiles and affectionate hugs. The church atmosphere included a sense of human warmth that had been previously unknown to me, and it was not long before I was enjoying a pleasant camaraderie with my companions there.

All of this sustained me that year. I was learning new things about the Bible such that other things—things I already knew—took on new meanings. I was seeing verses in a new light; everything now seemed to contain something practical for everyday living that I had never seen before.

On December 9, 1954, when I was almost twelve years old, I had an unforgettable experience. I had already been attending the Baptist Church of the "Once" regularly for almost a year, but on that day, during the evening service, I was seated on a bench near the back of the church auditorium and participating in the usual evening service. I sang, prayed, read from the Bible, and heard as if from a distance the message preached by Pastor Pluis. Upon reaching the end of his homily, he asked the choir to sing a hymn.

I was listening to those first few notes when suddenly I felt my entire being overwhelmed by a sense of conviction I had never felt before. The choir was pronouncing the words of a hymn that seemed heavenly to me:
"Come home, come home,
Ye who are weary, come home."

I was convinced that God was calling me, personally. For me this hymn was the audible voice of the Eternal One who was inviting me to go with Him. I knew perfectly well that this call was unavoidable and that I had to obey. I sensed a deep love embracing me as tears flowed from my eyes.

When Pastor Pluis gave the altar call that night, I was the first to respond. There, at that altar at the Church of the "Once", with my tears falling on the carpet, I accepted the Lord Jesus Christ as my own dear Savior.

He felt so real to me! It seemed like I could see Him looking at me with an expression of tenderness and overwhelming and overpowering love. It was impossible for me to escape. What place could I go to get away from the Presence of God? I let myself be dragged and immersed in that river of love whose waters, even to this day, have not ceased to satiate my soul.

CHAPTER 7

CHURCH OF "EL ONCE" NEIGHBORHOOD

The Baptist church pastored by Mr. Lorenzo Pluis was located at 370 Ecuador Street in the neighborhood called "el Once" ("Eleven") of Buenos Aires. At that time, the evangelical community of Argentina was extremely small. However, the fame of Pastor Lorenzo extended beyond his own community. He was well known and respected by both his own people and those outside the church. He was a man of Dutch descent. His ancestors had been part of the first wave of European immigration, arriving in Argentina around 1876, and his accent was unmistakable.

His Spanish set him apart and gave him an air of respectability, which could also be said about his style of clothing. He was in every way a gentleman. His English-style added a sense of authority to everything he did. The suits he wore were of varying styles and sober shades, but the shirt was always impeccably white. His felt hat, his cane, and his briefcase were inseparable parts of him. Also, the pocket watch and chain that hung from one of the belt loops on his pants gave him an air of singularity.

He was a serious man. His sincere smile almost always conveyed a wisdom and kindness. He seemed almost to measure his words as he spoke.

This man would have a great influence on the young people who attended his church. In fact, he soon taught us how to conduct a worship service. After gaining a little practice in leading praise and worship, he had us learning the art of homiletics. He was truly a pastor of pastors. He instructed very many of us. Almost thirty pastors were the result of his training during the years that I knew him. We learned from him how to tend to and soothe a flock.

The Baptist church building was of simple construction, composed of a main hall, a few adjacent rooms, and a second floor with several more classrooms. A separate parsonage was built behind the church, where Pastor Lorenzo lived with his wife, Julia.

For almost every Argentine family, whether or not of Italian background, Sunday is a day for pastas prepared in huge pots with special sauces. Sunday is the ultimate family day, and the Pluis family made no exception, gathering after the morning service for their traditional pasta dinner. Their family meal usually included their seven sons and daughters, as well as their spouses, boyfriends or girlfriends, and sometimes a guest or two from the church.

Another boy and I soon learned that Mrs. Julia rose very early on Sunday morning to prepare the day's food. There was a huge pot already containing the sauce, including the sausage and a variety of tomatoes, placed over a very low fire so that after the church service ended, the meal would be almost ready to serve. Because the entire family attended the church meeting, the parsonage was left empty while the pot emitted its tempting aromas. It was easy for us to sneak into the house, Sunday after Sunday—well, at least on three occasions—during the break after Sunday School. We would sneak in through the back door of the house, find a piece of bread, dip the bread into the exquisite sauce and savor it while sitting on the floor of the living room.

It was quite an accomplishment for us to partake of that Italian meal ... until my brother discovered us.

I think that he himself would not necessarily have declined to participate in the same felony if he had been in our place, but he was, after all, the boyfriend of the pastor's daughter, so he was obliged to reveal our wrongdoing. As a result, he became a true hero in the eyes of his fiancée and her family—and I received a harsh reprimand that even to this day makes me blush in shame. My childhood misdeeds were few because, truthfully, seriousness about life dominated everything I did. I had a growing sense of the fear of God, sharper each time, prompting me to carefully think over any actions that might have the stamp of evil.

It was at the age of twelve, during a meeting of the Youth Society on a Saturday afternoon, that I presented my first exercise in homiletics. My pastor had assisted in the writing of the sermon. Perhaps because I was speaking in front of my co-disciples, the event did not seem very noteworthy. There were a few of us of us learning the art of preaching. Several great preachers came out of that Youth Society, making it truly an important source of spiritual awakening for Argentina.

However, I will never forget my first experience of preaching during Sunday morning service at church—an assignment that made even the most polished student nervous. I will never forget that experience. I was about 15 years of age. Every six months, the Youth Society was given charge of the main service on Sunday morning, and the members asked me to deliver the sermon.

I arrived earlier than usual. I wanted to pray and ask God for his help. I was feeling extremely nervous, even though I had written out the entire sermon word for word, learned it by heart, and then recited it over and over again—I don't know how many times—taking great care for matters of diction, mannerisms, timing, posture, etc.

I had been very impatient for that day to arrive, and when it finally did, the complete opposite was true. I wanted the morning to be put off forever. I was overwhelmed at the thought of my own inadequacy, but there was no way to turn back the clock. The day and the hour had arrived.

After Sunday School, all of the congregants met together in the main hall of the church. For this special service, the young people were seated in a place of honor. While my companions were taking charge of the worship service, I was looking at the people seated in front of me. A large majority of those people were acquaintances of mine. But even so, they looked to me like judges preparing to carry out a sentence.

Everyone was dressed in their Sunday best, and I was wearing my best-fitting suit. My hands were sweating when I heard my name and it was time for me to step to the podium. But with a short leap I was behind the pulpit. What a moment! I believe that no preacher has ever forgotten that moment. To fully observe the entire church from that place, to realize that suddenly you have become a point of contact between God and men, that you have the responsibility of sharing the message of the Almighty, that before you there is a multitude of eyes and minds hanging on every word you say—all of this is a precious experience. Yes, our legs tremble and our hands sweat! The throat suddenly chokes. The heart seems to jump out of one's chest. But once the limits of our physical bodies have been reached, and our first words spoken, it seems that strength infuses us with the courage, the daring and the anointing to continue presenting in carefully chosen words the beauty and power of the Gospel.

My twenty minutes of preaching suddenly seemed like only five. I suddenly realized that I was giving the altar call. That was when I saw the blessing of God. On that morning there were twelve professions of faith. It was as if the Lord had torn open the veil and revealed a glimpse of my future.

The same scenario has repeated itself time and again throughout my entire life, but that first moment indelibly marked the vulnerability of my heart.

CHAPTER 8

THE UNAVOIDABLE CALLING

I had a favorite place. It was a chair in a room at the back of the house.

If that chair could talk it would reveal all the strange things that I dreamed of there. It was a very old piece of furniture, upholstered in velvet, and it fit me perfectly. That well-worn chair molded to my body was an excellent invitation to nestle with a book and lose myself in reading.

I always remember having that chair. I am unaware of when my family purchased it or even when it was discarded. I am certain only that it was there, in that place, where I was able to envision the most precious scenes of global evangelism.

My love of reading did not stop during this time of spiritual growth. On the contrary, it became more intense. Now, in addition to the books that we owned at home, a new world was opened to me through the books loaned to me by my pastor.

On many occasions I didn't just read, but devoured the volumes that came into my hands. For me, reading became a need that at times felt insatiable. My best reading was done during that stage of my life. My imagination took flight with each printed page. I would be filled with its flavor, its smell. I experienced the adventures of the protagonists. I felt their pain, their joy, and their sorrows. I also sensed the impact of being confronted with their message.

The Christian novel *In His Steps* (by C. M. Sheldon) presented a new way of thinking about the ordinary routines of daily life. There was Pastor Henry Ford with his style of preaching; Edward Norman, who managed a local newspaper; Virginia Page and her question: "What would Jesus do with a million dollars?", and the privileged voice of singer Rachel Larson.

Another question gripped my soul for days, maybe even years: "What would Jesus do in my place?" Even though it was only a novel, the impact of its message on my heart was not diminished. That book taught me about the reality of God's will, and a thirst for it sent me on a never-ending search through the darkness. I knew that the men who were close to Him somehow understood that the words of God were directed to humans who desired His presence and His power. I went to them with an open heart. I absorbed every biography I could find. I wanted to see on those pages how God acted. With time, I began to realize that each person responded in a unique way, according to His eternal and marvelous sovereignty.

I walked with Dwight L. Moody, the shoemaker and traveling salesman, through his native land of Massachusetts, then through Illinois, the British Isles and London, and ultimately through his massive campaigns in Brooklyn, Philadelphia, and New York City. There were so many cities, conventions, retreats, campaigns, seminaries, and schools! It is said that Moody traveled more than a million miles and preached to more than 10 million people. I traveled along with him by way of the biographical narrative left to us by his son. My soul was stirred to make myself useful to the Lord. Our abilities and our talents do not matter to Him. God transcends our weakness or lack of wisdom; He raises the simple to humble the proud.

I traveled with William Carey, the "father" of modern missions, another shoe salesman, another man destined for failure if measured by human standards. But God has the last word when the heart is willing. Carey's firm determination to see the results of his vision, and to not let himself be defeated by numerous obstacles, strengthened my weak spirit, so timid and filled with doubts. I suffered as I read about the life of William Carey. However, I realized that God is the one who triumphs at the end of the road, leaving an indelible mark on the world in which we live.

The diary of David Brainerd was bathed in my tears as I read on page after page of the desperation, the loneliness, the illness, the apparent futility of his efforts. Seeing those twenty-nine years of his life spent trying to reach the native peoples of North America, dying for them, having only a tiny glimpse near the end of his days that those Indians were starting to believe, changed my way of thinking and sharpened my spiritual sensitivity. When I finished the last page of the diary, I put my hands on my tear-stained face and sat there for a long time, thinking about what it means to serve Jesus.

The lives of the Judson family were a blow to my childish soul. How is it possible that they suffered so much for the work of God? Our calling ... could it be an illusion springing from false emotions? Why must Christians, especially those who sow the seed of the Word of God in inhospitable places, suffer so? Are the servants of God more likely to experience spiritual desolation, as when Adoniram Judson experienced desperation in Burma, exclaiming these deep words: "God is for me the Great Unknown. I believe in Him, but I cannot find Him."

Through books, the lives of the great men of God paraded before my eyes: Henry Martyn, David Livingston, E. Stanley Jones, Charlotte D. Moon, A. B. Simpson, Charles Haddon Spurgeon (and his *Collection of Sermons*, *The Treasury of David* and *Daily Meditations*), Andrew Murray (and his *Christ in the School of Prayer*), and R. A. Torrey.

John Wesley, the founder of Methodism, also passed before my eyes and found a place deep inside me with his immense capacity for work. At eighty-eight years of age he still preached five or six times a day. One day when he was called on to preach only twice, he called it a "day of rest." His orderliness, his great work of evangelization and his sermons made my heart burn with fervor.

"My dear friends: With all my heart I would preach until midnight, until I could not preach any longer, just to do good to you. Oh, if I had a thousand lives, if I had a thousand tongues, I would use them all to invite sinners to come to Jesus Christ! Come; let me persuade some to come with me." I also wanted to preach that way, to have a similar passion for calling sinners to repentance.

I was about thirteen years old, and I was gulping down these sermons. I devoured those of Spurgeon, so broad-based, cerebral, and filled with arguments. I think that my love of reading from a young age helped to prepare me to understand these voluminous works. And more than just understanding them, they also prompted incomparable emotions in my soul. I, too, wanted to run to the fields to minister to the unconverted. I, too, wanted my mouth to be full of the words of God and to speak them along the highways of the world.

An entire kaleidoscope of experiences that I was going through without ever leaving my chair began to fill my heart until it overflowed in visions and dreams of evangelizing work.

When I had in my hands the books of Dr. Oswald J. Smith, above all his *The Passion for Souls*, I could no longer resist. That same passion was kindled in me, one that has never been quenched. That is when a vision for world evangelism took root deep inside my being.

I read "But there are those who see the entire world. They see Europe, Asia, Africa, North and South America, and the islands of the seas. They see God's vision and that is the vision that He wants us to have: a global vision."

But someone might say: "Why go to those other countries before everyone has been saved here?" I answer that with four more questions: Why did David Livingston leave Scotland and go to Africa when where there were still people in Scotland who were not Christians? Why did William Carey leave England and go to India before every person in England had been evangelized? Why did Judson leave the United States and go to Burma when not every person in the United States had been brought to Christ? Why did the Apostle Paul go to Europe before Palestine had been won for Christ? My friends, there is only one answer and it is found in the words of the Bible: "The field is the world" (Matthew 13:38).

One night, while in my ancient chair, worn and discolored, I was feeling discouraged. For months I had been fighting in my heart about the will of God, a struggle so intense it was making me ill. I was in a cold sweat. My entire body was trembling uncontrollably. But that night something happened. Suddenly, I sensed the room filled with a pleasant Presence. I felt light, joyful, and with a precious ability to meditate on God.

Suddenly, my mind was opened to a beautiful vision. I saw multitudes of people standing on immense fields. I was seeing their faces, and I saw myself standing in front of them, preaching to them. My heart was ablaze with a remarkable intensity. I knew that the Lord was calling me. I could not resist. My eyes were emptied of abundant and uncontrollable tears. I sobbed uncontrollably. The presence of God felt so real that only with stammering words was I able to say: "Yes Lord, I cannot resist anymore. I will do your will. I will preach your Word! I love you, Lord, I love you!"

CHAPTER 9

THE LARGEST SEMINARY IN THE WORLD

The entire gamut of emotions and spiritual experiences conveyed to me through a constant reading of the Bible and any Christian book that I might find along the way, was intensified by the preaching and experiences of any a man of God who crossed my path.

My life at church was filled with continuous work. I did whatever I could --from picking up a broom to preparing a sermon-- and I felt true pleasure at doing one thing after another.

My desire to become a Pope was now stored away in the archive of memories. Now, with my calling to preach, my motivations were completely different. One of these was to prepare myself. The growing need of my heart was compelling me to learn and know more about God in order to present a more convincing, more useful, more accurate message in a way that would see greater results in terms of lives and hearts converted to Christ.

With this conviction, whenever I heard about someone coming to share experiences and preach a message, I would be one of the first to arrive. I never wanted to lose an opportunity to hear from any servant of God. I was of the belief that any detail about the lives of these men, especially anything concerning the will of God, was a light that could illuminate my path.

Also, every time that I heard one of these men speak, my heart burned. My soul was ablaze with a desire to see similar experiences in my own life, to know that I too could be an instrument used by the Almighty God.

I shuddered in the depths of my soul when our pastor spoke of the killing of five missionaries at the hands of the Auca Indians deep in the jungles of Ecuador. How could these things be possible in our day and age? However, that was only a small part of their story.

The Baptist Youth Association invited an Argentine preacher who had been to Colombia, Mr. José Bongarrá of the Free Brethren Church. Pastor Bongarrá told us that during the time when he was there, religious persecution in Colombia had reached one hundred and nine martyrs who had given their lives for Jesus. The dramatic experiences that he went through when he went there to preach made our hair stand on end. In my heart, I felt certain that God was instructing me through these men, His servants.

Later on I would have an opportunity to enter seminary. But during those days, to know and to learn from the wisdom of those men of God with whom I was becoming acquainted became, for me, the greatest seminary in the world.

I was learning Biblical arguments, listening to lectures, lessons, and exegesis of the Old and New Testaments, not from instruction presented by a magisterial docent, but rather from pure experience. It was theory made pragmatic. On several occasions, from the same field of action, some of the most moving and persuasive lessons the human ear could possibly hear were developed. What relationship could there be between a knowledge of the existence of Evil in the universe and a belief that the Good will always triumph in the end, when we were hearing of killings and crimes perpetrated without pity on those who are children of God? If they died, how could one really say Good triumphed?

However, when the narrative or experience is placed in its appropriate context, you can exclaim with Tertullian, who said: "The blood of the martyrs is the seed of Christianity." Then, with the whole picture becoming clear, one can see the behind the scenes work that God does through those faithful believers, those who have considered their own lives as nothing if only they can serve their God.

So much teaching was delivered by these itinerant preachers! To see them, to hear them in their own words, to be moved at the reflection of their own passion! It was marvelous that the Lord allowed me to witness such a loving outflow of His will.

When I learned that an elderly Dutch woman, almost eighty years old at the time, who had rescued hundreds of Jews from the clutches of Nazism using her home as a secret place of refuge, would be coming to Buenos Aires, I was eager not to lose the opportunity to meet her. The impression that I gained of that elderly woman of slow gait, with grey hair neatly combed, keen blue eyes shining with intelligence behind her crystalline eyeglasses, with a soft-spoken manner charged with a sense of drama that I had never before experienced, was utterly captivating for me.

The events of World War II, the concentration camps, the killing of the Jews, the unimaginable cruelties, and the atrocious crimes that should have engulfed the heart in perpetual hatred, in that elderly woman had been turned instead into a blessing from on high. "Every human loss is used by God for His glory," she exclaimed with deep emotion.

What loving warmth did I perceive in Corrie Ten Boom! Her dreams of assisting the needy, her vision of evangelizing the entire world: now they were mine. On my bench, spellbound, with tears clouding my view of that lovely elderly woman, I felt seized by God's compassion for the world.

Blessed be that elderly woman who demonstrated such love incarnate in the concentration camps! Blessed be God for transforming the utmost evil into a cloud of blessings! I left deeply touched in my heart after listening to that woman, but yet another event would stay with me from that period of my youth.

One day I began to see and hear everywhere announcements of a Crusade that would be held by a preacher visiting from Toronto, Canada, Dr. Oswald J. Smith. Imagine how my heart went crazy! I could hardly believe it; the author of *The Passion for Souls* and *The Country I Love Best and How to Get There*, the founder of the largest church in Canada, *The People's Church*, the visionary of world evangelism, one who had already held evangelism crusades in more than sixty-six countries, with thousands of people having accepted Jesus through his mediating role. It was this man himself who was coming to visit the land of my birth.

There were days of anticipation before the crusade began. In those days in Argentina the evangelicals were very few. Evangelistic work was little known, to a degree that never before had there been a crusade like the one they were proposing to hold, much less in a public place. However, God in His grace allowed it to occur. The stadium at Luna Park was rented for this event. For the first time the Protestant people united their efforts to carry out this crusade. And everything about it was a blessing.

During the days that Brother Smith was there with us, being used by God, he made our hearts explode. In addition to the people who packed the place and the decisions that were made for Christ, Dr. Smith expressed a love of evangelistic action that energized our souls.

On the last day of the crusade, his sermon ended with the story about Dr. Duff. Dr. Smith's baritone voice could be heard in his native English resounding through the speaker system, with long pauses for his interpreter to give the Spanish language version.

He told the story of Dr. Alexander Duff, that great veteran of missionary work in India, who had returned to Scotland to die. He was speaking before the general assembly of the Presbyterian Church and made a heartfelt invitation, but no one came forward. In the middle of his altar call, Dr. Smith explained, Duff fainted and had to be carried away for medical attention. The physician leaned over him to examine his heart. At that point the very sick Duff opened his eyes.

"Where am I?" he inquired.

"Do not move," said the practitioner. "You have suffered a heart attack. Do not move."

"But," said Dr. Duff, "I have not finished the call. Let me return. Take me back. I must finish the call to the missionary work in India."

"Do not move," the doctor repeated. "If you get up, it will be at the risk of your life."

But, Dr. Smith explained, despite the protests, the old fighter stood to his feet with great effort and, with the doctor holding him on one side, and the moderator of the assembly holding him on the other, he climbed the stairs to the pulpit. When he appeared on the platform, the entire assembly paid homage by standing to their feet. Once the congregation was again seated, the old man continued to speak, saying: "When Queen Victoria calls volunteers to go to India, hundreds of young people respond, but when King Jesus calls, no one goes."

There was a pause. Absolute silence.

Again he spoke: "Can it be true that the fathers of Scotland no longer have sons to give to India?"

There was another pause. The silence continued.

"Very well," the veteran concluded. "As old as I am, I will return to India. I can lie down by the shores of the Ganges River to die there, and tell the people of India that Scotland did have one man who loved them enough to give his life for them."

In an instant, throughout the assembly, young men leapt to their feet, exclaiming: "I will go! I will go!"

At this point, Dr. Smith turned his captivating story toward us. "My friend," said Dr. Smith, looking into the crowd of Buenos Aires, "will you go? Has God spoken to you? Have you heard His call? Don't you want to respond: 'Lord, here I am, send me'?"

I could not wait any longer. I sprung from my seat and joined the dozens of young people kneeling at the front of the platform. My heart, beating loudly, would not stop shouting: "Lord, here I am! Send me, Lord, send me!"

CHAPTER 10

"LET THE SILVER TRUMPET SOUND"

My life around the church was very active. Our pastor, truly a visionary leader, had the grace to allow us some freedom in our actions. He knew how to manage with affirmation the bottled up energy of young people. For each project we presented to the pastor, seeking his consent, he always knew how to give tactful advice, guidance, and suggestions. Moreover, in this environment of liberality we were able to develop talents and vocations for the good of the work.

For me it was a pleasure to work at the church. Our group of adolescents was so unified that team projects became a blessing. Out of this group, more than thirty pastors would emerge to fill the ranks of ministry in the Body of Christ. Several others would rise to management level positions at parachurch ministries serving the continent.

The church was experiencing a revival. There was a bustle of activity. There was always something to do. What I liked most were the open-air meetings. Every Sunday afternoon we would go to a nearby plaza and hold evangelistic meetings. Almost twice a month, the pastor would have me preaching.

Our movement had several churches throughout the country. We often had joint projects. One of them involved organizing youth conferences. Young people from the entire country prepared year after year to travel to the capital city to carry out the mission projects that were planned.

In Argentina, the evangelistic work was small, considering the size of the country. These conference events hosted about 2,000 young people. But the gatherings had a lasting effect on everyone who attended. The events were a marvel of coexistence and the messages—given with anointing from on high—caused us to experience days of intense Christian fervor.

I had the impression that if I ever missed a day of our regular and special church events, I would miss out on some knowledge from some teaching given in the Sunday school class, or would not hear some message that would never again be presented. I believed the omission would forever impair my preparation, so if there ever were some reason beyond my control preventing me from attending church, I would feel an enormous sense of anguish. I preferred, then, to never miss anything that happened at or was related to our church.

Soon I felt a desire to teach a Sunday school class, so I went to the superintendent and made the request. In the church's Youth Society, I began to climb the ladder of various leadership positions. At one time I was in charge as president not only of the society at my church, but also of the association that represented all of the youth groups in the greater Buenos Aires region.

Our work was quite varied. There were diverse drama works staged at Christmas and during Easter week; invitations to well-known people in our area, pastors and professionals; camp meetings; social gatherings; conferences; evangelistic campaigns; teachings on a variety of subjects, even lessons on etiquette. Everything that we thought might be of benefit for the group's advancement, we put into practice.

Amid all that, what I remember most were the annual conferences that we held under a huge tent that we would set up on a property adjacent to the old seminary building at the intersection of Ramón Falcón Street and Bolaños.

What joyous anticipation we had in the days leading up to the conference! There was so much to do: the programs, the invitations, the awards, organizing the young people who would be arriving from the provinces, the lodgings, and the food. How many organizational details we had to pay attention to!

On the inaugural day, when most of the attendees were sitting in chairs listening to the opening message, our hearts were also open to immense spiritual expectations. The workshops and the contests kept us all engaged. The messages at night ignited our souls. We experienced a gamut of emotions and challenges.

One of those conferences had as its slogan and general theme: "Let the silver trumpet sound." The well-known speaker who gave the final message was upright and highly regarded. His personality seemed somewhat dry; you might even say a bit strange. I think he was a man ahead of his time. He was intelligent, a visionary, appearing to have emerged from some revival of the past century. From his appearance one could compare him with someone like Müller, perhaps a Torrey or a Spurgeon. He was Santiago Canclini, the father of Dr. Arnoldo Canclini , and the son-in-law of Mr. Juan Vareto (renowned throughout South America as one of the luminaries of American Christianity). Those three men, along with many others of that era, were among the elite leadership, people who were passionately surrendered to the Lord of glory, who blazed new trails and set new milestones in the history of Christianity in their own country and beyond.

This man, Santiago Canclini, was a living treasure. It was he who brought us the final message based on Jeremiah 4:19: "Oh, my anguish, my anguish! I writhe in pain. Oh, the agony of my heart! My heart pounds within me, I cannot keep silent. For I have heard the sound of the trumpet; I have heard the battle cry."

I was sitting there, listening to this elderly saint, not wanting to miss a single detail. It was already Sunday night, and the electric light bulbs illuminated the platform and the farthest corner of the tent. We had experienced several days of intense heat, but it was cooler that night because of the wind so characteristic of the climate of Buenos Aires. The tent was filled to capacity. Many people remained standing, and each young person had been given a candle without knowing what its use would be.

The voice of the preacher took us along Biblical paths of the weeping prophet Jeremiah's description of the living conditions of his time. A man totally committed to his calling, Don Santiago knew how to immerse us in the passion of the prophet, so that we vicariously experienced the critical state of his emotions, produced by the cruel experience of an inhuman and merciless world. But he also showed us how, transcending the prophet's circumstances, was the Omnipotent Invisible God who can lead His people to the reality of His grace.

Yes, the heartstrings are pained whenever we see so much sin around us. Our souls roar like the voice of God, who uses the Jeremiahs of each era in history to rescue the lost and to shelter His own with tender love.

"Young people," Canclini cried out, "hear the trumpet of God in your heart! It is time for your souls to proclaim with loyalty and firm conviction the salvation of our Lord! Hear him, hear him!" These words, saturated with spiritual anointing, resonated throughout that place and beyond, penetrating to the bones and marrow of those present.

I had taken to heart every word. I felt like I was Jeremiah, and that the trumpet had sounded with a strong blast. My emotions were intense.

At a specific time, all the lights in the tent were turned off. From various points around the room, the candles began to be lit, one by one, until the entire room was illuminated. What a beautiful sight! The tiny lights in each hand flickered. When the call was given to dedicate ourselves to the service of the Lord, hundreds of young people went forward to the platform. There we raised our right hands holding the lit candles up as a sign of total devotion. A profound emotion overwhelmed me; with my face bathed in tears, I cried out sobbing: "Lord, Lord! Here is my life. It is yours. I belong to you. Make use of me as seems best to you."

For me this was not a game. This was a matter of utmost seriousness. I knew that God was real. We had experienced moments of intimate communion during which we seemed to breathe the very atmosphere of the Kingdom of God. It was as if we entered with fear and trembling into the Holy of Holies, stood in front of the Ark of the Covenant—an archetype of the throne and the presence of the Almighty—and fell on our knees, humbled and broken, waiting only on the mercy and the grace of our Lord.

As long as I live, I will never forget that conference. The Holy Spirit used that event to fill my heart with the message of God for me.

Yes, the powerful silver trumpet was now beginning to sound! The resonance that God awakened on that occasion has never ceased to reverberate. The pain I feel in my heart for the lost has never been extinguished, because I have heard the sound of the trumpet ... and I will not be silenced.

CHAPTER 11

NOEMI, MY LOVE

How intricate are the ways of love! One never knows at what moment or in what place Cupid will shoot his arrow at one's heart.

My sentimental life, to some degree, was determined by my way of thinking. Too soon I became aware of the vital importance and significance of romantic relationships among young people.

Apart from school and doing our homework, most of our available time was dedicated to the church. Almost every day we had some church activity to attend, which developed close ties among the young people. This fostered friendships in our youth group among the members of both sexes. It was nothing unusual that romantic relationships would develop.

I noticed that romantic relationships required mainly a lot of time, but also money and a good dose of maturity. When I thought about these things, I would feel very mature for my age. From childhood, life had placed me on a very serious path. Willingness to take responsibility for all of my actions was the outstanding hallmark of my character. I would be overly anxious if some task placed in my charge was not carried out because I had somehow failed in my responsibility. It is natural then that this fastidious trait would make me think seriously about the relationships between young people. In terms of money, I had little. As a son living at home, I was completely dependent on my parents. Moreover, I did not feel I could afford any excessive spending requiring an increase in the paternal allowance.

In addition to all that, time was my least available asset. My school and church duties occupied all my time. I thought that to have a romantic relationship, I would necessarily have to cut back on some of my other activities. I would not be able to give myself one hundred percent to the things that comprised my vision. These sobering thoughts caused me to stay away from romantic relationships.

It is worth adding another paragraph to reemphasize my conviction that God, sovereign of all, had to be of fundamental importance in my search for the person who would be my spouse and life companion. That is how I thought, and that is what I put into practice.

Every time that my heart became interested in some young woman, I would first discuss my thoughts with God in prayer. Even though my platonic love sometimes lingered, often, when I least expected, my feelings would suddenly be forgotten. And that is how the time passed. Later I decided that it would be good to remain without a girlfriend until at least the conclusion of my career preparation, which, according to my plans, would happen at about age twenty-five. And it might have all gone according to plan... if I had not attended that picnic at a park in Ezeiza.

The members of the Youth Society of my church had agreed to set aside a day for outdoor sports and recreation, and it just so happened that Thursday, December 8, 1960, was a holiday we could use to schedule that activity. The parks of Ezeiza are located near the International Airport of Buenos Aires. We rented a bus and everyone, each bringing his own food, arrived at a spacious setting of trees and fields, with tables and chairs and grills for roasting the meat.

Together we played soccer, volleyball, and many other games. Because there were other Christian groups there who had also had the great idea of having a picnic, we got together and organized some great sports competitions. At a time when I was not participating in any games, I decided to look around for my friends to see that they were doing okay. I was walking across the green fields when, suddenly, I noticed a young woman sitting at a table reading. Sensing that someone was staring at her, she stopped reading and stared back at me.

What is this power that eyes have to reach directly into one's soul?

I don't know, but one thing is certain: That tender look, sweet, from those large and shining eyes, made its impression very deep inside of me. We looked at each other for a few seconds. We smiled at each other with youthful shyness. And that was all. Each of us returned to what we were doing, but we were never the same again.

Almost as if I had been given wings, I felt like I was flying. My brain was suddenly torn to shreds by countless thoughts. For some mysterious reason unknown to me, the mental picture I had of that slender woman with long hair, dressed in a pleated skirt and white blouse, impelled me to walk, run, stop, laugh, and jump. If anyone had noticed how I was acting, I am sure that person would have thought I'd gone crazy. I was happy. I had seen a precious young woman. And she had looked at me and smiled.

But almost immediately upon seeing her, my mind was filled with questions: Where is she from? What group did she come with? Will I see her again? Is she a Christian? What is her name? I searched stealthily among the different groups there, scouting to find her again, but she had disappeared from my sight and I could no longer see her.

The picnic ended and we were preparing to return. We found our seats on the bus and I, from my seat by the window, was still helplessly trying to glimpse her among the people outside, but without success. Our encounter had lasted only seconds and I was already feeling the pang of her absence.

Soon we were on the road home. The rowdiness of the young people from my church, their jokes, their songs, seemed far away to me. My mind was on that young woman with the big brown eyes.

We had gone quite a distance when we saw another bus in front of us, parked on the side of the road. All the young people had gotten off the bus and were standing around, not knowing what to do. Our bus driver parked behind them in order to offer his assistance to a fellow driver. Because I was the person in charge of our group, I got out of the bus to find out what the problem was.

You can't imagine my surprise when I saw that the young woman who now occupied all my thoughts was in this very group. I jumped for joy—well, I did not actually jump. But I will say that my interest in resolving their problem suddenly became for me one of intense personal relevance.

"What happened?" our chauffeur asked his colleague, who was kneeling to get a better look at the motor of the bus.

He stood up and, very discouraged, said: "A belt broke and I don't have a replacement. I will have to go into the city to get one. Would you happen to have one?"

"No, I don't have a replacement, but is there anything else I can help you with?"

"Well, I don't know. The problem is that, if I go with you to the city to buy it and then return, it will take me at least two hours. And how can I leave these people here? It is already late afternoon and it will be night soon."

"This is certainly very serious. This place is very isolated."

During their conversation I was listening and trying to think of how I could also help. Knowing that two special eyes were keenly watching me, I mentioned a possible solution.

"Well," I said firmly, "what would you say if we all tried to go in our bus? It might be a little crowded, but I think that we can all fit. That way no one will be left behind. You can go with us and then come back later to fix your bus."

"If you'd allow this, I think it would be best," the other bus driver said with a cheerful air. Then he turned to speak with his passengers, telling them about the problem and the solution that we had agreed on. This, naturally, made me look like the hero to the girl. The group climbed joyfully into our bus and got settled. I was careful not to lose a single detail of the movements of that young woman with the big, shining brown eyes.

With much solicitude I took charge of accommodating our guests, "fortuitously" finding a place for myself next to the young woman of my dreams. The engine started and the bus was back on the highway heading toward the city.

"Well, these things happen, right?" I said, hoping to start a conversation and also trying to dissipate somehow my own jittery nerves that seemed to be exploding inside me at being next to this young woman.

"We were going along fine, when suddenly the bus lost speed and rolled to a stop," I heard her say, listening for the first time to that voice while concealing my ecstasy. "Then the bus driver came and told us what was happening. We were very worried. Thank God that you stopped, because if you hadn't, I don't know what we would have done. It would be dangerous to stay for several hours in that place, and it'll be dark soon."

I listened with careful attention to her kindly disposition. She seemed sincere, easy to talk with, and honest.

"What is your name?" I asked her.

"Noemi. And yours?"

"Alberto."

"What church are you from?"

We chatted and exchanged the normal pleasantries, all the while realizing that we liked each other and had some common interests.

Because Villa Ballester, the place they were from, was a suburb north of Buenos Aires, it was not far out of our way to stop and drop them off at their church. Before arriving, however, I asked her whether we could see each other again the following week.

"Yes, just tell me what day, except that it has to be after five o'clock. I am involved in a Vacation Bible School at our church and that's when we get out. I would have about an hour before I would need to be at home."

"Oh, how can I do that?" I tried to hide my disappointment. "I'm currently holding my first evangelistic campaign right here in Villa Ballester. I'll be preaching every night of the week and in the afternoons I'm busy."

"Oh! What can we do?"

"I don't know. Wouldn't you have an hour available in the morning?"

"That would be hard for me. The classes for our Vacation Bible School start at nine o'clock."

"You know, I'll see what I can do. I will try to rearrange my schedule, and I will see you at five o'clock. Where would I find you?"

"Are you familiar with the Plaza de Chilavert?"

"The one with the stone benches?"

"Yes! That's the one, exactly."

"Well, then at five o'clock next Monday. Agreed?"

"Agreed."

When we said our goodbyes we looked each other in the eyes, trying to let each other know of the great mutual interest that had been awakened between us. The warmth of her hand transferred a wonderful fervor that felt almost angelical to me. I left because I had to. But I would gladly have stayed there with my hand in hers until death did us part.

Promptly, at the agreed upon time, we met again. We spent an hour walking around the Chilavert area, an important German neighborhood located within the city of Villa Ballester. How many streets did we walk? I don't know, but we agreed to continue seeing each other. It was exciting to talk during those first days as we strolled along those beautiful streets lined with luxuriant shade trees. Our conversations about what we were doing, our memories, and our dreams about the future, were endless.

Noemi loved to talk. Her joy was contagious. Very soon my brain only held her image and the sound of her words. Those were days when I felt as if I were walking on clouds. I realized I was falling in love. I was eighteen years old, and there were still seven years ahead until, according to my plan, I could have my first girlfriend. Regardless… a few blocks from her house there was a park with a lot of trees and enormous flowerbeds. A granite bench there knew of our dreams.

Each time that I smiled or took her by the hand, there was an explosion inside of me. I experienced sensations that I had never felt before. I dreamed of her night and day. We could feel the inevitable evidence of our mutual attraction. We knew that that our budding relationship would go far beyond that of a passing friendship. We wanted to experience our future together. At just the right moment, under the shade of the trees, to the sound of birds chirping in the branches, Noemi and I made a commitment that has transcended the years, serving as the guideline that assured our happiness.

Noemi put her hands on mine. Feeling overwhelmed by deep emotions because I had just asked her to be my fiancée, my ears buzzing and a blush on my face, I waited anxiously for her reply.

"You know, Alberto, I feel I should say this, that we must always put the Lord first in our lives and in our relationship. Everything else, He will do."

The answer was a "yes" between the lines; nevertheless, it went straight to the core of how our lives would develop. God would be over everything, even over our emotions. If we obeyed, we would be establishing our future happiness. God was, both for Noemi and for me, our reason for being. Thus, it was right that He should have the first place in this, our fledgling romance. Noemi was right. And God has honored, even to this day, that commitment.

CHAPTER 12
BEGINNING OF THE PASTORAL WORK

One of the biggest problems and frustrations of my adolescence was that of wanting to correctly interpret the will of God. From the moment of my conversion, I did not want to be mistaken about what God might ask of me. I knew there was an eternal purpose for each life. I was conscious that I had a mission to fulfill. When I perceived the calling to serve Him, the consciousness of the divine will that many times I felt was overwhelming increased even more, to gigantic proportions.

I diligently read the Bible. I devoured any book that came into my hands. I searched through the biographies of the great men of God, and of contemporary preachers whom I had been blessed to hear, trying to understand the lights that illuminated the "thinking and doing of God."

I was determined not to make mistakes. In my prayers I pleaded for signs that would make me confident of the actions that I should take. I wanted to hear the audible voice of God telling me what to do, or see an angel of light appear in front of my eyes bringing me orders. But it was never like that.

For me, the Divine will was supreme in my life; to not understand it correctly was traumatizing. I experienced times of confusion. I was certain that God was interested in the mundane details of my daily life; however, why was it that on many occasions I felt like I was trapped in a dark tunnel or mired in a swamp?

But just as I experienced times of great confusion, I also realized that inside of me was a certain assurance that produced a sense of security and serenity. I did not understand it, but there it was, in the results that I was experiencing in the work of the Lord and in my personal life. Some nights I spent praying. The responsibility of the work of the church, and the preaching, weighed on me.

I want to say that even though in my denomination we never talked about or organized prayer vigils or fasting, I felt the need to do so. I felt certain that these were Biblical concepts and that in my readings I had discerned the value of these practices for closeness to and more direct dependence on the Lord. Naturally, I could see the results in myself. A greater freedom of action was expressed in the process of the work.

By this time I had immersed myself in a flurry of work and responsibilities. I was running around all over the city. After completing my secondary studies I was debating whether to pursue a secular career or go full time into the ministry. The latter idea was very appealing to me. However, I needed to secure my own financial independence. I began to work at a secular job. I found work as a salesman selling shavers from Remington and small electrical appliances. As a result of my contact with the public, I was afforded another opportunity that I could pursue at the same time, and that was collecting invoices for the publishing company Amauta. I was still a bachelor and therefore able to sustain myself perfectly. However, there was a "but" and it was the factor time.

I traveled in the subway, on buses, walked, and, at times, even ran if I was racing against the clock. At that time, 1960, I had two opportunities to enter pastoral work. One of those openings involved the church that Noemi attended in Villa Ballester, where the pastor had died and the church was orphaned. They urgently needed someone to take the pastor's place. The prospect was appealing, knowing that this was Noemi's church. That way I would be near her. However, at the same time, the Castrovince family, who were members of a church in San Justo, wanted to start a missionary work in their house. This alternate path, with the Castrovince family, would be an opportunity to plant a new church.

I evaluated both prospects and chose the second. The first opportunity offered the chance to be another assistant pastor. However, with the second opportunity I would be given full responsibility and would be starting the work from ground zero. I would be like the apostle Paul who built churches where there was no previous foundation. I was aware of my own lack of training and of my inexperience in pastoral work, but I would trust only in my great zeal for the work of the Lord and in my capacity to work hard. Everything else I would leave in God's hands.

With the consent of my pastor, Mr. Lorenzo Pluis, I began making the journey to the simple, humble home of the Castrovince family. Invitations were sent to neighbors, relatives and any others we encountered along the way, asking them to attend the initial small group meetings. Soon I became aware of the blessing of God. The congregation began to multiply by 30 percent, 60 percent, and then 100 percent. Although I was nervous in the beginning, soon we found ourselves in dire need to find our own property for the construction of a church building.

There were days when the people could not fit inside the house. Any folding chair or other seating the family had available was put to use, so it became very crowded. Even though crammed full, we lasted a little more than two years in that house. As the congregation grew, it began to make demands that I, not being an ordained minister, could not satisfy. I continually had to invite ordained pastors to fulfill certain obligations: child dedications, water baptisms, Holy Communion, etc. I was not adequately prepared for those duties, and, for that reason, it became essential that I begin my studies at the seminary.

I presented my application and enrolled at the Baptist seminary, and soon after I began attending classes. Since I had already spent many hours reading the Bible and books about the Bible, and because of the training I had already received from my pastor, and the constant practice of preaching in churches and on street corners, at Youth Society meetings and conferences, the classes at the seminary seemed easy to me.

Even so, there were professors whose lectures remain permanently etched in my mind. Precious knowledge of the Scriptures and of the Lord was shared with me during my youth and it has never disappeared. Soon I was ordained for the ministry.

The secular work, the evangelistic work and the romantic relationship kept me constantly going to and fro, like a frantic yo-yo. From Palermo, where I lived, I had to travel north for about an hour to visit my girlfriend. To the south of my home, also an hour away, was the place where I worked. And about an hour and fifteen minutes to the west was the location of the church. With such a wide distance between my places of responsibility, I often spent almost the entire day and part of the night traveling. It was tremendous. The days would disappear like sand sifting through my fingers as I tried to find time for my studies, my job, my church pastorate and my girlfriend. When I went to bed at night I was exhausted. I didn't even have time to dream after my head hit the pillow—as almost instantly I'd hear the noise of the alarm clock announcing another workday.

CHAPTER 13
THE CALLING OF EVANGELISM

When I was twenty-one years old, I was invited to hold two crusades in Ecuador. At the appointed time, in September of 1963, I left for this great undertaking. When I arrived at the airport in Quito, the capital city of Ecuador, a committee was there to welcome me. A senior missionary later confessed to me his first impression when he saw me stepping out of the airplane. Surprised at my youth, he had said to another colleague: "That's the evangelist? I thought he would be older. He's a just a boy."

The truth is that some people had recommended me highly. They believed that I could hold a major two-venue crusade (one at the Cerrado Coliseum in Quito and the other at the Huancavilca Coliseum in Guayaquil), and on that basis I had been invited. But the reality is that the sponsors were not personally acquainted with me, and so there was certain awkwardness to our initial meeting.

On the first day of the crusade, while I was at the hotel where I was staying, with only two hours to go, I was suddenly seized with a great fear. With the thought of a multitude of 12,000 or

15,000 people flashing through my mind, I began to tremble from head to toe. The job seemed too big for me. My legs became wobbly and I fell to the floor, totally powerless. I thought of running away from that place. I wanted to escape. But during that exact moment of emotional crisis, the room was slowly filled with a sublime Presence. The air seemed to acquire an exquisite quality. The restlessness that had recently gripped me gradually began to disappear, replaced by a lovely peace that invaded every inch of my being. A glorious sense impressed my consciousness. I knew that it was God. And, suddenly, a thought came to my mind, as if I were hearing an audible voice.

"A new flame will blaze throughout the continent. I want your life to be the fuel for my plan."

The atmosphere surrounding me was such that I had no doubt that it was the voice of God, so it was not hard for me to stammer, with tears flowing: "Lord, here am I. Use me, please."

In that hotel room in the capital city of Quito, Ecuador, I received from God my calling to mass evangelism. This calling was so potent that, even though my heart was passionate about the pastoral duties at the Church of Haedo, this experience defined the starting point of a strong and powerful evangelistic fire that still consumes my being every day that I live.

God's calling is not just any calling. One does not have the option of doing or not doing. Never! It is life itself. There is an energy inside of me that is always ready to take off. If for some reason I were to not act according to the calling received, this energy create so much pressure that I feel myself at the point of death. I would be suffocated if I could not set free its potentiality. On the other hand, when I do exactly what I have been commissioned to do, I feel surrounded by a deep and inexhaustible peace.

This calling to mass evangelism became a blazing passion, consuming my bones and my flesh. I knew that my life would have no meaning if I did not obey my Lord, and that my service would be given at any cost, even if it were necessary to give my life.

The calling was so powerful and defining that I would have stopped people in their tracks and paid them to give me a few minutes of their time just so I could communicate to them the love of Christ. Yes! I would have paid people if necessary, just so they would listen to me, so that they might hear about the salvation that can only be found in the Lord.

After I got up from the floor of that hotel room and dried my eyes and my face, I was never again the same person. My heart was ablaze. I had been on Mount Sinai standing in front of the burning bush that is never consumed. Now I had to come down. The pulpit at the Cerrado Coliseum in Quito, Ecuador, was waiting for me. A multitude of people would hear me share with passion, with love, with the tenderness of heaven, the story of the Savior, the Son of God, the story that has been retold millions of times.

A few months later, on February 18, 1964, Noemi and I were at last united in holy matrimony. It was a day of insufferable heat. The weather was unbearable. The humidity saturated the pores of our bodies. Nervous though we were, we made our way to the Civil Registry that afternoon, along with a group of close friends. As night approached, and after our signatures were stamped, we headed to the church, beneath a rainstorm that flooded Buenos Aires. That storm caused quite a few automobile accidents—some cousins suffered a mishap, and the car that was carrying us didn't escape the impact of the weather either. Our brakes gave out and we had to drive onto the sidewalk to stop the car.

Even so, with all of these calamities, the church building was bursting at the seams. My pastor, Mr. Lorenzo Pluis, was the messenger of God who united us with his blessing.

Thus a beautiful relationship began under the shelter of the Almighty, one that will last until death may separate us. Two sons would arrive later to complete the family: Marcelo and Martin.

The Mottesi-Mazzarielo family was marked by the divine seal and determined to follow in the footsteps of the Galilean, even when they led me to prison itself... in Devoto.

CHAPTER 14
THE DEVOTO PRISON

Time for seminary work was never easy for me to find. I now had more responsibilities to fulfill. Often I would fall asleep on the subway or in the bus, and at night the books would fall out of my hands. My life, while I was a student, was a period of great sacrifices.

During the four years of my seminary studies, we were required to accomplish a practical ministry project. Most of the young people carried-out their project duties by helping some pastor in the local area. However, because I was already a pastor, I opted to fulfill my requirements by working as a prison chaplain serving the inmates.

For a long time I had intended to get involved in this type of ministry. I knew that this prison in Villa Devoto was a place with a great need for spiritual assistance, but few Christian people were interested in providing this daunting service. I obtained the necessary permissions and presented myself, along with two other seminary students, at the Devoto prison.

This experience would leave an indelible reminder in my heart of what the protection of God really means.

That prison, the largest in Argentina, provided food and shelter to a multitude of individuals who were the outcasts of society, representing the widest range of criminal behaviors. The prison was located in the northwest part of Buenos Aires, near General Paz Avenue, which divided the capital city of greater Buenos Aires, close to the neighborhood of San Martín.

After entering through the enormous steel doors and as we walked toward the interior of the facility, several doors would close behind us, one after another, producing an overwhelming sensation of fear and doom. The glances of the prisoners are a language with which they communicate with one another inside those walls. Their eyes were burning, scrutinizing us as if to discover the true intentions of these strangers who dared to tread within those grounds—grounds so filled with hate and evil.

To walk along those corridors to the place assigned by the authorities was always an experience fraught with tension. Our hearts would race while we tried desperately to maintain an appearance of equanimity. Every time we went inside we were surrounded by a large group of prisoners offering us things in exchange for money—or perhaps they simply wanted to see what the strangers were bringing. We noticed, quite quickly, that the only security inside the prison consisted of two guards with machine guns standing at the top of the walls.

The two other seminary students who went with me were also musicians—or at least that's what they said. One was a converted Jew who played the violin, but the sound he extracted from his instrument resembled rather a mewing cat. The other student played the accordion. The poor prisoners! With those two musical "virtuosos" and me as the preacher, it was enough to make anyone want to run to a faraway corner of Argentina.

We visited twice a week. One visit was in the evening, when we provided a devotional service with preaching. The other was the next morning when I went by myself to train and disciple any prisoners from the previous night's service that had shown an interest to surrender their lives to Christ.

This prison work created many offshoots. For example, as a pastor I was also called upon to minister to the families of several prisoners. I had many good and dramatic experiences during the time that I was serving as chaplain.

Inside any prison it is commonplace for prisoners to proclaim their innocence. Such was the case there, where most would tell us they didn't even know why they were imprisoned. There was one prisoner in particular whose story caught my attention.

He would usually join our group, just listening silently to what the others were saying or asking. I often felt his penetrating stare locked in on me. Later, after all of the others had given me their errands, he would approach me and say, with a booming voice:

"Pastor, help me get out of this place. You can talk to the authorities. They will listen to you."

"Why are you here?" I asked him at our first meeting, just to get to know him a little.

"Well, I don't know. They just grabbed me and threw me in prison. I have already been here for several years and I don't know why. I haven't done anything wrong to anyone."

His pained expression, the tone of his voice, would make anyone suspect a possible injustice perpetrated by the authorities, even though I knew his pledge of innocence was suspect.

"Very well; let me look into this and see what I can do," I said, thinking maybe there might be some truth to what he said.

"I will be very grateful to you. I want to get out of here and help my family out of this disgrace. Believe me, they will listen to you. Here inside this prison they treat us like animals and forget that we exist. Well, pastor, I await your news. Have a good day. We will meet here next week. Thank you very much."

And he left, blending into a crowd of prisoners who also "did not know" why they were there.

Because of the promise I made to him and his seeming sincerity, I spoke to the authorities in order to learn more about his case. But was I in for a surprise! This man was imprisoned because he was convicted of 19 murders. In fact, they called him the "razor boy." He simply entered any house at random, grabbed the women in the house and slashed their necks. And yet the man had the audacity to complain that he didn't know why he was in prison.

In spite of encounters like that, God allowed me to guide many prisoners, and even some of their relatives, to the feet of Christ. In spite of our rudimentary training, God prospered our efforts.

As a pastor, I was in charge of a block, which was a section of prisoners. This cell block had been designed to accommodate seventy-five people, but at the time I was serving there, the place held more than four hundred men. The overpopulation of the prison had dire consequences. Upon entering the prison and walking along its corridors, it was as if one was suddenly assaulted by an enormous, violent, evil rat. The environment became palpably malignant and perverse.

Then one day, a dramatic event occurred. For some reason that escapes my memory, I was not able to attend to my duties that week. There must have been something indispensable, because my tenacious diligence in attending to my responsibilities meant that I always fulfilled my commitments. From a very young age I had developed a strong sense of responsibility, and throughout the years I have always fulfilled my obligations with painstaking commitment. This makes the story seem even more dramatic and highlights the divine intervention on my behalf.

On exactly the day and time that I should have been there inside those walls teaching the prisoners, there was a prison riot. Several guards were taken hostage. They were made to kneel; guns were pointed in their faces, and they were shot point blank in the head, shattering their skulls.

From that moment the prison was shut down and no one was allowed to enter or leave. The situation was out of control and extremely tense. The prisoners were placed under siege, deprived of food and water, or of course, visitors. The difficult situation lasted for several days while the authorities carried on a shouted dialogue with the prisoners, trying to reason with them.

A countless number of policemen and soldiers surrounded the prison, where the prisoners were beginning to suffer the pangs of starvation. Finally, under those desperate conditions, the police convinced them to surrender, promising that there would not be reprisals.

Once the rebels had surrendered, they were placed in a large room and, without a trial or hearing, mercilessly executed by a firing squad.

This cruel episode became one of the most deplorable incidents of all of the prisons in the Republic of Argentina. All media outlets talked about this episode for several weeks afterward. For me it was impressive to see the marvelous protection of the Lord. I should have been there fulfilling my duties as chaplain on the first day of the riots. I had never before missed. I would have been inside, because that was exactly the time scheduled for my responsibilities. How great is the Lord in all his mercy. I praised the Lord together with my congregation for his divine protection for several weeks after that national event cast a terrible shadow on the prisons of my country.

CHAPTER 15
THE THREAD OF FAITH

How can it be that I, being a boy with a lot of fears and issues, having grown up with a pessimistic outlook, half backward and half naïve, would be chosen by God for matters of faith? This still surprises me. I believe that He should have called someone else, someone who already had faith and was already prepared for the battles of spiritual warfare.

In reality, if I had been the owner of a business to which young Alberto Mottesi had applied looking for a job, I never would have hired him. As soon as the interview had ended, I would have said: "Alberto, go home and relax. I will call you later." Then, after leaving the office I would have thought: "I'll never call this young man. If I were to place him on my payroll, I'm sure that he would wreck the business."

At this point I see fulfilled in my life the verse that says: "But God chose the foolish things of the world to shame the wise; God chose the weak things of the world to shame the strong" (1 Corinthians 1:27). I fit perfectly into this picture. I preach because of this Biblical passage. If this verse did not exist, I would not be able to teach God's Word. God is the God of wonders, of marvels, of magnificence, of the extraordinary. He accomplishes things that man could never do.

After about two years of selling electrical shavers and collecting the payments, I had the opportunity to begin a new job. I began to work with my denomination's Commission of Radio and Television. In this job I was often required to travel to the interior of the country. The radio ministry in Argentina in 1964 was very small. The financial needs of the new Mottesi-Mazzarielo family merited my inclusion on the payroll with a regular job. As a pastor, I didn't receive any economic assistance. My only support came from this job which, even though it was Christian work, often deeply divided my time. I was always on the run. The needs of my church demanded more and more from me. I felt that my duty was to be fully devoted to it. I was in turmoil with the burdens of my work for the Commission, my seminary studies, the church and my family. In addition to all of this, in my inner self I had a great fear. I was afraid of fatherhood, and I didn't want to have children.

At times this phobia seemed to intensify. There was the precedent of my own childhood, the hang-ups of my upbringing, the traumas that had induced my pessimistic outlook on life, which now reappeared as an unhealthy apprehension about having a family. When I looked at the outside world the thought would come into my mind: "Dear God, what will I do if I have children. The way young people are these days, and the way so many of the youth are lost, it is better not to have them; I do not want to have children just to lose them!"

One day when I had some time off, I decided to take the opportunity to meditate on God, and He clearly spoke to me: "Alberto, serve Me, and I promise that I will take care of your children."

This promise flooded me with a peaceful feeling.

Little by little, that tormenting fear began to dissipate, and I would see the fulfillment of this divine promise with the passing of time. But the pressures of the church were also causing a lot of anxiety. I saw that my job was getting more and more demanding. The thought of devoting my life full time to the pastoral ministry grew in my mind.

The restlessness grew stronger. Even though the work for the Commission of Radio and Television was Christian work, I never ceased to be frustrated with having to spend entire days at the office. Finally, the moment came when I could not take anymore.

It was only one month before the birth of our first son. The emotional implications of that situation were at a boiling point. At the same time we were preparing for the Christmas festivities at our fledgling, humble, and financially poor church. We did not have a large number of faithful attendees, but we were able to manage any problems that arose with the help of the people we did have.

It was during that time that I approached my wife and said: "Listen, Noemi, for several months now I have been wrestling inside with a decision; I feel that the Lord is calling me to full-time service at the church. I believe that He wants me to devote myself fully to the pastorate. But if I do that, I will have to give up my job at the Commission of Radio and Television."

My wife, even though she was in an advanced stage of pregnancy, gave me a very understanding look and said pleasantly: "Well, if it is the Lord who is calling you, there is no problem."

Her support felt as if someone had removed a huge weight that had been holding me down. The next day I presented my letter of resignation, telling them that I would only work one more month at the Commission. That was on a Friday, and I said nothing about the matter to anyone.

On that Sunday we went to church as usual. We carried out all of the duties of the service that evening and, finally, I asked the congregation to stay for a few moments after the service ended to discuss the last details of an evangelistic campaign that we were planning to hold the following week.

And that is what we did. I was speaking to the brethren about their responsibilities when suddenly one of them asked to speak.

I agreed, believing that he had something to add to the discussion about the coming campaign.

"Pastor, I don't know what has happened to me, but during the past week, I have been burdened with the thought that the time has come for you to give all of your time to the pastorate."

I stood there frozen and speechless. Soon, eleven men were saying the same thing. When that finished sharing their thoughts, I told them, almost trembling, about my letter of resignation and my desire to devote myself completely to the pastorate. I added that until that moment I had only told my wife, and that the decision had been completely personal. But now, having heard their voice, I had not the slightest doubt that the Lord was behind all of this. The brethren, new converts, with simple faith, asked me to step out of the room for a few moments. I left, while they remained to discuss the matter. After a few minutes they called me back in and told me that they had pledged to give the rest of the money necessary so that their pastor could devote himself full time to the ministry.

This was my first true step of faith, the beginning of what I call my thread of faith. Throughout my entire life, even to this day, events have occurred that continually reveal the abundant provision of God. Step by step, patiently, the Lord has been saying to me: "Here I am." The church never failed to fulfill its pledge. When my son Marcelo arrived we had an automobile, even though at that time it not easy for a pastor to afford one. I do not remember, honestly, ever suffering economic hardships.

Not long before I became a full-time pastor, we decided that the church lacked the funding needed for a better building and for some expansion of the capacity that we considered appropriate. We all knew that as members of the convention of churches to which our congregation belonged, we could ask for assistance, which meant participation in the convention's funding program for local churches.

There were churches of thirty years' existence and older that continually, year after year, had been beneficiaries of that plan. We, as a church, thought of asking for the same assistance.

I went to see them and learned to my surprise that they had just suspended the program for one year. The reason they gave was that the plan would be reorganized. Moreover, in the interim they would not be accepting any requests. They told me to come back the following year and then there would be no obstacle to helping our congregation.

Throughout that year, strengthened by the way in which God had responded to my leap of faith even without my having asked, and together with those new believers, we dared to trust God and his Word.

Less than a year later, I was talking to some members of the convention's funding committee and they told me that it was now possible for us to obtain financing. All I needed to do was submit an application and they would process my request in a short while.

But my response was negative.

"Dear brothers, I told them, we no longer want the assistance. Do not think that I am saying this out of resentment or bad feelings; no, it is simply that after we were unable to get economic assistance last year, we decided to simply believe the Word of God. And the results have been marvelous. In no way would I want us to go backward. We would not want to set aside this attitude of faith that has begun to develop; we will continue, then, depending on the resources of God."

I believe that we Hispanics need to learn to pay our own bills. We should conceive and carry out our own projects that honor the Heavenly Father. About fifty years ago the evangelical community in Argentina was tiny; however, we threw ourselves into doing the work of the church and paid our own way. I had decided to devote myself full time to the pastorate without knowing whether this poor church would support my determination. It was as if God had said to me: "Alberto, do not expect to see any tangible proof in front of your eyes before doing my will. Rely on the Name of my Son Jesus, and I will always support you."

Sometime later, I heard someone say that our ministry was like someone putting his feet in the waters, even if the waters were cold, deep, and threatening. If God had spoken saying that He would part them, then we would always go and immerse our feet and ankles and anything else necessary, knowing that the Word of this marvelous God will never fail. Throughout our entire history, we never did anything just to have the concrete results in our hands, but only as a response to the promptings of the Holy Spirit expressed in words.

God had said to go forward and He would part the waters. Even though the waters may have seemed imposing and exceedingly cold, we put in our feet with abandon. For a few moments, we felt the coldness of the water causing our bodies to tremble, but God, always attentive, parted the waters in His time.

We worked in Haedo for eleven glorious years, surrounded by churches that were supported by missionaries, or with pastors who supported themselves with secular jobs. I supported my family and raised my sons in an environment that was not wealthy, but not deprived. I saw with my own eyes the construction of that church auditorium in front of the main plaza of our town. We lacked for nothing. We experienced the reality that God is a God who faithfully fulfills His Word.

CHAPTER 16

THE FIREMEN AND THE BAPTISMAL TANK

From the beginning of my pastorate at the home of the Castrovince family, my main purpose and goal was one hundred percent focused on evangelistic outreach. I taught the first members of our fledgling church to work continually to reach the lost for Christ. My new converts readily accepted this lifestyle. For me it was nothing unusual. I lived with that passion. My mission to propagate the Gospel anywhere possible, whatever the venue might be—under a tent, in the park or on a bus—was something contagious.

During the early years of my ministry I met Pastor Juan Florio, an utterly simple man, a worker with no intellectual pretenses. He was pastoring a church in the outskirts of Buenos Aires, in the neighborhood of San Justo, located in the neighborhood of La Matanza. He had one lovely and healthy Christian virtue: he was passionate about evangelism. He had a good-sized tent and on several occasions I was invited to preach under his tent. At each campaign that was held, he would come looking for me and I gladly lent him my support. At the same time, whenever

I needed his tent for campaigns in my district, he never refused me. We developed a great friendship. Brother Juan Florio had a wonderful influence on my life, reinforcing an emphasis on evangelism that would continue throughout my years in the pastorate and in my current ministry.

Such was the overflow of my passion for evangelism that during one year our small congregation hosted twelve campaigns, each lasting an entire week. Moving forward at full speed, we were active throughout our district. We would use anything that might serve as an instrument of evangelism.

The congregation continued to grow from the time when we organized all of the faithful as active participants. It was exciting to see each day that everyone was excited about their activities. Each one enthusiastically embraced his commissioned responsibility.

Continued growth had required us to think about buying land to construct a building for the Lord. We began to pray, work and live with the idea of obtaining our own place of worship. This dream became a reality in Haedo, a suburb in the western section of the Greater Buenos Aires metropolis. With a main plaza directly in front, we felt that our location was optimal. It offered all of the conveniences, including a wide variety of transportation options and a generally quiet residential neighborhood. So we began with the construction of a wooden chapel on a piece of land and later we purchased another piece of land in front of the main plaza.

We inaugurated the auditorium, a simple building. The consecration service highlighted our inner satisfaction at seeing the fulfillment of a spiritual dream. Surrounded by a small flock, having left behind the grind of the secular workplace, I myself, kneeling in prayer and with the shedding of tears, continually sought the help of the Almighty. I knew that only the Lord "… added to their number daily those who were being saved" (Acts 2"47). This accomplishment did not cause us to rest on our laurels. We also knew that, with a willing attitude, we could be instruments that God would use. That is why we maintained a distinctive vision, clearly stated, for our small Church of Haedo: a vision for evangelism and constant work.

But one day, without any advance warning, something unusual happened.

On the first Sunday after the inauguration of our new building, we had decided to hold our first water baptism service using the baptistery that had only recently been completed. Because the auditorium was newly built, we never thought about testing the water pressure. We assumed that the water flow would be what we were accustomed to in other parts of the city.

We arrived that morning and turned on the water faucet, thinking that by the afternoon the baptistery would be full enough for the baptisms. Then we promptly forgot about it and went on with our Sunday morning routines. We left to eat lunch and returned that afternoon planning to hold a good baptismal service.

Imagine our surprise when we saw that the water didn't even reach the ankles of those who were planning to be immersed in the baptistery. We saw that it was getting late, that the congregants were arriving and filling the seats of the church auditorium, and that the candidates for water baptism were already making the last-minute preparations, yet the tiny baptistery was still almost empty of water. Worried, I put my hands on my head, despairing in front of some brothers who also were disconcerted about the situation.

"Dear Lord! What are we going to do?"

Brother Federico Shuster, treasurer and a great team member, one who did everything he could to help during my eleven years in the pastorate, said calmly, with great assurance and confidence: "Don't worry, pastor. I am a friend of the firemen in this city, and with one telephone call I will solve this problem."

Immediately, Brother Shuster turned around and went to the nearest telephone.

Those of us who were left there looked at each other, perplexed; asking ourselves what was it that a few firemen could do to solve this baptistery problem at our church.

Not long after brother Shuster went to the telephone, we began to hear the sound of fire truck sirens. Within a few minutes the piercing sound of the sirens grew louder and louder in the streets around our church building. The fire trucks were coming at high speed through the streets of the town and quickly arrived at our front entrance. Expertly, they unwound and dragged the huge fire hose into the church building, all the way to the baptistery. In less time than it took to recover our composure, the captain of the firemen, with a big smile, said to me: "Ready, pastor? Your baptistery is full. It was an honor to serve you."

The only thing that could come out of my mouth was a very sincere, "Thank you."

What I had not noticed before the captain of the firemen left was the big swarm of curious onlookers that had gathered outside the front door of our church. The loud whine of the sirens had attracted a large crowd of people who perhaps thinking that the new church building was burning, had come running to see the supposed calamity with their own eyes. So God used this humorous episode to make our new church known to our neighbors. We did not need to stage a publicity stunt to call attention to our church; the Lord knew how to use his own advertising agency that surpassed anything we could have done with our human efforts. From that moment on, several other events happened that would make known the Church of Haedo not just in the capital city, but also throughout the entire country of Argentina.

CHAPTER 17

THE MANTLE OF THE SERVANT OF GOD, TOMMY HICKS

During the early part of 1954, a man of Anglo heritage was traveling from Chile to Argentina with a vision deep in his bones. This vision had been born two years earlier in Tallahassee, Florida, when Tommy Hicks, during a time of prayer, looking at a map of South America, saw a vision of an immense field of ripe wheat, ready for the harvest. While looking at the wheat crop swaying in the wind, the stalks suddenly became human bodies that, with hands raised high and eager eyes, exclaimed with urgent voices, "Brother Hicks, come! Help us!"

Hicks faithfully interpreted the calling. After several other events had confirmed his vision, he was now stepping out of an airplane, filled with an intense assurance that God was about to perform something awesome.

Already, with a question to the flight attendant during the flight, he had verified the identity of the man with whom he would need to speak. He was none other than the president of the Republic of Argentina, Juan Domingo Perón.

It seemed crazy to even think such a thing. The general, even though he was no longer at the height of his political power at that time, still exercised power that reached into every corner of the country. His leadership for eight consecutive years had been exercised in a hard-handed way, dictatorial, yet this was the man to whom Hicks wanted to direct his inquiries. Surely it would not be easy.

Brother Hicks was persistent in spite of the many obstacles that interposed themselves along the way. Finally, his perseverance was rewarded when the Minister of Foreign and Religious Affairs agreed to receive him, a possible opening to an audience with the president himself. On the scheduled day, after a long wait but confident that perhaps this visit could mean the fulfillment of his purpose, the Minister announced that on that day the President had run out of time for personal appointments. The reason given was that Peron was preparing to meet with the president of Panama, who would be arriving in the city of Buenos Aires that afternoon.

Brother Hicks was standing there, listening to this discouraging and frustrating news, when the Minister's secretary entered the office. Immediately, Hicks noticed that the man was badly limping, obviously due to some problem with his leg. The secretary asked the minister for permission to take some time off due to the pain he was experiencing. He raised his pant leg, showing a bluish limb and a swollen knee. Before the minister had a chance to give his consent, Hicks spoke up, suggesting to the secretary that they could pray for him to receive his healing.

"Even if Jesus Christ himself were here," the man said, "he would not be able to cure this leg."

"Allow me," said Hicks, approaching the ailing man.

He knelt and, placing his hands on the injured leg, he prayed. The pain disappeared and the leg in an instant was restored to a healthy natural color. Stunned, the secretary looked with amazement at the Minister, who could not believe what he was seeing with his own eyes.

"May I speak with the president?" Hicks asked with calm assurance.

"I will take you there myself," the Minister answered resolutely.

They walked through the lavishly decorated halls until arriving at the presidential office of the Casa Rosada (Presidential palace).

Juan Domingo Perón, a man of swarthy complexion and wide shoulders, was seated at his desk, elegantly attired in light grey. He glared with inquisitorial air at this minister who had dared to enter his presence accompanied by a *gringo* unknown to him. But after being told of what happened, he became friendly and cordial during the length of the short conversation. When it was about to end, Hicks requested that he be allowed to pray for them before leaving. With reverent attitude, they let him lift a prayer. It is said that Perón had eczema on one of his hands and that he also was healed at that time.

What is certain is that after Hicks left, having gained the full support of the president, the ministerial assistant was given orders to grant the preacher anything that he might request. Hicks obtained permission to hold an evangelistic campaign at a huge stadium and also obtained free access to newspaper and radio publicity—an amazing accomplishment.

The campaign lasted fifty-two days and there were great miracles of God witnessed there. The power of God had an impact on a national level, and the event was a milestone in the history of the Gospel in Argentina, with results that continue to have repercussions, even to this day.

I never imagined the influence that this event would have on the subsequent development of my life. Even though at the time of Hick's crusade I was only twelve years old and knew very little about it, I cannot say the same about myself at age twenty-six.

In 1968, I organized a camp meeting for the youth of my church. We wanted to take advantage of the Carnival holidays, which are held every February in the city of Buenos Aires. We decided to use that time to go out of the city, to a place called Hurlingham, to a country house leased by the Terranova brothers, who had generously loaned it as a venue for the retreat.

The house was like a residence for nobility, very beautiful and sumptuous from any angle it was observed. Stunning gardens meticulously tended surrounded the house, which was of colonial architectural style. There were several rooms luxuriously decorated with landscape paintings enclosed in golden frames, lovely vases, heavy drapes, countless fine porcelain ornaments, and intriguing ethnic antiques, which became our constant companions during those days. The place was so large in terms of land that there were several forests surrounding it. The landscaping was magnificent. We watched in joyful ecstasy the sun rising in the early morning and gloriously setting at dusk. It was a splendid place to seek the face of God, surrounded by those views of nature that encouraged meditation. A few women from the church came along with us to help with food preparation. Our agenda included several sporting events, hiking, bonfires, contests, lectures, and time for prayer.

From the time when we arrived on the buses that took us there, joy was ubiquitous on everyone's face. After quickly settling in to our accommodations, we began with some recreational activities. On the first night, we gathered around a campfire in a clearing near the house, with a large stockpile of wood nearby to keep the fire going. We could see the stars shining brightly in the dark night sky. The country air felt fresh and the soft sounds of tree branches, barely perceptible, induced a feeling of relaxation. The fire crackled and we felt its radiant heat on our cheeks. The flickering flames were reflected in the attentive eyes of the young people listening to the voice of the preacher speaking peacefully about God, and about His renovating power in the lives of those who were willing to surrender themselves to Him unconditionally.

There were several young people around the campfire, sitting on the green grass, or on a large stone or piece of wood they had found somewhere, or perhaps on a blanket spread out on the ground, where several girls sat in reverent silence.

An attitude of reflection had fallen upon those present. The musical sounds flowing from the guitars and the accordion, and accompanied by the many voices of all of the young people praising their Creator, slowly faded. One could sense in the atmosphere a Presence overwhelming the souls of those gathered in that place.

Months earlier I had noticed that the spiritual disposition of the young people was different than that of the adults. It had seemed necessary, I would even say urgently necessary, to plan this retreat out in the countryside. And what was happening that night gave me the assurance that I had not been wrong in my assessment. God wanted to speak to the youth of my church.

It was getting close to midnight. We had shared songs, testimonies, preaching and times of fervent prayer. I stood up, intending to dismiss the meeting.

"Young people, it is time to go and rest. However, those who would prefer to remain here for a few more moments of prayer are welcome to do so. My only request is that you do so quietly, so as not to disturb those who will be sleeping."

To my amazement, no one moved. Everyone wanted to continue praying. I did not insist on closing the meeting even though it was very late and the day had been very strenuous. I thought that perhaps in another hour the exhaustion would send them off to sleep.

They organized themselves into little groups. Some were hugging one another. Others knelt, weeping and sobbing. The blessed presence of the Holy Spirit surged into and overflowed throughout those hearts thirsting for God.

I heard voices pleading for holiness, consecration, and revival. The latter was an impassioned cry: "Renew us, Lord! Renew us!"

Without noticing, the hours went by. At some point, I became aware that rays of sunlight were starting to appear on the horizon, signaling a new day. We had spent the entire night praying! But the most extraordinary thing was yet to happen. We had no intention of stopping that divine breath. Truly, we had experienced a Pentecost. The Spirit of love had control over everything that was happening in such a way that we barely noticed the passing of time.

At midday they called us to eat, but no one went. The food got cold. It wasn't until later, in the afternoon, that we began to descend from this, our "Mount of Transfiguration."

How often my spirit had been deeply moved in the past, when after reading about great revivals and men of God visited by the supernatural power of the Lord, I had longed for and dreamed of those moments of glory. Now I was experiencing these things in my own flesh. I had spent almost twenty-four hours submerged in the holy and blessed Presence of God.

How incredible and impressive it was to see more than two hundred young people, eyes swollen and faces reddened from weeping, totally absorbed in prayer. They were disheveled, their voices hoarse. Ah, but the smiles. They looked like angels. Their faces shone with holiness. The love of the Almighty flowed in the hidden corners and penetrated every pore of their bodies, now committed as never before to their King and Lord.

This camp meeting radically transformed the life of my church. I did not have to say: "Do this or do that." It was as if an ocean wave was coming down so forcefully that if I did not go along with the flow I would be dragged along by the momentum. To work for the Lord, to preach, to tithe, to testify and open new evangelistic fields, to disciple, all of these were the product of the fire that now consumed the renewed hearts of the members of the church. In time, several of those young people would become torches in the ministry, holding key positions of leadership, both inside the country and elsewhere. The flame that had been lit in that little corner of heaven would not be extinguished. On the contrary, it would continue burning brightly, producing worthy fruit for the Giver of all good things, our beloved Jesus.

One significant factor that was stunning to me was learning that the mansion in Hurlingham, which had been loaned to us for the camp meeting, had also been loaned fourteen years earlier to that servant of God, Tommy Hicks. He had spent many days there in fervent prayer, saturating his life with power from the throne of the Heavenly Kingdom. How amazing that those were the same rooms that had been silent witnesses of the passion of a man fully surrendered to the vision he had received in 1952, in far-away Florida. Argentina became the recipient of one of the greatest blessings of the Almighty, and all because of the faithfulness of Tommy Hicks. This man of God, who by the time of our event was living in California, seemed to have left his mantle behind, in that exact place, and we, on that retreat, had picked it up with trembling hands, finding shelter in the protection of the Almighty. It was as if the power of God was already there and ready to be taken by anyone who wanted it. We wanted it, and in no way were we disappointed.

We were treading on holy ground. We took off our sandals in reverence. And God provided an abundant supply of manna, to such an extent that the spark of Pentecost that engulfed our humble lives then still continues to blaze.

CHAPTER 18

A VERY MODERN SOLUTION TO THE
PROBLEM OF MARRIAGE

"Wait! Be patient! The report will be on the air soon." I was trying to calm down the high spirits of my family and several members of the church. We were all anxiously awaiting the news report by Héctor Agulleiro, one of the best reporters on TV's Channel 11.

"But will they put it on the air?" said one of the young men, his face sincerely reflecting doubt.

"Of course," answered another. "Didn't you see the camera and the reporter working at the scene?"

"Yes, but … because it is a religious matter, perhaps they will not do it."

"Stop doubting. You will see it on the air," said Mr. Alberto Pets, an elder of the church who was a gift of God to my life during the years of my pastorate.

There were no less than eighteen people waiting for the broadcast of those television images reflecting scenes from the event that had seemed to us of singular effect. We were meeting afterwards there at the church, chatting about many things over cups of coffee, but without taking our eyes off of the television.

The preparations had begun months earlier, and now we anxiously waited to see the culmination on television, because we knew God had allowed these circumstances.

Three couples had come to me at different times and in different circumstances asking me to marry them. The dates they had scheduled were more or less during the final days of December or early January. This gave me the idea of hosting a multiple wedding ceremony at the church. However, there was a problem with that thought: the limited space of the Church of Haedo. Because of the spatial constraints, it would be impossible to hold this event at our church. We estimated at least one thousand people would attend, but the capacity of our auditorium would allow perhaps only half that number inside the building. Then, we thought of holding the event outside, in the open air. The designated place was the side of our church building located directly in front of the main plaza of the city. The marriage candidates loved the idea. We submitted an application requesting the appropriate legal permits, and sent a press release to all of the local media outlets, inviting them to cover the remarkably unusual event.

What unforgettable moments we are given as sweet gifts from the Lord!

"Hey, hey, wait!" cried one in our group. "The local news is about to begin. This is when they will probably air the report."

We all crowded together in front of the screen, with bated breath and in keen anticipation.

In fact, the TV reporter almost seemed to know what the audience was waiting for. He started by saying "*We have noticed, kind viewers, that in Argentina some events are being organized that draw attention because of their uniqueness. This is one of them. It is possibly the most modern solution to the problem of marriage.*"

The broadcast started with scenes showing a crowd gathered in the park in front of the municipal offices in the city of Haedo. There were chairs arranged and lanterns shedding light on the area. The seats were all filled and many people were standing, their faces expressing joyous expectation. Several pedestrians walking nearby had noticed the commotion and stopped to watch the proceedings and satisfy their curiosity.

"*Starting at the curb, a purple carpet stretched between two columns of chairs until reaching the improvised altar. This was located at the center and toward the back of the garden. It was a wooden platform with a wooden pulpit on top, and a microphone. The platform was beautifully adorned with drapes, drawing all eyes to that specific location. Music from an organ and a clarinet could be heard in the background. They were playing the music of "Holy, Holy, Holy, Lord God Almighty." Flower vases filled with white gladiolas were the ornaments arrayed down the aisle.*"

"*The ceremony began with great display of emotion from the people in attendance. There was an environment of intense spirituality in that place. In his Oxford gray suit, Pastor Alberto Mottesi addressed the audience.*"

"Brothers and dear friends," I watched myself say on television, "who have joined us here tonight for this ceremony in which three couples will take the sacred vows of marriage, under this ornate roof of twinkling stars, a temple of nature, I invite you to pray and give thanks to God for this wonder that He allows us to experience, praying that He will be manifested not only in the lives of these future spouses, but also in each one of those in attendance, to bless their lives."

"*A little while later, the bridal trio slowly approached the altar to the strains of Mendelssohn's "Wedding March." There were three handsome young men in formal attire and three beautiful brides, radiant and yet visibly nervous, in their white wedding dresses. There was a sense of excitement in the crowd. All of the people stood to their feet as the couples walked down the aisle. Some raised their hands, others expressed their joy. Boys and girls were milling all around; young women holding their babies and men of every age strutting around in their best outfits. An unusual outdoors experience it was, that prompted a security officer to watch from his headquarters across the street to not miss a detail of what was happening.*"

Despite the multitude that made it necessary to block traffic, it was not necessary to add extra security. Everything was done orderly. The people in attendance enjoyed the event."

"In words tinged with emotion, Pastor Mottesi spoke to the crowd about the holiness of marriage and the love between man and wife. At the end of his sermon he called each one of the couples forward and led them in the traditional marriage vows."

"Eduardo, Graciela, do you want to be united in conformance with the ordinance of God in the holy state of matrimony?"

"Ricardo, Martha, will you love, comfort, honor and care for each other in times of sickness and of health?"

"Norberto, Lidia, will you renounce all others, saving yourself only for each other as long as you both shall live?"

"They all answered with a definite "I do" complete and unhindered. The prayer of blessing, said with the affection based on love, was the contribution of the audience. The hands of the Pastor were extended toward each one of the couples in loving gesture, sealing each one with a kiss on the cheek. There were tears streaming down the Pastor's face and the faces of several in the audience. A deep emotion overwhelmed hearts in this social act where sincerity was manifest in its most pure expression."

"Handel's "Hallelujah" added a touch of majesty to the event, setting an upbeat tone for most of the audience. Hands held high, eyelids tightly squeezed, exclamations honoring the Creator, all of these occurrences seemed quite normal at this spectacular event."

"Radiant and happy, the new spouses walked back toward the street accompanied by the music of the Wedding March. There was applause and blessings for the couples. The music blended with the sound of laughter, of chatter and hugs while children darted about."

As they were leaving, the vibrant emotion-filled voice of the Pastor was little by little drowned out by the growing roar of the crowd: "We praise you, oh Father. We glorify you because your Spirit is present here...."

"It was a warm evening under the Argentine stars of the Haedo community, where a handful of evangelicals decided to take to the

streets to manifest their faith and show the world their simple way of living in community."

"*This synchronized matrimonial event has been,*" the TV announcer summarized with his resonant voi*ce, "to eyes around the world a demonstration that where there is a will, things can be done well. Don't you think that this could be 'the most modern solution to the problem of matrimony'?"*

"Bravo! Magnificent! That was good!" exclaimed one of the church members watching with me.

"Thank God that they did it," said the one who had earlier expressed doubt.

"See, I told you they would do it, didn't I?" answered Mr. Alberto Pets. "Besides, they structured it well, in a way that made the whole event shine."

"Well," it was my turn to speak, "now let's go home and rest. This day has been a lot of hard work and very emotional and we are all very tired. Good night, everyone."

"Good night!"

That Sunday the triple wedding was the talk of the town all day long. The main newspapers devoted space to it. The radio stations discussed the event during early morning broadcasts. The TELAM agency also spread the story all around the country.

My heart felt very pleased at the outcome. When I sometimes looked into the eyes of Noemi, my wife, I saw there a little smile of satisfaction as well. The Church of Haedo had overflowed its four walls. Even though it was only a social event, we never lost the most important feature: the opportunity to proclaim the King of our lives.

This experience taught us that any aspect of our existence can become a vessel for communicating the great love of God to humanity. That night in Haedo gave us undeniable proof.

CHAPTER 19

THE CHURCH GOES TO THE STREET

During the eleven years of my pastorate (1961-1972) the Church of Haedo was often named as one of the fastest-growing Christian communities in Argentina. From the moment we held our first worship service, the burden of my heart was for this to be an evangelistic church. My aspiration was that soon our small group, meeting in a family home, would become a large congregation, meeting in its own building. There was only one way to accomplish that goal: through evangelism.

In addition, evangelism was a passion that flowed in my blood. My work had begun as a young person preaching on the streets and at outdoor events. I valued the power of prayer and fasting. I knew, from the books I had read, the spiritual benefits of these methods. Now that I was beginning this new work, these factors would naturally become part of my new congregation.

Evangelistic campaigns at the church, in parks or under a tent, became the norm for us. Lots of people began to visit our place of worship, and many stayed and became active members.

During the decade of the 1960s new winds of spiritual renewal began to appear in our country.

After the great campaign done by Tommy Hicks in 1954, things had changed radically. A sense of openness had begun that had never been seen before in the land of Argentina. Almost as if the flow of living waters had broken a rigid resistance, the evangelical testimony flooded the streets and suburbs of the city. Many new churches were formed and new forms of worship were adopted. Revival winds were sweeping across Argentina.

My church (and I in particular) was deeply affected by this infusion of divine breath. I was well informed about all the discussions and events taking place in connection with spiritual renewal. I think I expected it all, or perhaps it is better said that I was deeply desirous of spiritual renewal. My past readings about the great servants of God in history were now bearing fruit in surprising ways: God was acting on a supernatural level.

My background was very conservative, but through the years God had been preparing me for a purpose that at that time was completely unknown to me. This movement of the Holy Spirit began to overflow in my church, causing its members, as never before, to enter into a beautiful revival that had very significant results for the glory of God.

What profound lessons did our Lord impart to us through it all! He took away the value that we might have attached to a name or a denominational title. Instead, He made us delve deeply into the truth of the invisible Body of the Lord Jesus Christ. We are one in Him!

In us was birthed a firm conviction about the love shared by the Heavenly Father with every Christian brother of any denomination or ministry who has been washed and purchased by the precious blood of the Lord Jesus.

From that time on I was reluctant to label myself with any denominational title, but not because I considered the denominations a bad thing—not at all! I am aware that God has used denominations in the world and throughout the ages as glorious manifestations of the divine process in the salvation of mankind.

I knew that it was God who raised up each movement or denomination. God raised them as one more expression of the greatness and multi-faceted expression of who He is. He had transcended the weaknesses of humanity and with His power turned them into a blessing for His people.

That wave of revival took my church along new pathways. We became fruitful. We had only one desire: that Christ would be accepted by all of the people.

For this reason our church, along with many others, went out to the streets. Even though the evangelical movement in Argentina was very small at first, the Lord was giving us the strength and the courage to go to the streets.

That was the place where we would find the beggar, the prostitute, and the alcoholic. There we found the rich man, the professional, the worker, the student, and the housekeeper. We eagerly poured ourselves, taking advantage of any circumstance to expound the Lord of Lords, Jesus Christ.

That is why private ceremonies were transformed into public manifestations, as for example the joint marriage ceremony for three couples, or the firemen called on to fill the baptistery. We also strengthened the spiritual atmosphere and kept it thriving, such as when we had the camp meeting at Hurlingham. And then, there was the contract that I made with television's Channel 13. You see, there are sometimes unusual things that God does for his children.

One day, without knowing how or why, I was hired by the most important television channel in my country. They invited me to become a part of the regular staff at Channel 13 to bid the audience farewell each night, at the end of their broadcasting day. I would not be alone in this task. There were also three or four Catholic priests, a rabbi, and perhaps one other evangelical pastor. The men who were part of this group were mature people, some of them quite aged. In fact, I was a boy in comparison with them. I was a "kid" in the midst of those elders. This catapulted me to the forefront of public opinion in Argentina and, by default, my congregation as well.

Each month I appeared on television six or seven times preaching the Gospel for a few minutes. During the nightly farewell to the audience I would tell the viewers to sleep and rest with Christ.

This represented an important milestone for my church, and also for me as a young pastor. It was important because at that time the outlets of mass communication were closed. And I should point out that the television channel actually paid me to proclaim the Good News. I was surprised to see how God performs miracles for His children, in order to carry out his work. Blessed by our God and Heavenly Father!

This huge collection of experiences that we shared, my church and I, for eleven years made our lives so deeply woven together that it would not be easy to break our relationship. We were so passionate about one another, yet God had another task to fulfill, and it was necessary to obey.

CHAPTER 20

A DIFFICULT DECISION

Ten years had gone by, and I was in the eleventh year of my pastorate at the Church of Haedo. We had worked very hard together. We had become one of the largest congregations in Buenos Aires. During that time, we had rejoiced greatly to see the victories of the Lord. The congregation was experiencing revival. The Spirit of God was freely working his will within each member of our community. Joy and happiness were continual. The evangelistic work was outstanding. The church had gone to the streets and these events had placed us in the minds of the people of Buenos Aires, and of the entire nation. It can be said with good reason that it was a very successful congregation.

Its faithful and hardworking members had given themselves body and soul to serve their Lord. Despite my constant traveling to preach in other places, they continued to grow to the point of self-sufficiency. My departures had always been with full trust that they, the body of elders and deacons, were fully capable of carrying out the work of the church in every detail that might be necessary.

I was experiencing at this time a beautiful romance with my church. I saw that it was strong and on solid footing. Its atmosphere was one of love and freedom.

All of these thoughts were on my mind for several months during my eleventh year in the pastorate. On several occasions they filled me with anxiety, because weighing in my mind was the idea of submitting my resignation to my beloved church.

I strongly resisted this thought. I saw the church as a daughter born of my own being. It had been the subject of the tears I shed; the object of my travails in prayer, the cause of my perspiration in teaching, Bible study and preaching. I had given the best years of my youth to this church; all of my energies. Even the first years of my marriage were surrendered to the church when, instead of finding comfort with my wife and children, I used my time to feed my flock. I had given it my all.

It was not easy to embrace the idea with any delight, so resignation became a difficult decision to consider. How can a father abandon his daughter? How can he leave her and perhaps never care for her again? How could it be possible to leave behind something that was so intrinsically part of my being? Although I reflected on this idea for a long time, it seemed impossible to accept such a prospect, such determination.

I talked this over with myself, with my wife and with God, and I could not bring myself to abandon this piece of my heart. But then God dealt with me in a personal way: "Alberto, if you do not respond to the calling of evangelism, I will not continue to support you in the pastorate."

This telling signal went off like a bomb in my conscience. God was clarifying for me a principle that I will never forget. I realized that if I did not resign as pastor, the church would start to be damaged by my stubbornness. I learned, with the help of the Holy Spirit, that one can have a very blessed ministry and be fully immersed in success, but if God calls you to do something else and yet you close the doors to what He wants to accomplish, then it would be foolish to expect God to continue His blessing on what you are doing. This gave me a tremendous shock, because not only would I not be doing a good thing that was God's will for me, but also the Lord would take away any good things that I had done. I never doubted again. I resolved to announce my decision to the church.

When I made public the news of my resignation, some people cried, and others were stunned or simply did not understand. The most mature believers accepted my decision, saying: "Evidently God has called him to evangelism. We know that he is an evangelist. We should not hold him back; our pastor must devote himself to his mission."

It was an extraordinary thing. That congregation, with eyes wet with tears, demonstrated a supernatural understanding of the situation, and manifested its great love in a way that brought serenity to our lives.

Needless to say, my congregation never accepted outside money for its maintenance. The church was built from nothing during a time when there was no revival in Argentina. Because their confidence was in God, they pulled down treasures from Heaven with prayer and fasting, in order to distribute these to their neighbors with a passion, and that's what they proceeded to do with me.

"Pastor," they said to me in a voice quavering with emotion, "you will continue to receive your monthly salary for quite a while. Don't worry about coming here; we will send it to you wherever you are."

That broke my last reserve of strength. Deeply moved, not because of the gift itself, God knows, but because of the generous outpouring of hearts that loved us so abundantly. I cried with each one of them. We prayed with deep fervor for one another. We blessed each other abundantly in the only Name that could grow such love between brothers in the faith of Christ.

I will never forget that day, as long as I live here on this earth. The Church of Haedo. My going away. The pain of leaving. And the joy of a future not yet revealed.

In the months that followed the Lord surprised me with his gift. The Church of Haedo, faithfully, for two full years afterward, continued to send my salary. But I am aware of the rest of the story. The pastor who replaced me also received his salary and, in addition, there was help for missionary works in other parts of Argentina. This demonstrates to me that a church in Latin America, however small, is never an underdeveloped church if the magnificent Presence of Jesus is at its heart.

We do not need other resources than those that come from the Lord. Our resources do not come from dollars or from computers. Our resources come from the LORD our God, who made the heavens and the earth.

CHAPTER 21

SOJOURN IN CHILE: THE BITTER SIDE

During 1973 and 1974, we took up residence in Santiago, the capital city of Chile.

Those were very important years in our lives. They were the cheese between the slices of bread. Before 1973, we had always lived in our native country, Argentina. After 1974, apart from a short sojourn of eight months in Buenos Aires, we have lived –and continue to live– in Southern California, in the United States of North America.

From age sixteen I knew of a man of God who would be a permanent influence on my life: Dr. R. Kenneth Strachan, a prominent Presbyterian missionary full of the Holy Spirit. His ideas and his labor on behalf of evangelism saturated my mind. Later, I would have the opportunity to meet him personally, and the brief encounters that I had with him would leave an indelible imprint on my life. His "Evangelism of Saturation," which later would be developed as the International Institute of In-Depth Evangelism (INDEPTH), would become a real "revolution in evangelism."

Kenneth was a strategist and a visionary in the field of mass evangelism. I devoured his messages and his writings; I kept myself up to date on what INDEPTH was developing in Nicaragua, Costa Rica, Guatemala, and in all of Latin America. The principles elaborated by this man of God would mark my basic vision for the church as having direct responsibility for the salvation of men by means of the complete mobilization of lay workers. Many of his ideas I put into practice in my own pastorate and the results were always very positive.

I remained in direct contact with the INDEPTH movement even after the death of its founder. The directors maintained the same philosophy and with that my friendship with them was sealed. Because of this relationship, I received an invitation to collaborate on certain projects. After I resigned my pastorate, it seemed natural for me to work with INDEPTH. My heart clamored for evangelism to the masses.

I was asked to live in the Republic of Chile because of my knowledge of that country's geography and church structure, since I had been, for several years, visiting that neighboring country. I can even say that I was more familiar with the land of Chile than with my own country. There were many times that I traveled throughout Chile, from Santiago to Punta Arenas, from one end to the other. I especially remember the city of Concepción, and the island of Chiloé, places whose natural beauty always enthralled me. The times that I traveled across the Andes Mountains from Argentina to Chile, whether by train or plane, were always times of inexpressible wonder. I exulted in the magnificent landscape, including the cone of Tupungato, a gigantic volcano that rises to a height of over 21,600 feet and, on the other side of the valley, the breathtaking panorama of Aconcagua, the highest mountain in the western hemisphere.

We moved to Chile in early 1973, a year that was to be of great significance in the country's history. Chile's "doctor turned into president," Salvador Isabelino del Sagrado Corazón de Jesús Allende Gossens, was the man who commanded the national destiny of this South American country, but his presidential mandate, which began in 1970, was coming to a violent end. The first experimental effort in South America to turn a democracy into socialism would dissolve in a military coup d'état on September 11, 1973. That was a catastrophic time for a political system that did not succeed.

During the days preceding the military seizure of Chilean sovereignty, people were experiencing difficult conditions. I remember that frightful morning when I was walking with my son, Marcelo, who was barely eight years old, to the offices of INDEPTH. The office was located in the capital city, across from the Plaza de Armas and the Portal Fernandez Concha, on the seventh floor of a building that housed the restaurant Chez-Enri, a place where I learned to enjoy the famous seafood of Chile—the shrimp, abalone, crab, and clams were delicious.

My son and I were about to cross the Plaza when suddenly we heard the sinister blasts of firearms all around us. Startled, in instinctual self-preservation mode, we threw ourselves to the ground and squeezed underneath a parked car to wait for that devil's dance to end. From our improvised observation point we could see terrified people running along the street. We heard malicious orders being shouted and uncontrolled wailing. The scene was like something out of a Hollywood movie that we were forced to watch with extreme anxiety. We stayed there motionless for several minutes in a state of acute tension. After the sound of gunshots had ended and the police had taken control of the situation we could hear the whining sirens of patrol cars and ambulances. Trembling, we emerged from our hiding place and quickly walked toward the offices with dry lips and hearts leaping inside. That was quite a fright, what we experienced that morning.

In the following months, these violent outbursts became commonplace. Several times we had to walk forty or fifty city blocks to get home from the office because the entire city was paralyzed with gunfire or its aftermath. The situation was simply chaotic at that time in the country's history.

On the evening of September 10, my parents arrived from Argentina to visit. As it happened, within hours of their arrival the military coup d'état took place. On the following day the president of Chile, Allende, would lose his life at the presidential residence, the Moneda Palace. What a welcome to give my elderly parents!

For several days afterward we remained secluded in our house. What little news we heard was of complete chaos around the city and country. Military repression was at its height; civil liberties were suspended. Martial law was an oppressive reality that limited human freedom.

A week later, when we were able to leave our house, we were stupefied at the horrific sights all around us. The city was a disaster. Damage caused by bullets and cannons was everywhere. During the following months, on several occasions, we saw with amazement, in the middle of the Mapocho River, dead bodies of men and women floating in the current.

On the slopes of the San Cristobel Mountain, which overlooked our home, overnight there appeared cadavers of people who had been killed in various ways. In fact, it is estimated that several thousand people died or disappeared during the repression.

Those two years were filled with tensions and danger. All of the work of INDEPTH, the projects and everything else, suffered. Nothing could be finished properly. The civil disorder had caused immense disillusion and frustration. Nevertheless, you could also say that this was a learning experience that taught us some tremendous lessons on a personal, family, and ministerial level.

I had come from a successful pastorate where each day I had experienced a continual flow of the Spirit within the church, and precious fellowship with pastors of differing theological backgrounds and persuasions, but united by the Holy Spirit and the Word of God. Now I had entered a completely new dimension, one where the separation between movements, councils and denominations was the overriding emphasis characterizing the evangelical church in Chile.

Truly, the situation in Chile was a big disappointment for me. I had embarked on an adventure that was not edifying and which brought me to a spiritual wasteland where I was overwhelmed by persistent doubts. Feeling compelled to reinterpret everything that I had experienced and known until that time, I sank into a deep depression. I felt like I was only hanging by a thread of salvation. That was the only thing of which I was certain of, my salvation. Everything else in the church was giving me a nauseating sense of insecurity.

In this state of spiritual despair I was able to look upward and glimpse a tiny beam of divine light descending, and by the mediation and strength of the Lord I was able to rise out of my depression. Fortified by my intimate relationship with my God, I climbed back step by step and was again able to experience fullness of life as a servant of the Lord Jesus Christ.

I had made a two-year commitment to serve with INDEPTH ministry and those two years were about to end. I had not the slightest desire to renew the contract. Even though they pleaded with me to continue working for them, I had decided it was time to draw to a close.

During the last two months of my stay in Chile two things occurred that made my decision clear. In the midst of our preparations to leave, packing suitcases and saying farewells, I received an invitation. Pastor Javier Vazquez, a fine person with whom I had a beautiful friendship, extended an invitation to the inauguration of his church building, which would later be named the Evangelical Cathedral, the Pentecostal Methodist Church of Jotabeche. Jotabeche was the name of the street on which the church was located, on a corner at an intersection of the most important street in Chile, the Alameda (or Bernardo O'Higgins Avenue). The building, with its magnificent façade and imposing size, was impressive. Several times over the years I have preached from the pulpit of this church.

On the day of the inauguration a multitude of between 20 or 30 thousand people arrived at this place. There were so many people that the main avenue was jammed. People from within the country as well as from other countries were trying to enter the building.

To my surprise and without my knowing it, the invitation that I had in my coat pocket was special --so special that when

I showed it to the ushers, they quickly opened a way for me through the crowd and led me to a door that would take me directly inside the building. My reserved seat was directly in front of the pulpit on the first row.

A little while later, two very important officials of the Chilean government arrived. One of them was none other than President Pinochet. He was ushered to a seat, along with a general who was one of his advisors, to my left. At my right was the executive secretary of the Bible Societies, Pastor Isaias Gutierrez. Only one seat separated me from General Pinochet.

The meeting was a bit strange. The purpose was the dedication of the new building; however, the entire program seemed to focus on oratorical praise of the person and activities of Augusto Pinochet.

The event ended with a sea of comments, greetings, hugs, and laughter. I shook hands with the president, an obsequious grin on my face. Later I, being half dumbstruck, half speechless, and with a very naive mindset when it comes to the processes of political dimension, spoke with Isaias Gutierrez.

"How tremendous everything was! Right? What a good meeting!" I exclaimed.

But Isaías was angry. Not with me, because we were good friends, but at what we had just witnessed. He answered: "What are you saying? What do you mean, *good*? Didn't you notice that there was not one prayer, not one Bible reading at the dedication of a Christian church building?"

My eyes were opened. And with that question, just like a ray of light, illumination flooded my brain. I did not need him to say anything more; I fully understood why Isaías was angry. Quickly, I reflected on the program and the message, if you could call it that, given by Bishop Mamerto Mancilla. I realized, frightened, that everything had been an exaltation of the president, and there were innumerable promises that had a distinctly political tone.

That experience, along with other incidents that I experienced during my time in that country, taught me about the terrible and dangerous error that is committed whenever the church makes alliances with political powers. That event had consequences that, in my judgment, were disastrous; and the experience taught me an object lesson about the deep truth of the words of our Lord Jesus Christ: "Give to Caesar what is Caesar's, and to God what is God's" (Matthew 22:21).

Another unforgettable experience, one I can now look back on with humor but did not seem so funny at the time, occurred while I was preparing to leave Chile.

Around the time of the inauguration at Jotabeche, I was afflicted with a toothache. And what a toothache it was! It was so painful that I was compelled to visit a dentist.

The doctor, a very large Argentine man, gave me some reason that I cannot recall for not being able to extract the tooth. He told me that he could only extract it by breaking it—what a dreadful dentist! Stupidly, I submitted to his professional opinion. That man, with an iron instrument and a huge wooden mallet, struck my tooth and broke it into pieces, but it was then that something awful happened.

One piece of the tooth became embedded in the gum, and then, no matter what methods the dentist tried, he was not able to find it. I watched in a daze as he placed the pieces of my tooth on a table, one by one, placing the bits together like a jigsaw puzzle until it was clear there was one piece missing. Even though he searched my mouth for a while, he never found it, and so this dentist promptly declared the surgery over and sent me home.

The pain, of course, did not cease. The extraction of the tooth was quite a calamity in my life. I will remember that dentist as long as I live. The pain continued for months and months; almost a year. Later, in the United States, it took minor surgery to extract the ghastly piece of tooth.

With all of these experiences on my mind, I bid farewell and ended my work in Chile. My goodbyes were said with a tinge of bitterness. I was leaving extremely disappointed, feeling very empty as a consequence of my spiritual wasteland and on top of that my tooth had been hammered. That was the last straw. I left Chile with a mantle of sadness, even though it was a country that I had always loved and admired.

CHAPTER 22

SOJOURN IN CHILE: THE SWEET SIDE

However, not everything in Chile had been an arid desert. Not at all! It would not be fair if I described everything in those two years as bleak and bitter. That stage of my life was difficult and stressful, true. However, I learned some extremely important lessons. Several very relevant events happened there in terms of the work of the Lord.

One of these came from observing the disorder then prevalent in the ecclesiastical situation in Chile: the petulance, the arrogance, and the divisions in some of the evangelical churches. There was, in reality, a state of anarchy. Amid all of that confusion, my wife Noemi noticed, with better discernment than mine, the strange mood in the local church, and she asked me not to commit her to get involved.

Rather, she devoted herself to organizing small groups for Bible study and prayer in the neighborhood known in the Chilean capital city as Barrio Alto. That urban neighborhood was home to many professional and business people; these were people with the economic resources for good living. This was a class of people who, at least at that time, never attended Protestant churches. Evangelicals kept their distance from them, and the rich people saw the Protestants as poor people to be scorned.

The former said this kind of people did not want anything to do with the Gospel, which was not really true. The latter didn't want anything to do with the stereotypes or anomalous forms of worship; but they were hungry and thirsty for God. How impressive it was to see these people seeking God with all their hearts! This became one of the most beautiful experiences that we had in Chile. Noemi organized several groups. I helped her whenever I had spare time after fulfilling my responsibilities at INDEPTH. At the meetings for married couples we reached many people from the highest social class of Chile.

Out of those cell groups, there were some young disciples, mere boys at that time who, when we left them, did not seem to have much in their future, but have since become formidable servants of God, making a tremendous difference in the history of Chile. The Mottesi family remembers with much pleasure the case of Nora's mother, the wife of a Navy captain, a family of high society, with famous surnames, expensive jewels, and sumptuous mansions. Nora was caring for her elderly mother, who was suffering from terminal throat cancer, when the two of them began attending one of the study groups led by Noemi. They converted, surrendering themselves completely to the Lord. The elderly woman, upon reading her Bible, learned about the need for water baptism, and she purposed to obey this ordinance of our Lord before the cancer consumed her.

Noemi explained that we could not baptize her at that moment because, even though I was an ordained minister, I was not pastoring a local church at the time. Our work was to provide assistance to the churches, and we could not in any way circumvent the local church authorities. Noemi suggested that she could go to an established church and speak to the pastor about her need to be baptized, and also, afterward, to be enrolled as a member of an assembly of Christians.

She very solicitously followed the advice and inquired at one church, but was told that they could not baptize her unless she attended their services for a certain amount of time, and also attended their discipleship courses, a requirement that would take weeks, or even months.

At that point Nora went back to my wife, Noemi, and said: "Look, my mother will probably not live long enough to fulfill the pastor's requirement of completing the classes for water baptism. I am sure of it. You and I know that she has converted. My question is: is there anything that prevents her from being water baptized? If your husband Alberto could do it, I would be very grateful to you. Ask him to make an exception, even though he is not pastoring a church here; please take into account that my mother is in the final days of her life."

I really would have preferred to abstain from complying with her request because I am very respectful of the local church. However, I considered this situation an exception to the rule. I called a local pastor and explained to him the critical state of the elderly woman's health and my decision to officiate at the water baptism. He told me: "Do it. I don't see any problem, understanding that these are special circumstances."

Noemi organized a small group of women from the family's social circle. Together we went to the foot of the mountain, quite high on the slope, to a place where a river flowed slowly and the water was deep and, expectedly, very cold. And so it was that this isolated and unanticipated site was chosen as a place for the baptism of the elderly woman.

Dressed in clothing appropriate for the occasion, I stepped into the river while the gathered group of women sang. The water, flowing from thawing snow on the high mountain, was extremely cold. Suddenly I felt my extremities starting to freeze, my hands and feet quickly turning purple. This was truly liquid ice. I debated in my mind whether to continue or to call off the water baptism. I thought: "Surely the elderly woman will die on me in this place. When I put her in the water she will not be able to resist death, but she has been so insistent." I feared she'd go from these frigid waters straight to the Kingdom of Heaven. Then I said to myself: "Well, let's go ahead in the Name of the Lord."

To make the ceremony as short as possible, I called her for water baptism as soon as I could. After the woman got in the water, instead of allowing me to immerse her immediately, she began to sing, and then she decided to give a testimony to those who were standing on the river bank, talking about what Christ had done in her life. Meanwhile, I felt like I would die from the cold. When she stopped speaking, I baptized her, and at that instant --I don't know how to explain it in theological terms-- the elderly woman was completely healed of her cancer.

We left that place feeling an indescribable happiness. We forgot about the coldness in our bones. We went to a house nearby, home of one of the women in attendance. We drank hot tea and ate with joy, and that elderly lady lived several more years in perfect health as a powerful testimony of the mercy of God.

These events were the sweet and buffering side of what God did for us in Chile, so that we would remain faithful and without grievances s about the ministry that He had given us to do. It was a lesson from heaven that we would never forget.

CHAPTER 23

AN ASSOCIATE OF PAUL FINKENBINDER

While we were still in the country of Chile, another unusual event became one of the most glorious moments of my life. It had been some time since I had had the privilege of meeting Paul Finkenbinder, popularly known in Latin America as "Hermano Pablo." Even though I already knew of him, it was in 1971 that I had occasion to meet him personally. In that year, his campaign coordinator, Brother Izy Vega, arranged some meetings for me in Southern California. During those visits I stayed at Paul's house, under his roof. Our relationship immediately deepened. His office in Costa Mesa was a pleasant place for me.

During that same time, Paul had to travel to Mexico for the purpose of preaching at two conventions, one in Monterrey and the other in the capital city, in the country's Federal District. He invited me to go with him, and I was not averse to the idea. The scheduled dates were not a problem for me. My speaking engagements would be over by then and, from Mexico, I could continue my journey back to my country.

During the international conference in Monterrey, halfway through the service, I noticed Paul and another American man walking toward the place where I was seated. Suddenly, in short order, they had placed hands on me and Paul was saying: "We feel that the Lord wants you to be the preacher. Take my place."

I stood stiff as a board while they prayed for me; my thoughts were colliding in my mind. In only a few minutes they would be calling the preacher to the podium, and these two noble brothers had decided that I should be the preacher.

I picked up my Bible, all the while fervently imploring the assistance of the Holy Spirit, and then confronted the task at hand. I believed that God had spoken to them. I felt the anointing of the Father and proclaimed what He inspired in me. That opportunity was a beautiful blessing.

The same thing was repeated again in the Federal District of Mexico City. Paul was to speak at a meeting in an area near the capital city, in a theater. However, he was so hoarse that he asked me to replace him in the pulpit.

During those days of close fellowship with Paul, he invited me to work with his team. I informed him that I could not because I was working with INDEPTH. That was the time when, during several months of 1971 and 1972, I was working part-time for this ministry from Buenos Aires and traveling continually to Chile.

Then in 1973, after I had taken up residence in the nation of Chile, we invited Paul to speak at a crusade hosted by INDEPTH. While the crusade was being organized, I was discussing the ecclesiastical situation and my disappointment with my experience there, and Paul repeated his request that I work with his association. I was committed to INDEPTH, however, so I once more I rejected his invitation.

The following year I received financial assistance from Paul so that I could attend the Congress of Evangelism in Lausanne, Switzerland. During this world congress I received blessings and instruction, and Paul once again insisted and stressed his desire that I work alongside him in his evangelistic efforts.

By then, I was feeling inclined to accept. The idea had been beating around in my head for some time, even more so now that I was experiencing a spiritual drought in my own life. Paul's invitation at that time seemed like refreshing water on a hot summer afternoon.

INDEPTH was flesh of my flesh and blood of my blood. It was what had given me a vision for discipleship, for the mobilization of the church, and for conceptualizing evangelism in a way that is still the mode in which I operate.

Truly, those were my people, my family, those with whom I fellowshipped and shared similar ideals; but deep inside of me, I was feeling like a little ant trying to move a dead elephant. I perceived that God, and I say this with fear and trembling, was not at that moment breathing on these denominational structures. My co-workers at INDEPTH asked me to continue working with them. We had a wonderful relationship and my ministry among them was growing more and more, nevertheless, something was calling me out, something was telling me that God did not want to use me only as a coordinator, as a promoter, as a motivator, but that He had other plans for me. The Heavenly Father was calling me to a new world, and also to be dependent only on Him.

So, finally, I accepted the invitation to work with Paul. The transition to his ministry seemed natural because of the repeated invitations, the beautiful friendship that we enjoyed, and the deep respect and admiration that I felt for him. In addition, Paul's ministry was being carried out in a non-denominational setting, and I saw an enormous potential for expanding my own ministry by working at his side.

Now as part of Paul's team—Hermano Pablo, as we called him—I returned to my hometown in Argentina, where we lived for the next eight months. I traveled constantly throughout Latin America and the United States, until we realized that moving to Southern California was a necessity. Noemi and I took whatever we could fit in suitcases and moved the family to the "great country of the North."

Once settled, I began to work at the offices of Hermano Pablo in Costa Mesa as director of the pastoral department and as an associate evangelist. I learned so much from Hermano Pablo! Only God can fully repay his generosity. He showed me the secrets of preaching on the radio, the personality of a man of God, the humanity of a ministry, and so much more.

However, after almost two years of working with Paul, I began to experience a renewed feeling of spiritual drought. I had a sense of disappointment about the things that I was doing. My office hours began to be a burden. Even though I maintained a work level that produced more or less acceptable results, I was not happy. It was as if I had entered a freezer that was slowly paralyzing my nerves and muscles. I felt a spiritual coldness. I held personal devotions only now and then.

I already knew about the kind of life that can arise in the spiritual realm. Just as in Chile, I again began to be aware of the rigors of entering a spiritual wasteland while still in ministry. I felt alone, devoid of strength, crushed.

I believe this was the method that God used on those two occasions, to signal that it was time for me to move from the place where I was standing. He had other purposes for me and this was His way of telling me. But naturally, the experience was very distressing for me.

My own ministry was growing alongside that of Hermano Pablo. Like a son that reaches maturity and wants to seek his own destiny, feeling that he must take charge of developing the necessary aptitude for independence, and then jumps into a vacuum without knowing what will be the consequences of his fearless deed; so it was for me. Almost without resources, without acquaintances in a country of strange customs and an unknown language, with children to support, my family took a step of faith. Very deep inside of me there was a certainty that God was standing behind all of this, and that if He is involved in the matter, there is no risk or danger. He would bring us into safe harbor.

Noemi and I got the idea in our heads of starting our own evangelistic association. It was bold to think of such a thing when we had so many limitations. Economic resources? Zero. Relationship with local churches that could provide support? Few. Working with Hermano Pablo had seemed to us like a utopia, but nonetheless I resigned my job. He and I had a relationship of complete understanding. He wisely understood my need. There was no rift between us or anything of that nature; on the contrary, I left with his blessing.

Hermano Pablo, from the very beginning of our ministry, has been a permanent member of our Board of Directors. His counsel, his vision, his love for the Lord, all has remained as a continual fount of instruction and a role model to be imitated. Paul has been and continues to be one of my heroes in my Christian walk.

Soon after I decided to establish the evangelistic association, my spiritual strength returned. Now I could palpably sense that God was returning to His place at the center of my nervous system. And this would be confirmed to me some time later, but, before that, several events would occur.

CHAPTER 24

IN A CHURCH PARKING LOT

I was meditating on the idea of establishing my own ministry one day at mid-morning, while driving home alone in my car, when I was overcome by anxiety about the future of my family and my ministerial work.

"If I stop being an associate of Hermano Pablo," I found myself worrying, "I will be alone in a country foreign to me, lacking a command of its language, with few acquaintances, without churches to support me, and in a very difficult economic situation. On top of that, I would need to take sole initiative to create the evangelistic association. "All of these thoughts made me want to pray.

As I kept driving, I noticed a church building ahead, and drove into its parking lot. At that moment I did not see one soul walking in that place. There were only birds flying from one tree to another. The weather that day was warm. There in the car I was talking to God: "What should I do, Lord? What do I do?"

I knew that my prayer was filled with anguish. This burden was very heavy.

In the silence and solitude of that parking lot, the Lord spoke to me: "I want you to start your own evangelistic ministry."

I heard the Voice of the Lord speaking so clearly, that I was filled with a precious calm. I noticed how the anxieties and concerns flew away, making room in my heart for the wonderful peace of God.

I no longer had any doubts. The promise of God was so real to me that I left that sunny place filled with deep joy and serenity. I praised and adored Him while thick tears flowed from my eyes.

So, on a Friday near the end of September 1976, I submitted my resignation, leaving behind the work that I had been doing for Hermano Pablo Ministries. This job had provided my economic support for two years and it was over; now I would depend only on God. One of the ways that I, as a traveling evangelist could continue supporting my family financially was by preaching at the churches that invited me and accepting an offering from them. Here, once again, was the need for the thread of faith.

By that time I had been living in the United States for a year and a half, and the salary that I received was enough to comfortably cover the family's expenses. However, now that I had left the job at Hermano Pablo Ministries to build my own ministry out of nothing, I trusted that God would provide for his servant.

On Sunday, two days after I submitted my resignation, I had an invitation to preach at a church in Los Angeles, California, at the People's Church shepherded by Brother Mike.

I went there along with my entire family, and the service, with a good number in attendance, was agreeably in progress. The spiritual atmosphere was pleasant. The hymns were sung with great enthusiasm. I participated in every part of that worship service from the place designated for me on the platform and, with barely five minutes to go before I was to walk to the sacred podium, I suddenly heard an emphatic voice saying to me: "Look at your wife." I obeyed, extending my gaze to the middle of the auditorium where Noemi and my two sons were seated. Again I heard the same voice: "Now, look at your sons. Study their faces."

I saw them and watched their little faces, tender and sweet, waiting for daddy to begin preaching. Then I heard the voice, in a critical and serious way, once again directed at me. "You will be the cause of their disgrace. The decision you have made will put your family to ruin. Your sons will suffer. They will not have money enough even to eat."

Immediately I realized that this voice was Satan. It could not have been God. He had already spoken to me and called me to His service. The demon was restlessly trying to trouble me, using what would pain me the most: my family.

Having discarded in the name of Jesus that entire line of negative reasoning, I began to present the morning message. The Lord helped me with his anointing as I gave bread from heaven to his people. I concluded by turning the service back over to the pastor. Then he announced that they would be taking an offering.

"Well, my brothers, we will be collecting a missionary offering, but I want to tell you that this one will be dedicated to a missionary pastor who has recently arrived in this city and is only passing through. Brother Mottesi lives nearby and we always have him with us so we will not give him the offering this time. Is that alright with you, Brother Mottesi?"

What could I say? This was my test of fire. Later, the demon would batter me all over again, corroding me from the inside out: "See! See, I told you so!" I lowered my head and prayed to my Heavenly Father. This act of obedient prayer—this, and only this—was the thing that I knew I must continue do.

This was the first Sunday that I preached after submitting my resignation. Now that I was going to depend on God, Satan would tempt me and Pastor Mike's decision was used to test the reality of my faith. Was it God or the offering? What or who was really my source of sustenance?

Blessed be my faithful and generous Father! Tenderly He placed in me the right perspective. He has never, never left us without help. He has always provided and continues to provide what is necessary, so that his servant and his family will lack for nothing. And even more, with the great responsibility that was placed on my shoulders: to go forward with the Alberto Mottesi Evangelistic Association.

CHAPTER 25
THE FIRST BABBLINGS

The first step was to initiate the paperwork necessary to establish a corporate presence for the association. While this was going on, I did not lose any time. Invitations from churches began to arrive, so that my schedule started filling up.

My office was at my house. Noemi and I typed the letters and the newsletters that we needed to send. At every church that I visited I mentioned our new project. I encouraged people to support the work, and soon we began to hear from the first supporters of our fledgling association. I never failed to keep them informed from month to month about the work done and the projects yet to be done.

Brother Jorge Garcia and his wife Marilys joined our organization, and began to work with us as a team. They were a blessing come down from heaven.

From the very beginning, the association had been organized with the idea of adding a team of godly men who believed in our ministry, who were wise and experts in various areas, but, above all, who loved us greatly, enough to be honest and speak to us as father to son, so that things would go well with us and we would remain in alignment with God's purpose.

During the early days of January 1977, we were given the official permit for the Alberto Mottesi Evangelistic Association. Thus my work began under the legal framework of the North American nation. The first receipts for the tax exemption of our donors were mailed out with great joy.

And meanwhile churches continued to invite us. Our working territory continued to expand. In addition to engagements within the state of California, we held campaigns in Chicago, Illinois, in Texas, and in Puerto Rico. The public impact of those meetings was great and glorious, and we saw a great many people surrendering themselves to God and finding a new reason for living. One man, whom I was able to guide to the feet of Christ at a moment when he was emotionally shattered, was completely transformed. In less than two months he had the joy of having won his entire family for Jesus.

While I was on my way to a preaching engagement in San Francisco, I had an unusual experience on the airplane. A voice inside of me said: "Why are you working and working without rest? Why are you asking people to help you in this endeavor?"

Suddenly, I lost control over my emotions. I felt a chill, and then became feverish. The flight attendant was offering me something and the woman sitting next to me wanted to strike up a conversation, but I could not speak to them. The Presence of the Lord in my body was so strong that, stammering in my mind, without being able to hold back the tears in my eyes, I answered: "Lord, You know why I am doing this. I feel a fire inside my bones. You have poured out Your love in my soul and I cannot remain silent."

This passion is what takes me from place to place, from one church to another. With a full schedule and without much rest, I travelled to Canada, Mexico and Puerto Rico. The experience of seeing people surrendering to Christ is always our comfort and our strength. To see so many happy faces overflowing with new life becomes the reason not to faint or grow weary.

One day God stirred in me the idea of beginning a radio ministry. I had already preached on radio and television on many occasions. However, God wanted me to develop a permanent media ministry, continuous and lasting. One evening in October 1977, I sketched a plan. I put everything down on paper and convened a meeting with my Board of Directors to present the proposal for their approval.

When the meeting was in progress, I declared to them with great enthusiasm:

"My brothers, we will be going into radio."

"Very good!" some of them said, almost as if I had told a joke at a party.

I continued.

"In the coming year, in the first week of March, we will begin with daily broadcasts on 20 radio stations."

There was a sepulchral silence. No one said a word, although I do believe that some were thinking: "Poor boy! Surely he must have a fever! It is good that his work as an evangelist going from church to church is growing, that—thank God—he is able to earn enough to support his family, but daily broadcasts on 20 radio stations? Please!"

Six months before the launching date, I had prepared the pilot programs and began the job of finding contacts at the radio stations. When the first week of March arrived, our daily broadcast did not begin at 20 radio stations. We had 68 radio stations that had agreed to begin broadcasting our program: "You and Alberto Mottesi!"

It was extraordinary to see the hand of God made manifest. Soon afterward the number of radio stations climbed to 100, to 200 and to 300, in several countries. At present, there are about 2,000 stations broadcasting our program throughout Latin America, the United States, and Spain.

And with this change and growth, the work intensified. There were very late nights when I worked nonstop to record 24 programs in one session. It did not matter that we were sometimes overwhelmed by physical and mental exhaustion. At those moments of intense fatigue, we experienced the Spirit of God giving us the necessary strength to complete the task.

This had been another evidence of the thread of faith—from the moment of awareness that God was ordering us to carry out this work, through not knowing, or even imagining, how this expense could be covered. I simply drafted a plan and scribbled some directions, trusting that the Father would support me. I had presented the challenge of 20 radio stations, but my faith was no match for God's provision. I believe that at that particular point in the thread of faith God could have said something like this: "Ah! You made a mistake, Albertito; there were not just 20 stations for you but 68!"

So, one day I sent a letter to my supporters with the following message:

"Today I want to share with you some information about the radio program. This is a very important part of the ministry (and a very costly one!).

The process goes more or less like this: We begin with the writing of each message. Then we do the recording at a studio in Whittier, California. This takes hours of intense work and prayer.

When we receive the master tapes, we listen to the recording again to make sure that it has been edited correctly and to determine whether pertinent corrections need to be done. Then, we send the master tapes to another company that duplicates them onto cassettes to use by radio stations for four weeks of programming. Everything is then mailed to our office and we finish the processing there. We have to stick labels on the tapes, put the tapes in plastic boxes, print the address labels, prepare any paperwork required by customs inspectors, and affix proper postage on the packages. At that point, everything is ready for mailing to the radio stations.

We recently renewed all of the contracts with the radio stations. In the process of doing so, we received some very valuable information about the impact of our program at each station. The programming directors have evaluated our production and made some helpful suggestions. With this information, we have discontinued some radio stations and added others.

The program airs Monday through Saturday. According to estimates, about 15 million people listen to our program each day. One important detail to note is that we are not asking for financial help or giving out any address on the program. We are hoping that the people of God will collaborate so that the program will be completely evangelistic."

How could anyone doubt that God was behind all of this radio programming labor? Day by day it kept growing for the glory of my Lord.

One day, while traveling on an airplane, which for me was and is almost as common as driving an automobile, all the emergency signals suddenly went off. The voice of the captain sounded brusque and a bit hurried over the speakers: "We are experiencing an emergency and we must return to the New Orleans airport." The next thirty minutes were extremely tense, and time seemed to stand still. Some passengers feigned indifference. Some laughed, but the laughter sounded phony. Others maintained an impenetrable silence. The night before I had concluded a glorious bilingual campaign at a Nazarene Church in El Monte, California, and had spent the entire night working at my desk to leave several matters in order before leaving on this trip. My eyelids ached with sleepiness.

The airplane could not land and we were circling the airport. Unexpectedly, the air conditioning stopped working and everyone began to perspire in the suffocating heat.

After having traveled so many times by airplane, this was the second or third time that I had experienced a small scare of this kind. "Lord," I mused in my thoughts, "if the time has come for me to go and be with You, may it be as You will. However, I feel badly for my family. And, besides, there are so many things still to do! So many people do not know about Your love! And, Lord, would our dreams be left unfulfilled? What about the crusades with which we want to reach all of the nations? And the Schools of Evangelism? What a huge impact they have had! What a great need there is to train and mobilize every Christian toward a deeper and more consecrated life! And the Pastoral Institutes? And the literature? The series of booklets that we recently published are having a greater influence than we imagined possible. And the radio, Lord? Are You aware of the hundreds of radio stations that are broadcasting our program? You did this miracle! And the television? Don't You believe that if we could put a regularly scheduled program on television we could reach many millions more? Are You aware of this, Lord? My life is full of dreams. These are dreams of serving You, of loving You, of preaching Your Word, of stopping people on the road of life and telling them that their existence can be different if they will surrender to the love of God."

My eyes were wet with tears. Finally, I exclaimed in my heart: "I love You, Lord. You know that I love You. You know all things … and, all is well."

CHAPTER 26
TELEMUNDO: AN UNUSUAL EPISODE

One of the dreams that I cherished during the early years of our evangelistic association ministry was to produce our own television program, and this plan gradually became a reality. Before we knew it, we had already produced the first pilot programs.

Naturally, God prepares us long in advance for the ways in which He desires to use us. Whenever I was in front of television cameras, I thought about those times when, as a young pastor in Argentina, night after night I delivered a goodnight message to the television audience. That experience was the beginning of my familiarity with the technological advances of our era. After those initial babblings on the medium of television, I'd had several other opportunities. However, the television ministry had not yet become a permanent feature.

Now it seemed to be God's timing. The programs were sent to the television directors in several countries who knew of our ministry. The director at one radio station in Cuenca, Ecuador, wrote to us: "We are very happy with your radio program, which has a great audience and public impact. I want you to know that our company also owns a television channel and we would like to offer you free broadcast time for any television programs sent by your ministry."

Truly, this was our motivation. We understood the significant potential of television for massive distribution of the gospel message. It would not be easy, however. One major obstacle stood in our way: the high cost that television programming represented, and our own lack of funding.

At the most, and with great financial sacrifice on our part, we might manage to produce a few programs; however, the cost in terms of airtime was out of the realm of our human possibilities. We did know, on the other hand, that if God was in the matter, then no one and nothing could prevent the fulfillment of this dream of proclaiming the Word by means of television broadcasts. For that reason, when we had the first television programs ready and sent to television stations that had offered free airtime on their schedules, it was a cause of great rejoicing in our lives. We manifestly saw how God opened doors so that his Gospel would be proclaimed through this powerful broadcast media.

Surely you can imagine the great physical, mental, and economic toll taken by this new facet of our ministry. But that was the least of our concerns. The obstacles were vanishing by the power of God, and we were discovering, for the benefit of our spiritual strength, new paths and opportunities that we had never dreamed of achieving.

One of the experiences that intensified our boldness and enthusiasm for reaching goals in the Name of the Lord happened in Puerto Rico, on one of the most important television channels of Latin America.

Telemundo, a network serving Spanish-speaking Latin-America, is an important enterprise, a power player in the broadcast industry, the most important channel in Puerto Rico, the "Isle of Enchantment." To think of entering that market, of wanting to participate in its programming when one has no money is an unimaginable dream, a utopian ideal.

Only companies with vast resources are welcome. People like Alberto Mottesi, a street and church preacher, without big bills in his pocket, are left on the outside.

However...

One day, I visited the office of the programming director for this television station in Puerto Rico. The executive looked me over from head to toe, taking in every detail of my appearance, trying to detect what kind of person had the audacity to make contact with him, because, of course, the time afforded by these people can be measured in pure gold. Needless to say, if the man who dares to approach does not project a business image, it is a waste of time.

He listened attentively to my detailed explanation of our television program and its production. The program's focus was on the problems of the family and the city, attempting to provide Biblical and Christian solutions.

"My predicament, Mr. Director, is that I do not have the funding to purchase the airspace. I would like Telemundo to provide us with free space.

"Please, Mr. Mottesi! Here, even the Catholic mass pays! Believe me," and he raised his hand in front of me, then moved it down horizontally, as if cutting the air, "everyone, absolutely everyone, pays. It is impossible to agree to your request. I am sorry but we do not have free space."

I persisted, trying to make him see the moral value of the content of our production, and, besides, the urgent need for this type of material in a modern society so steeped in depravity, suicide, divorce, drugs, alcoholism, etc.

The director of programming remained firm, however.

"I truly am sorry, Mr. Mottesi, but it is completely impossible to agree to your request."

"Then do me a favor. Look at our materials, evaluate them, think about it, and give me another opportunity to meet with you. We will talk about it then. I am sure that you will change your opinion."

"I don't believe so. The policy of this company is categorical.

Nevertheless, I will not lose anything by looking at your program. Leave it with me and I promise to review it. Come back tomorrow."

I cordially said goodbye. The executive gave me a patronizing smile, as if he were an understanding father thinking: "This poor lad is a dreamer. He is crazy if he thinks that he will get on the air without paying."

The next day I arrived punctually for our appointment, but this time his attitude was different. He seemed more agitated. He was shouting orders here and there, moving papers around on his cluttered desk, the telephone attached to one ear.

"Excuse me, Mr. Mottesi. I will be with you in a moment," he said.

"Don't worry about me. I can wait."

I noticed his flurry of activity, his conversation filled with television industry jargon. His office was a collage of paintings and photographs of television celebrities, graphic designs, and calendars.

"Now we can talk, Mr. Mottesi. Please forgive the delay. There are so many details to fix that I scarcely have time."

Without giving me a chance to say a compassionate word, he abruptly continued to speak:

"As I promised, last night I was able to watch your program. Congratulations, your content is of very good quality and very professionally done; but I cannot give you free time."

"Mr. Director, it is a matter of great urgency that the people of this community find answers to their problems. Television is the ideal medium for providing this service. Please make an exception."

"I cannot. Believe me, Mr. Mottesi. My programming calendar is crammed. We have a long line of companies who want space and we cannot give them space because our contracts do not allow it. Forgive me. If paying for the broadcast it is hard to get a space, it's about impossible to get it without money."

I ended my plea, contemplating this obstacle that seemed so impossible to remove. I had done my best to persuade him with my words, I had tried to conquer that huge barrier, but he was unmoved. Slowly, I stood to my feet, preparing to leave. The man, impeccably dressed, did the same. We shook hands. A grimace on his face seemed to say "not a chance." I was walking toward the door, on my way out of the room, and reaching for the doorknob when, suddenly, I turned halfway around and looked him straight in the eye, speaking with great authority.

"You are a father," I said, assuming so based only on his age. "You know as well as I do that our children and our families urgently need a program like this."

I am certain that God used those words. What impact did they have on the mind of that unconverted man? I do not know. But what I did see next was something marvelous.

The programming director bowed his head, staring intently at the glass panel covering his desk. He paused for a few moments, motionless. Time seemed to stand still. The silence in that office was transformed into a language of the conscience, a place where individuals are rarely allowed to tread, at the risk of diminishing human liberty. What was he thinking? What mental images were shaking his strong will? What changes should be made in the programming schedule? To pay or not to pay? Why has this preacher come here with this request? Do my children really need this program? Will these truths help many people? What would my superiors say about such an addition to the lineup?

He raised his eyes and said the following: "Mottesi ... you are right. The space is yours."

Hearing those words was like hearing the angels speaking to me. That entire moment of emotional tension awaiting his verdict was transformed into an expression of sincere gratitude: "Thank you, Mr. Director. Thank you very much."

I left that office savoring the precious and unspeakable answer of my Lord. He had done everything. He is the one who changes hearts. He waits until the last moment so that it will be very clear that these things are coming from Him. My heart never ceases to thank my God for His love, His blessing, and His power.

That was the beginning. We now had free airtime for programming on the most important television channel in Puerto Rico, Telemundo. The work of establishing a permanent presence on the airwaves was about to begin.

The change in the schedule of programs affected one journalist who for many years had hosted a talk show interviewing guests. Her airtime was shortened to half an hour. The poor woman was very angry with those responsible for the program scheduling, with me, with the television channel, with God, with everyone. I was very consciously aware that I was facing a battle at the television channel and that I needed to do something in order to keep the program "You and Alberto Mottesi" on the air in Puerto Rico.

And that's when I had an idea.

I have never told anyone, but I organized an unprecedented campaign of handwritten letters addressed to the director of programming at Telemundo's Channel 2. Because I had so many friends at local churches, I distributed to the faithful congregants some sample letters containing possible texts that could be adapted and penned in their own handwriting for mailing to the television executives. Often, the church attendees also asked people in their neighborhoods to write letters to Telemundo. Soon an avalanche of hundreds, perhaps thousands of letters, arrived at the office of the programming director.

"We congratulate you on the program, 'You and Alberto Mottesi.'"

"What a good idea!"

"We have needed a program like that for a long time!"

"Thank you. My family has been greatly influenced by this program."

"We fervently support this airtime."

"Alberto Mottesi is a great preacher. He should be kept on the air for a very long time."

"Very good! This program has been very good for my family."

Those who wrote the letters were common people, and their letters were not filled with religious language.

One day I was again visiting Telemundo's department of programming, where quite a few people working in the room were in a state of constant activity. When I entered, great was my surprise to see that all the employees stopped what they were doing and stood to their feet to greet me. It almost seemed as if General MacArthur had entered that place and not Mottesi; all that was lacking was a military salute to complete the picture of conquering hero.

Then I found out that they were very impressed by the avalanche of correspondence that was arriving at that office. They thought I was a real celebrity. The director cordially welcomed me with a hug. Later, I learned that the journalist whose program had been cut short had angrily appealed to the director of programming to reclaim the scheduled airtime. He told her: "Look," opening several boxes to show her the letters, "this is just a portion of the correspondence that we have received about the program from Alberto Mottesi. Even though you already know this, I will repeat it. We, as a broadcast medium, are influenced by what the public wants. Here is the proof. Alberto Mottesi's program will remain on this channel."

In fact, we remained on the air for more than a year. Hundreds of testimonies were the result of those television programs. I saw that when one desires something and works hard to accomplish it, overcoming any obstacles, success can be achieved, even more so if beyond the hard work one has faith in the One who can do all things. My spirit had been tempered from my childhood by a continuous struggle to accomplish goals that might honor my God. In that occasion He had supported me in a very unusual way, for the benefit of people whose lives were shattered by evil.

CHAPTER 27

DON'T WEAR NEW SHOES WHEN
TRAVELING BY AIRPLANE

At the beginning of my evangelistic ministry in the United States, cultivating good public relations was very important. It was essential to know a large number of leaders, so that at some future time they might invite me to preach at some campaign. For that reason, when some of my friends, pastors in California, mentioned the name of Humberto Cruz, pastor of one of the most successful churches in South Florida, and told me that it would be very important for me to know him. I knew beforehand that he was a very distinguished man, very well known, one whose work has transcended the area of his local influence. The idea did not seem disagreeable to me. The occasion presented itself during one trip that I had to make to Puerto Rico. I was on my way to the Caribbean island, and it was easy for me to spend an extra day in Miami, where our Brother Humberto was residing. To have the pleasure of meeting him, and sharing our experiences during a few hours, would be a wonderful experience. Later, we became great friends, but at that time I was a perfect stranger to him.

I made the necessary arrangements so that I could stay over in Miami. I would spend a day there and on the following morning resume my journey to the "Island of Enchantment."

On the day of my scheduled departure, I got the idea of buying new shoes. I went shopping with my wife and we chose a pair of Jarman brand shoes that felt very comfortable. After I got home with my new shoes I decided to wear them for the trip. I chose the newest pair of pants that I owned and in the mirror the combination looked perfect.

As always, Noemi took me to the Los Angeles International Airport. While I was waiting to board the airplane nothing important happened. I passed the time reading and jotting down some ideas for campaigns that would be held in Puerto Rico. I didn't notice anything strange about myself that would make me feel uncomfortable.

At the scheduled time, I boarded a huge Pan Am jumbo jet. My seat number placed me in the middle of the airplane, in the nonsmoking section. I saw that there were passengers on both sides of my seat; I noticed the airplane would be filled to capacity on this flight. A mixed crowd of passengers was engaged in endless chatter, little by little settling into their respective seats. I felt as if I were imprisoned, trapped in a parrot cage.

The flight attendants prepared us for takeoff with the security instructions. Soon we were on the runway and a few seconds later we were rapidly slicing through a cloudless, blue sky. The great city with its maze of freeways was behind me, and we were flying over the rough open spaces of North America.

The captain of the airplane informed us that our estimated flight time was approximately five hours, which would be plenty of time for me to enjoy reading, and writing some notes. I might even write some letters that I needed to mail upon returning to the office.

We were served our lunch, which I quickly dispatched. I wanted to make good use of my time on the flight. But by this point my feet were feeling tired. It's a long flight, I found myself thinking, so it would not hurt if I were to take off my shoes. With a little wind blowing from the air conditioner, surely I would feel more comfortable. As soon as I thought of it, I went ahead and kicked off my brand-new Jarmans. I could smell the scent of new shoes, and now my feet were feeling the cold air. With my extremities unconfined, I plunged fully into the activities I had planned.

The time passed to the characteristic purring of the jet engine. The rest of the people stretched out in resting position—some sleeping, others chatting softly, but most of them watching a movie or listening to music with headphones placed over their ears. Once in a while, someone would stand up and walk to the back of the airplane to find the lavatory, where the flight attendants discreetly assisted those people who solicited their services.

Suddenly, the voice of the captain was heard, shaking us out of our reverie. He was announcing that we were 45 minutes away from our destination. Time to put the shoes back on, I thought to myself. I collected my papers and placed them back in my briefcase. I set the little tray table back in its place and felt around for my shoes to put them back on. I searched for them with my own feet, and tried to slip them on without using my hands, but to my utter distress, my feet felt quite fat. I struggled, but was not able to fit my feet into the shoes. I bent over to use my hands, but still my feet wouldn't fit. Now I began to struggle with increasing desperation, seeing that all of my efforts were in vain. The shoes had staged their own rebellion and were refusing to contain my feet, which were now perhaps a little swollen. "Dear God, what should I do?"

I began to perspire and became very nervous. My neighbors were becoming aware of the battle. I felt very uncomfortable and decided to pick up my shoes. I got out of the seat and walked toward the back of the airplane, to the lavatory area, thinking that since there was a little more space there, I might be able to maneuver with greater dexterity, to get my swollen feet inside the rigid new shoes.

At the back of the airplane was a long line of people, waiting for their turn to use the facilities. Using the back of a seat for support, I attempted my struggle again, but it seemed futile as I realized much to my great consternation, that my feet had developed a tremendous resistance to the shoes. Perspiring, I paused to wipe away the sweat that dripped without permission off my forehead. A flight attendant approached to offer help.

"What seems to be the problem, sir?"

"Ma'am, I have been trying for a while now to get my feet into these shoes, and I cannot."

"Let me help you."

The kind lady tried to force one of the shoes onto my foot, but without success.

"I think that with a shoe horn we could get them on," she said, "but ..." And she paused then to think for a moment, "I don't think we have one here on the airplane. If we were to substitute a spoon instead, perhaps that could be the solution. Let me see, I'll be right back."

The attendant went to the front of the airplane and returned with a stainless steel spoon. Once again we tried to get the shoes on my feet, but it was not possible.

By that time, the people around me were becoming aware of my battle with the shoes. The flight attendant, realizing she was unable to do anything else, picked up the telephone and called the captain in the cockpit. She explained my problem to him, and he said: "Let him walk around; that might make his feet smaller."

I did not waste any time obeying that order. I began marching up and down the aisles of that huge jumbo jet, three and four times around from end to end. I noticed a thousand eyeballs starting at me, but it didn't matter. The important thing was that I put on my shoes. I didn't even want to think that I might have to walk off the airplane barefoot, carrying my new shoes in one hand. How awkward!

When I arrived back at the place where the flight attendant was waiting, I saw she had summoned another attendant, and they both tried to help. However, we realized disconsolately that the remedy of walking had not produced the intended result. They even tried again to use a spoon as a shoehorn to no avail.

Once more, the first flight attendant got on the telephone to discuss our problem with the pilot. He answered: "If walking didn't work, then have him run. With a little more exercise, I am sure that his feet will get smaller."

Once again I paced the aisles of the airplane, trotting from one end to the other. The people who earlier saw me walking, and had stared at me in disbelief, were now smiling at the sight of me running. Jovially, they expressed encouragement, some even applauded. I seemed to have become a real show, and my face was starting to blush with embarrassment. I was dripping with sweat, my heart was beating wildly, and yet my feet still were not yielding to my efforts to return them to their normal state.

We realized, the flight attendants, those who were standing in line for the lavatories, and I, that the shoes were not suited for feet as swollen and sweaty as mine. Filled with consternation and feeling dejected, with the announcement of the plane's imminent landing, I got the idea of going into the bathroom. I got in the line and when it was my turn, I took off my socks, and in the cramped quarters of that airplane lavatory, one by one I placed my feet in the sink and bathed each with cold water—a blessed solution!

Within a few minutes the swelling had gone down. Happily, I saw that the shiny new shoes were finally back where they belonged.

When I emerged from the bathroom, people saw that my feet were now shod in their Jarmans, and they smiled. I thanked the flight attendants for their help and quickly returned to my seat to prepare for landing at the Miami airport, ready to meet one who is now my great friend, my fellow pastor, Humberto Cruz.

The moral of the story: Never wear new shoes when traveling on an airplane.

CHAPTER 28

ESTABLISHING FOUNDATIONS (1977-1983)

"*To the work! To the work!*
We are servants of God,
Let us follow the path that our Master has trod;
With the balm of His counsel our strength to renew,
Let us do with our might what our hands find to do."

I always remember this old hymn from my youth. We sang it with other teenagers whenever we went out to preach on the streets and plazas of Buenos Aires. From time to time, the old hymn still comes to my mind. When it seems like my strength is failing, the Holy Spirit always brings renewal. It truly has been a rough battle throughout the years since I accepted my calling—work without vacations, a constant exercise of ministry in a zealous pursuit of human beings for God. How I wish I had a thousand lives, so that I could dedicate them all to Jesus Christ!

A position on the battlefront provides a comprehensive visual perspective. You can study the strengths of your enemy, his ferocity, his intelligence, and his resources. With such knowledge, you have a greater awareness of the enormous needs to counteract his forces. We should be there, at the frontlines! However, we spend most of the time whining because our resources are so poor and useless when measured against the massive amount of effort required. However, it is not our own work that we must do with all of our strength; it is the work of God, for which He uses His servants and endows them with power, so that His plan is carried out and His will is fulfilled.

All of those years, from 1977 to 1983, were years of laboriously developing the ministry of the Evangelistic Association, of going to and fro, from church to church. The traveling ministry was gradually building up. I held campaigns and seminars for pastors, produced for radio and television, spoke at camp meetings and workshops, etc., anything possible to set free the captives of Satan.

During the first few months, the Association operated out of a small office at a business located in Westminster, California, generously loaned by a friend, Robert De Hoop. He served a key role in the establishment of our association and the development of our ministry. Later, we would move it to the home of Jorge Garcia who, with his wife Marilys, would become a precious gift to our ministry. For the first few years they were our inseparable companions, always at our side, and they dedicated much of their lives to the Lord through our Association.

The office work has always been vital. The first letters written to people who were interested in our organization helped to develop a wonderful family of associates who yielded themselves to the vision of evangelism. The supporters of our ministry have been aware many times of our helplessness to confront the huge challenge of taking the work of God upon our shoulders, but they have also rejoiced with us to see the great wonders that the Lord has done through the efforts of this team. God has used the generous hearts of our supporters to carry out projects that at first seemed like madness.

The schedule of activities was, and continues to be, one of constant travel. Although we began in the region surrounding Los Angeles, we soon expanded to include most of the United

States, mostly places where there were large concentrations of Hispanic people.

Puerto Rico has been a second home to me. I have grown to love those people dearly. I have visited my precious "Island of Enchantment" numerous times. Some of my first campaigns at churches and broadcasts on radio and television were in that country, and I am deeply indebted to the wonderful people of Puerto Rico. From there, as if God were loosening the reins little by little, I was sent to Canada, to northern Mexico, Costa Rica, Venezuela, and Honduras, among other places, until I had visited every country of Latin America.

During those first years, the ministry established its place within the Body of Christ, His Church. It was in the local churches—churches of all kinds—that my evangelistic work would begin to harvest its first fruits. There were evangelistic campaigns lasting three days, or even an entire week. We organized Schools of Evangelism where we taught about the price to be paid in doing the work of God. It is sacrificial, yes, but remarkably joyful to know that we are placing our little grain of sand at God's disposal.

The Lord sharpened our focus on the Spanish-speaking world. And what a challenge it was to begin communicating with English-speaking people!

I remember that the first time I spoke with an interpreter was in Northern California, at one of the churches in the outskirts of San Francisco. The brother who was assisting me with the translation of my sermon and I had a friend in common who was perfectly bilingual. He would be in the audience listening. Doubtless he would be a good judge of the interpretation and could rigorously evaluate the quality of the interpreter's work. We gave the message, and at the end of the service we ran over to him and enthusiastically inquired about how the message and interpretation had sounded to him. He answered very calmly: "Oh, very good! I liked the two messages very much."

In another occasion, I had an experience of translation at Biola University during which I nearly started a small world war. I have preached at that college several times. The first time was at the gymnasium, in an auditorium filled with more than 2,000 students. The assistance of an interpreter was obviously essential.

The placed looked beautiful, filled to the brim with the upturned faces of university students listening to the message. I clearly saw their eagerness to hear the Word of God as presented through this man from Argentina. The message was dramatic. With words and phrases tinged with emotion I painted landscapes from the Bible as I retold the story of the war between the people of Israel and the Philistines. I never thought about the tremendous problem that might arise among the international students at the university. At about the time that the preaching was reaching its climax, while I was talking about the battle between David and Goliath, I exclaimed: "And the people of God were fighting against their enemies … the Philistines."

My interpreter translated it this way to the audience: "And the people of God were fighting against their enemy … the Philippines."

Alas, even though I have received invitations to minister to other cultures and languages, I am very certain that my calling is to the Spanish-speaking people. I know with certainty that my heart is continually emptied before the altar of the Lord, as I endeavor each day to gain more souls to obtain redemption and to know my God and serve Him. I am certain that there are millions of Latin people throughout the entire region of Latin America who need the knowledge of the true God. If the Lord has sent me to them, I want to work for them every day that I live on this planet, whether traveling along the jungle pathways of Tabasco, or on the expansive range of the pampas, or climbing to "the roof of the world" in Bolivia, or walking the cobblestone streets of Guatemala. I can say with Paul the Apostle, "Though I am free and belong to no man, I make myself a slave to everyone, in order to save as many as possible. I have become all things to all men, so that by all possible means I might save some. I do all this for the sake of the Gospel that I may share in its blessings." (1 Corinthians 9:19, 22b-23)

CHAPTER 29

THE TESTIMONIES OF THE ASSOCIATION

In Puerto Rico, I was invited to meet a man who was emotionally unstable, and God allowed me to bring him to the feet of Christ. When I returned two months later, that man, now completely changed and rejoicing, had won his entire family for Christ.

On another occasion, in front of a church building in the center of Los Angeles, a young man approached me and said: "Brother Alberto, you don't know me. But let me tell you about an experience I had." Without giving me time to respond, he continued speaking in a youthful and excited voice, "I purchased a recording of yours several months ago. I am the closest assistant to my pastor at our new mission. One night our pastor was not able to arrive on time for the service and unexpectedly I was given charge of the meeting. It was almost time for the message and I did not know what to preach about. During the meeting I got the idea of playing your recorded message on the sound system when the time came for the sermon. That night, two people were converted and two married couples who were on the verge of divorce decided to seek public reconciliation." Moved by the words of this young man, I embraced him and said: "Thanks to God for His blessing!"

On yet another occasion, at a service where I was preaching, there was a man in the audience who had the bearing of a business executive. Far from where he was, within the huge crowd attending the campaign service, was a woman wearing a print dress that had obviously been purchased from a high-level fashion boutique. These two people had once been married but were now separated, and precisely that week they would be receiving the paperwork finalizing their divorce. Neither of them had had any connection to churches, nor were either of the two aware of the other's presence at the meeting.

When I made the invitation, both accepted Jesus Christ. Each one said the prayer of a repentant sinner and came to the front during the altar call. When they saw each other standing side by side at the altar, they reconciled publicly, right there. How beautiful it was to see them the next Sunday at church, with their small children in tow and smiling together!

On another occasion I was in San Cristobal, Venezuela. The weather was cold and rainy. The campaign was being held at an outdoor amphitheater, a bad omen in that continuously rainy climate. It did not stop raining all day. That evening, my guide was very late arriving at my hotel to take me to the venue. When he finally arrived and drove me to the site, it looked like the service might have to be cancelled. My brother in Christ who was driving the car, Pedro, stopped near the place and told me: "Brother Mottesi, wait here so that you do not get wet. I will go and see if someone is there and I will be back right away."

"Very well," I answered.

"What a shame," I thought to myself with sadness. A few minutes later, Pedro came running. His face was shining.

"The meeting will be held, Brother Mottesi! There are at least 500 people in the rain waiting for the message."

I had never seen anything like it before. Under that persistent drizzle, 160 people came forward, their tears mixed with the raindrops. The microphones, the Bible, everything was wet. I myself was dripping wet. But that night we strongly felt the power of God working among those people. On the platform, some pastors hugged me and burst into tears, because God had visited San Cristobal.

Another time, a group of 50 adolescents who called themselves "The Tambourine," with shining faces and great rejoicing were prepared to participate in our campaign at Country Club, Puerto Rico, where there is a church shepherded by my great friend and advisor, Pastor Carmelo Terranova. The group had come from the town of Bayamon. A young girl in the group, with glowing face, introduced "The Tambourine," saying into the microphone: "For me this is a special night. I am very glad that I can attend this campaign. I received the calling of God to serve Him under the ministry of Brother Mottesi, and yesterday I began my studies at the Seminary."

I was listening to this from where I was standing, far away from the platform. My heart beat loudly, and there was only one thought deep in my soul: "Thank you, Lord!"

Without our being aware of it, there in the distance, outside the covered field in the Country Club, a more lackluster party was going on. It was a rainy night. One solitary man at that party was very bored. The salsa music that was blaring from a sound system at times blended with other strange and distant harmonies carried by the wind. The man wanted to know where those sounds were coming from. Leaving his shelter, he braved the stormy weather, looked around and then walked toward the covered field where the campaign was being held. When he arrived, he saw a lot of people, with smiling faces, chatty and obviously to him, very happy. So, he entered and sat down in a dark corner near the back of the field.

"What is this?" he asked himself. "God? They are talking about God!"

He found, quite unexpectedly, that he was very interested,

and he began to listen attentively to the message. After a while he said to himself: "God is talking to me."

When the invitation was given to accept Christ, he saw that from all over the place people were walking toward the center of the playing field. "This is what I need," he thought to himself before he, too, went forward, and there, in front of that roughly hewn square platform, he began a new life of true happiness.

During those years when we were establishing foundations, we saw several things that became increasingly clear and certain in our lives and for the Association: our Biblical and evangelistic convictions, our faith in the absolute virtue of the blood of the Lamb, and in the unchangeable Word of God, our submission to the Holy Spirit and our identification with the Body of Christ. Our convictions were also clear about having a Godly lifestyle and promoting holiness "without which no one will see the Lord." Our expectation of the imminent return of our King and Savior, and our total dedication to evangelizing the world is coupled with our decision to live simply and use every available resource for the proclamation of the Gospel. These thoughts were like a creed that solidified our vision of ministry.

After those first six years of life at the Association, being involved in a fertile and exhausting, yet joyful work, we had seen almost 75,000 professions of faith in Christ, our radio program broadcast 700 times each day on 400 stations in 19 countries, our newspaper called *In His Steps published,* with a distribution of 30,000 copies dedicated to the edification of the People of God, and the production of a television program, distributed to several TV channels in the Spanish-speaking world.

There were only five loaves of bread and two fish. Just like Andrew, brother of Simon Peter, many people thought: "What is this that it should provide for so many?" The multitude was composed of several thousand people. The difference came when those few pieces of bread and fish were placed in the hands of the Lord. There was enough for everyone, and there were even twelve full baskets left over.

They were only twelve men with our Lord! Some of them had no formal preparation, and one of them harbored in his soul the seed of treason. Another would deny his Lord at the critical moment. And all of them would abandon the Master, hiding in fear. However, when the Holy Spirit took possession of them, they were enough to change the course of history.

I am at the forefront of the battle because of that special verse in the Bible, in 1 Corinthians 1:27-28: "But God chose the foolish things of the world to shame the wise; God chose the weak things of the world to shame the strong. He chose the lowly things of this world and the despised things—and the things that are not—to nullify the things that are."

My heart leaps within me when I read these words, saying: "That is where I fit in." If God chose only the wise and the strong of the world, I would be left outside. However, praised be His Name because He chooses what men would not have chosen, so that "no one should boast in His presence." This is the only reason for my ability to stand on my feet and behind a pulpit, because this verse exists in the Word of God. If this verse were not there, this book never could have been written.

CHAPTER 30

1984: A SURPRISING MILESTONE (I)

On Sunday, January 15, I was passing through El Salvador, leaving the next day for Guatemala. We were making plans to hold major crusades and those trips were a way to expeditiously plan the details of how the next would be organized. I stayed almost a week in Guatemala. My planned departure, scheduled on a Sunday in order to arrive the same day in Managua, suddenly developed a glitch. Later, pastor friends would reconstruct the details for me, corroborating the protection of God.

During the week that I was in Guatemala, I stayed in a hotel that was almost empty. On the entire floor where my room was located, I was the only guest. That Friday, I sensed in my spirit a restlessness that began to grow until I was filled with an anxiety that would not leave me in peace. I decided to go to Managua earlier than I had planned.

After I left, a fire broke out on the floor on which I had been staying and the two Nicaraguans who set the fire were arrested by the police and taken to prison. As it turns out, these men had instructions to try to take my life. They were two Sandinistas who had left their country and traveled to Guatemala to prevent the "imperialist" preacher from arriving in Managua. However, the Holy Spirit had miraculously taken me out of that place.

When I arrived at the airport in Managua I was welcomed by some leaders who were working with the crusade. They all had sad faces. They were very disappointed because after all the work of planning and organizing that had gone on for several months, the event had been canceled by the Sandinista government of Nicaragua, on the eve of the inauguration. The Plaza de Toros, with a capacity of 6,000 or 7,000 souls, could, at its absolute maximum, hold up to 10,000 people, if we could use the areas around the perimeter and outside, but we were not allowed to use the Plaza. One day before the campaign was to begin, it seemed an impossible task to find another place. The organizing committee for the campaign explained to me some of the events and facts that the Sandinistas were manipulating to have the event canceled.

"Brother Mottesi, the government of our country has cited two powerful reasons for denying the permit. First, that you are an 'anti-Communist' preacher sent by the imperialist Yankees, to contaminate the minds of our people. Second, they have pointed out some physical and technical problems with the Plaza that could endanger the people attending the event at the Plaza de Toros."

I looked at them very calmly. Listening to their account did not worry me in the least. I well knew that for the past ten years the Sandinista government had not allowed any public appearance of the Nicaraguan church. Ever since the Crusade of Luis Palau in 1975, the church had been oppressed to such a degree that its activities were restricted to the four walls of its churches.

Now that we had openly publicized the event, rented the Plaza de Toros, and everything was almost ready for the Crusade to begin, the government wanted to shut everything down, putting the organizing committee in a quandary.

Immediately I said to them: "We will go and talk to the people at CEPAD."

CEPAD was an ecumenical parachurch organization that had a lot of clout with the Sandinistas. The members of the committee, flustered, with their eyes as big as saucers, answered: "Brother Alberto, we cannot go to them. They are Sandinistas."

"Precisely. We will go and talk to them and place the burden on their shoulders."

Although they were not very convinced about the instructions I was giving them, we went to meet with the leaders of CEPAD. On the grounds of the First Baptist Church, we waited for Dr. Gustavo A. Parajón and Sixto Ulloa, who would later become a Sandinista official.

I explained to them the situation that we were going through, and the need for their direct intervention. Sixto Ulloa picked up the telephone and spoke directly to a general, a member of the Government Committee. This man invited him to come to his house, so they could talk there. He agreed, giving us hope that he could arrange the permit.

Meanwhile, I went around visiting every government official that I needed to see, followed by a journalist from the secular news agencies, who was carrying a television camera on his shoulder.

"In no way do I want to say something bad about you. But these people," I said, pointing to the cameraman, "will tell the entire world that the Sandinista government has canceled the campaign." At that time, the government was very concerned about avoiding any negative publicity, a fear that, as it turned out, would have quite an effect later on.

At 4:30 in the afternoon on Monday our permit was restored. The campaign would start at 6:00 p.m., but of crucial importance was that they had changed the location of the meeting. The new location was the stadium of the Central American University, rather than the Plaza. We would have no lights and no sound system, but still, it was a huge space that could hold thousands of people.

The authorities had now taken charge of planning everything. With so much pressure exercised by us and by the international press, they had agreed to restore our permit but in such a way that would guarantee the event to be a complete disaster.

Someone connected to the government explained to us later, in private, what their strategy had been: "If we grant them the permit at the last minute, using a huge stadium that was not the advertised venue, they will end up looking ridiculous. The people would go to the Plaza, only to discover the event was somewhere else entirely. We can be certain that the event will start with maybe 200 or 300 people in attendance and ending, possibly, with a maximum attendance of 2,000. But with a crowd that size, the people will look like just a few in that immense place. In that manner, we give them what they asked for, but they won't have any impact."

It certainly was a reversal of situations. The people arriving at the Plaza learned the news that the event would be held at another place, so thousands of people went from there to the stadium. The service began a little after 6 p.m., because of the change. We were all stressed about the situation, and unable to conceal our anxiety. We were worried about the lack of lights and sound system, but someone found a megaphone somewhere and with that we made ourselves heard.

Remarkably, more than 15,000 people attended that first night. With all of the difficulties and the obstacles, this was a very surprising number, but everything that followed was surprising as well.

The daylight was gone very soon after we started. Surrounded by a multitude that was straining to hear the message in the twilight, I suddenly realize that two young men, their skin a copper hue, wearing blue jeans, their thin shirts unbuttoned, putting their bare chests on public display, climbed with great agility a tall concrete post behind me. Perched in the heights, hanging on without any security harness, trusting only in their own dexterity and the strength of their arms and legs, and using a simple razor, began to splice electrical cables and reconnect the stadium lights.

The sight was so amazing I almost cried. For a moment, everyone remained motionless watching this marvelous spectacle in the semi-darkness, holding our breath at the daring of these anonymous heroes. My skin had goose bumps watching those young men, and a deep respect for them was born in me. They were risking their own lives to solve this problem. I am certain that when they get to heaven they will be received with high level honors, a reception full of joy and homage.

When the lights began to shine in the stadium, even though only partially, there were emotional shouts and screams from the audience. Now, with an emotion that I could not contain, I preached under the anointing of the Lord. That crowd was hungry for God, and I had the responsibility of giving them manna from heaven with these unclean lips, yet sanctified by my God, anointed by the Holy Spirit. When I asked the people to make a decision for Christ, they literally ran toward the podium. We could breathe the pleasant odor of the Presence of the Almighty in that place. . And within that framework, we knew everything had been managed only and exclusively by God. He is the one who decided to give a spectacular end to the event, finishing the evening with a miracle.

While all of the people were coming to the front to make a public confession of faith and confirm their commitment to Jesus Christ as Savior and Lord, while I was praying over these penitent new believers, a blind woman who was known in Managua as such was supernaturally healed. She left the stadium with sight restored to her eyes, an event that was like an explosion circulating all over the city.

Each subsequent day, the attendance continued to increase. On Tuesday, it numbered about 20,000; on Wednesday, 30,000; on Thursday, 35,000; on Friday, 50,000; on Saturday, 60,000.

We lived each day of the crusade in a constant state of expectation. We knew that God was working. It was already a fact, from the very moment that we began, that the hand of God had surprised us. All of our expectations had been much too low.

We had planned for an attendance of about 10,000 or 15,000 people. The story of the Nicaraguan church over the previous ten years seemed to confirm this estimate. There was no precedent of a public meeting attracting large multitudes.

In addition, several barriers were erected to make our campaign efforts look ridiculous. But God surprised us all, and at the final meeting on Sunday more than 80,000 people arrived.

The attendance far surpassed our original estimates. The little Plaza de Toros would have been a monument to futility, because we never would have been able to proclaim the Gospel to so many, had we been given that venue, as we'd asked. Most of the people would have returned to their homes disappointed at not being able to find a place to listen. Nevertheless, God thwarted the evil designs with a most beautiful blessing. The "Sandinista Nebuchadnezzar" was used as a servant of God to carry out his plans. The government had wanted us to look ridiculous, using an immense stadium for a few people scattered here and there. But now, we were amazed to see that the Stadium of the Central American University was barely large enough to hold the huge crowds that were about to descend on it for the closing event.

On the other hand, our counselors were not sufficient to handle 36,000 decisions for Christ. We distributed the available literature until we ran out at about 25,000. Definitely, we were not prepared for this avalanche of great blessing that overcame us during that glorious week.

Meanwhile, each day more and more people came to the stadium for the crusade events. Throughout the day we had planned a variety of activities. One of these was a Pastoral Seminar, which would become the largest event of that kind in the history of evangelical Christianity in Nicaragua. About six hundred and fifty people attended, including four hundred and sixty-two pastors from all over the country. They came from Puerto Cabezas, Mina Rosita, León, Chinandega, Granada, Masaya, Del Rama, San Rafael del Sur. Some of them left their homes on Thursday to arrive in Managua by Monday. There were those who traveled by river and crossed mountains. They also came from Jinotega and from Matagalpa, areas that were war zones. Those were four glorious mornings of revival with the Word of God.

CHAPTER 31
1984: A SURPRISING MILESTONE (II)

Each morning, on the grounds of the stadium, it was like a celebration. People from everywhere anxiously approached, hoping to find a good seat. It was noticeable to me that most of the people were poor, the needy, from the lower social classes, as their clothing alone clearly identified them as such. These were people who had suffered. These people were seeking refuge after years of suffering during a ferocious civil war that held this nation on the verge of collapse.

Despite the governmental restrictions, such as the rationing of gasoline that limited each owner of a vehicle to 20 gallons per month, the people did not mind using their rations for this week; they didn't want to miss even one service.

After the services had ended and the people were event, the sight was a spectacle worthy of mention in the book of the Acts of the Holy Spirit.

You could see cattle trucks filled with people, literally like clusters of grapes hanging onto the sides, and the drivers praying, not for the individuals they were carrying, but for their vehicles. Their tires looked so worn that you could see the steel ribs reflected in the light of the street lamps, but these drivers prayed and pleaded with God not to let them burst on the road. And that is how they were able to arrive safe and sound at their destination.

Throughout the city, at about midnight, when the capital city of Nicaragua was a very dangerous place to be outside walking, you could see groups of people on the corners, brothers who were praying for the unsaved people they encountered on the way to their homes.

It was a precious movement of the Holy Spirit! We were witnessing a revival from the Lord in Nicaragua! And you could also say under his protection; thousands of angels were doubtless sent from heaven to work overtime on behalf of his chosen ones.

On Friday, in the afternoon, the so-called "divine mobs" arrived at the stadium on several trucks, in a frightening uproar and with palpable hostility. These men were part of a paramilitary group trained for battle, disciplined in violence to support the Sandinista government. One of the characteristics of this group was that they wore on their wrists, attached to short chains, balls of iron with razor-sharp points, with which, if they wanted, they could in a matter of minutes tear down an entire building. Another feature that obviously set them apart was their ferocity, which was already known from previous situations, such as the time that the Pope visited Managua, when their booing and shouts broke up a public meeting that he held there. These same men had decided to make their presence known at our crusade, not to hear the Gospel of love, but rather to obey orders to tear down at any cost this event that the Sandinista government was no longer able to control by legal avenues.

We began the service with congregational singing, and when the ushers outside saw the trucks driving up and the "divine mobsters" getting out; they knew exactly what those men wanted to do. The road leading to the entrance to the stadium was filled with these people brandishing their iron weapons and ready to spring into action with a lot of shouting.

All of the ushers, faced with the urgency of the moment, joined hands and stood across the entrance to the access corridor for the stadium. They closed their eyes and began to pray. It was impressive and moving, one of those moments when destinies are forged. Thousands of lives, among them my own, depended on these urgent prayers born in the deepest regions of their souls.

There were hundreds of eyewitnesses to what happened next.

Suddenly, there was a terrifying silence. The "divine mobsters" became quiet, and their expressions were firm and tense. Then in a twinkling of an eye, without opening their mouths, they returned to their trucks. The engines were turned on and they went away, never to return.

What exactly happened? Why did they change their plans? Who gave the order to retreat? Why did all of them, almost moving as if with one mind, without hearing any spoken command, silently return to their trucks?

Perhaps we will never know in this lifetime. There was no doubt, to all of those who remained inside the stadium, that God had protected us, just as in Old Testament times, when God turned the invading armies crazy and they killed one another.

What a night so filled with emotion and gratitude to God. He had saved us from the evil, that is, the so-called "divine mobs." It was clear the government could not stop what was happening any longer. God had taken them by surprise, just as he'd taken us by surprise. They thought that we would look ridiculous, but it never crossed their minds it was someone who was using these events for his own purpose.

Sunday was a feast of spiritual celebration, of jubilation overflowing onto the people with an intense sense of intimacy with the Presence of God. I preached and, feeling led and directed by Him, I invited the people to pray for peace in Nicaragua. I opened my Bible with absolute solemnity. This was one of those occasions when one takes the Word of God in hand with painstaking care, as if it were a fragile petal, that if carelessly handled could break. I read from the Bible, in front of a crowd of 80,000 souls, standing there, filling every nook and cranny of the bleachers and the field of the university soccer stadium. I said, "The weapons we fight with are not the weapons of the world. On the contrary, they have divine power to demolish strongholds" (2 Corinthians 10:4).

In my message I tried to bring this huge throng to an understanding of Who our God is, what Jesus has given us, and what He has placed at our disposal for confronting evil.

And at the end, after the altar call, I opened the Sacred Book for a second time. With trembling voice I read, after speaking of the calamities brought on by warfare, not only in Nicaragua, but also in every nation of the earth: "If my people, who are called by my name, will humble themselves and pray and seek my face and turn from their wicked ways, then will I hear from heaven and will forgive their sin and will heal their land" (2 Chronicles 7:14).

Speaking deliberately and with power, I placed a special emphasis on verse 15: "Now my eyes will be open and my ears attentive to the prayers offered in this place." Then I urged them to cry out to God, and the entire crowd of people fell to their knees to pray for the peace of Nicaragua and of Central America. On the steps, in the field, on the platform, in every corner of that stadium, not one person was standing. There was an overwhelming groaning of a people in disgrace, of souls who have lost loved ones to the bullets of fratricidal warfare, of the suffering that brings about misery, and pain, and sickness. They were conscious that their existence was hanging on a thread and that promises about tomorrow could be too expensive for the reality in which they were living. Amid this clamor to the Creator, wrested with the final strength of their souls, a heartfelt prayer was being released, greatly nourished in the crucible of suffering.

Eighty thousand people were praying, weeping, crying! The sight was impressive, and it was an outcry that parted the skies of Central America—a weeping that reached the ears of God Himself and changed the history of Nicaragua. In fact, it changed not only the history of that country but also of the church and of my own as well. From then on, we would never again be the same.

With such an impressive outpouring in which the hearts of the people are identified with their God, rage is ended; pride falls to the floor; egotism is torn to pieces; vanities give way to simple and sincere humility.

When that multitude of faces bathed in their own tears, wiping their eyes, again stood to their feet, and I with them, the first thing I saw off to one side, at the edge of the university grounds, climbing over a wire fence bordering a Catholic school, were several nuns in their white habits, jumping and overcome with emotion, shouting wildly and blowing me kisses.

I will always remember that scene. What made them break out into this demonstration of joy? Why were they blowing me kisses? I may never know. But the Holy Spirit is the Sovereign of every living soul. The only impression that remained in my consciousness was that when God moves within the hearts of the people, there are no prejudices that can resist Him, nor traditions that can block his way. He is the Lord of all the living.

In this crusade—and it's very important that I say this—God showed me irrefutably that He can touch entire nations, and that even if the entire population of the country may not be converted, there must be a change in the mindset of the church. Our God is capable of influencing and transforming history and the entire life of a nation.

When I remember in my mind the Crusade of 1984, I see a milestone, a surprising landmark in my life and in my ministry. I see with a new vision how God wanted to use me. The year 1984 would serve as a dividing line between a ministry of traveling from church to church, and a ministry of serving cities and even entire nations.

CHAPTER 32

EL SALVADOR 1984

Those three weeks of spiritual harvest in Managua are infinitely difficult for me to quantify. Only in heaven we will know the entire story. However, the crusade we held in El Salvador in 1984, would become another event that left its mark not only on the team that worked with me, but also on the Salvadoran church, and on the entire nation.

The event had been organized far in advance. We would hold a Pastoral Seminar, a Week of the Family, and then finally the Evangelistic Crusade. The pastors' seminar was held the last two days of August and the first of September, at the Tabernacle, an auditorium adjacent to the Bethel Bible Institute of the Assemblies of God. There were 755 pastors representing 16 evangelical denominations participating, making it the best attended evangelical pastors' seminar up to that time in the history of El Salvador. A total of more than 1,100 people participated in the conferences, workshops, and plenary meetings. God powerfully used our team to teach, not just with theories, but with living experiences from the field.

During those two weeks of intense labor before the crusade itself, there were several instances that made us restless. One of these, and perhaps the most worrisome, was the action planned by the guerrillas against the government. They had announced one of the largest offensive maneuvers of the ongoing civil war against the government. The republic of El Salvador, during the previous four years, had witnessed the deaths of 30,000 Salvadorans due to internal strife. A mountainous area located only 35 kilometers (less than 22 miles) away from the capital city was swarming with guerrilla combatants who were at that time impossible to control.

At the beginning of the Crusade, the Salvadoran government had imposed martial law in several areas of the capital city. The guerrillas were threatening public transportation; moreover, it was announced that during that week the means of public transportation would have an 8 o'clock curfew each night. The guerrillas had seized several radio stations in order to broadcast their own messages, and the mood was fraught with tension. In addition, a very strong tropical storm had required the evacuation of thousands of families from their homes. During that week, several bombs went off in the capital city, making people even more insecure about the idea of peacefully navigating the streets of their own city. With this upsurge of adversity, the campaign began.

And yet the attendance grew each afternoon, until on Sunday we saw a multitude of about 50,000 Salvadorans packing the Flor Blanca National Stadium. With every invitation to accept the Lord, we had witnessed the spiritual hunger of the people. Linda Pritchett accompanied us with her team to work with the children. A location three blocks from the stadium had been prepared for her ministry. There, more than 3,000 children heard the Gospel presented in Linda's special way, with the use of ventriloquism and the lion "Miguelito" (little Michael), to the delight of the little ones. On Sunday the children paraded around the stadium, which was completely full. They walked three times around the stadium while 50,000 people greeted them with handkerchiefs held high. It was a very beautiful moment, resounding with the joy of the Lord.

On that same day, without my knowing it at the time, someone had been commanded to murder the preacher.

He was a dark-skinned man, almost black from daily exposure to the strong rays of the sun. Costumed in a glaring white garment, he was walking around in the highest part of the national stadium. One of the pastors, César Augusto Ayala, saw him and noticed the two pistols half hidden under his guayabera shirt. Immediately, he summoned an usher and together the two men followed the man from a prudent distance. They noticed his anxious movements as he descended towards the soccer field and then walked around behind the platform where I was standing.

Pastor Ayala and the usher did not do anything to stop him, because they knew that he was a guerrilla and that it was possible there could be several other such men scattered in the crowd. If they had tried to stop him, there was no way to know what disastrous events they might have unleashed.

In the meantime, however, they did not lose sight of him. They continued to follow him discreetly from behind, to find out where he was going, ready and willing to throw themselves at the guerrilla and stop him if he were to reach for his pistols with evil intentions.

Without any idea of the danger I was in, I preached boldly about how the Lord wanted to put an end to the violence born in the heart of man and to give him a life of peace, of victory, of happiness in God. The man, who was nervously circling the platform, suddenly stopped in front of me as if petrified by some invisible force. He stood motionless, listening. On his face, the tears could be seen streaming down his cheeks. When I was making the call to accept Christ, he walked forward and surrendered his heart to the Lord. Right there, the counselor who approached to pray with him became the repository of the two pistols the man had been carrying all day, with the purpose of killing the preacher by orders of the guerrilla. This guerrilla fighter did not know that a Warrior more powerful than him, the Lord Jesus Christ, would take him and transform him into a new person.

Later I was introduced to him, and I, from within my being, glorified my Lord for his precious protection. How can there be any doubt? The army of heaven had come down to protect his own. It was while I was saying farewell to the people who were greeting and hugging me, that I was introduced to the man who had so recently been a guerrilla fighter. That's when I learned about the plans that had brought him to the Crusade. I hugged him and told him with a smile of affection: "Welcome to the Kingdom of God."

CHAPTER 33

AN OUTSTANDING 1985

From the very moment when we finished the work developed by the First Hispanic Pastoral Conference, held in Pasadena in March of 1984, we began to develop plans for a Hispanic Congress on Evangelism, as a continuation of the work of Amsterdam 1983, and as preparation for Amsterdam 1986. I remember that when I informed the committee that we would be holding the event at the Crystal Cathedral, they thought I was crazy. It was too expensive, they said, and it would probably not be rented to us, etc. The committee wanted something more affordable due to our limited finances, something like the Olympic Auditorium in Los Angeles, a building plagued with rats and cockroaches. I let them know that we would do everything that we possibly could to hold the event at a worthy location.

And so it was. We were able to rent the Crystal Cathedral as the site of this first Congress planned October 14-18, 1985, and our entire ministry became involved in this magnificent event.

During the days leading up to the scheduled event, as always, there were formidable obstacles. During Easter Week, I was preaching in Miami, where I heard the following story: "I have been a prostitute." These words, so unexpected and drastic, were spoken by a woman whose face looked very young. She was holding a young girl of angelic face by the hand. "But last night," she continued, "when you were preaching, the Word reached very deep into my life and I surrendered myself to Jesus Christ. Before, I felt two forces constantly struggling inside of me: one that inclined me toward the evil and the other that made me want to do good. The strength of the evil always triumphed in me. But now I no longer feel that force of evil in me."

She continued speaking in that same sweet tone of voice, with a markedly emotional emphasis, telling me about an experience that she'd just had that morning.

"When I got up, I didn't even have enough sugar to put in a glass of water for my daughter. I called a former co-worker from the profession and asked her to lend me 10 dollars."

Her co-worker answered, "Precious, this very night you can easily get the money on the street."

But the narrator in front of me had answered with firm resolution. That way of life had ended for her. "No! I will never do that again. Now my life belongs to Jesus Christ. My body is the temple of the Holy Spirit."

"However," she continued speaking, "hunger began to make its presence very real." She took an old toy wagon that belonged to her little girl, went outside and managed to sell it for 10 dollars.

Three days later, she phoned the radio talk show where I was ministering live. Without giving her name she told her testimony to the audience, as she'd told it to me. The thing that most impressed me was when she said: "Ever since I surrendered to Jesus Christ, I feel like a virgin."

How beautiful it is when the Lord changes lives! Seeing testimonies like this is what motivates our lives.

In July of 1985, Billy Graham organized his largest crusade on American soil. It was held at the Angels stadium in Anaheim, Southern California, and I was invited to deliver a short message before the preaching of Dr. Graham.

This represented a very important milestone for my ministry and myself, first, because Dr. Billy Graham has been one of my heroes since my youth, and second, because it represented an opportunity to place our ministry in the eyes and ears of North America. It was a tremendous honor, very significant in our ministry's history.

In that stadium in Anaheim, with an impressive number of persons coming from many neighboring cities and counties, a large part of the audience was Hispanic and it was possible, with broadcast technology, to provide a simultaneous Spanish interpretation of what was said in English. On the platform at the stadium, I was seated near Dr. Billy Graham. I was able to hear from his mouth encouraging words for our ministry. Later, before the preaching began, I stood at the podium and announced to those present the upcoming Hispanic Congress on Evangelism, promising that it would be the largest such event ever held in the United States.

"There will be 2,000 Hispanic leaders there," I said with visible emotion to the multitude. "We expect that this Congress will cause the largest increase of evangelism in our history. One of our goals is to reach two million Hispanic people for Christ in the United States."

I continued speaking while the public applauded: "I have a firm conviction: the destiny of the Hispanic world is not in the hands of politicians, nor in the hands of the military or the guerrilla fighters. Our destiny is in the hands of the Church of Jesus Christ."

The memory of the crusades held in Nicaragua and El Salvador in 1984 was still fresh and vivid in my mind. This additional presentation put a spotlight on our work amongst the millions of people scattered throughout the expansive territory that comprises the United States. The media outlets of mass communication immediately broadcast the news. And I will always be grateful for the honor of having been invited by Dr. Billy Graham, my hero, my elder brother in evangelism.

After that event we ministered for seven days in Spain, in the cities of Madrid, Valencia, and Barcelona.

The Spanish citizen, generally speaking, is very closed to anything that comes from outside of his own country. One afternoon while I was preaching in a public park, a voice inside of me was saying: "This is not going to work; the Spanish accent is different. They handle religion differently. Most of the pastors in Spain never ask for public professions of faith... " But when I began to give the invitation, I spiritedly declared within myself: "The Spanish may be different, but my Lord Jesus Christ is the same here as He is in Latin America."

And of course, He was! Many people began to come forward and surrender themselves to Jesus Christ, weeping! Jesus Christ is also Lord in Spain.

Soon afterward, we held two pastoral seminars for the relevant leadership, one held in Santo Domingo, in the Dominican Republic, August 1-4, with an attendance that fluctuated between 900 and 1,000 leaders. It was publicized as "the most important event in the Christian history of the Dominican Republic." After the seminar had concluded, our Evangelistic Association was unanimously invited to conduct a national crusade in that country in April of the following year.

Another event with historic repercussions for the unity of the Body of Christ was held September 3-7 in Bogotá, Colombia.

Months after our Crusade '86, I can point to what was said and testified publicly. I heard it, others heard it, and it has been written about as well; that as a direct result of our work in Colombia, the two largest evangelical organizations in the country, whose history went back many years, decided to merge into one organization, establishing what is now called CEDECOL. The two agencies, CEDEC and ACECOL, merged and are now working together as one organization.

What a great privilege it was for me, during September of 1985, so full of the Lord's Presence in our lives, that the ministry of Open Doors would invite me to preach at a series of three conferences called *Central America: We Love You*, held in Guatemala, El Salvador, and Costa Rica. What an honor it was for me to travel with the team led by my friend, Héctor Tamez.

Also participating was the legendary Brother Andrew, popularly known as "God's Smuggler." Those were glorious days bringing hope to a Central America that was at that time full of bloodshed.

However, the outstanding event of that year would be the Hispanic Congress on Evangelism.

We had already spent several months in the intensive labor of organizing the event. Now, the time for God to take over had arrived. Driving along the freeway from west to east, near the Anaheim stadium, one can admire the majestic sight of a glass building, completely transparent, one of the most beautiful settings in the world. The place is called the *Crystal Cathedral*. In that place, with 2,079 registered participants and another 1,000 part-time attendees, the dream became a reality.

Those who attended came from all over the United States, Canada, Puerto Rico, and northern Mexico. We also had delegations from 24 countries and their flags flanked both sides of the platform of honor during those five action-packed days.

As president of the Congress, I made a presentation introducing the Pact of Los Angeles 1985; others presented greetings and telegrams, among them from the president of the United States, Mr. Ronald Regan. The launch of what we were hoping would be an ongoing event, the *First International-Hispanic Congress for the Evangelism of the World*; the solemn celebration of the Lord's Supper; and, finally, the closing service when, at the conclusion of my farewell message, the altar and the aisles were filled with a multitude of leaders in attendance who came forward to renew their commitment to the Lord.

The setting was outstanding; the Presence of God majestic. One Mexican senator, weeping, embraced me and said: "I came to the Congress as a politician. I am leaving as a servant of Jesus Christ." In the same way everyone there, in one way or another, was renewed by the Spirit of God and changed in order to make us more effective in his work.

CHAPTER 34
GREAT CRUSADES IN 1986

We arrived one day ahead of schedule at the site of our Crusade in Panama, which was to be held March 16-23 in 1986, in the midst of a country experiencing social upheaval. On the day that we arrived, six bombs went off in the Panamanian capital city. One of them in front of the hotel where we were staying, destroying a woman's hand.

These events were very strange and out of the ordinary for that country. That night dozens of businesses were looted and destroyed. There was no gasoline. There were long queues everywhere. There was very little transportation available in the city and several workers' unions were on strike.

For four or five days previous to our arrival, the government had been threatening to declare a state of emergency, which would mean the suspension of the right to assemble.

One Nicaraguan who I encountered in that place said to me: "Brother Mottesi, I was at your Crusade in Managua. It seems that the Lord always takes you to places with problems." I just smiled and gave him a friendly hug.

We began on Sunday, the 16th, at the *Gymnasium New Panama* with an attendance of about 3,000 people. The attendance continued to increase as the days went by, reaching about 10,000 people in attendance at the Plaza in front of the Legislative Palace. A few days earlier, this plaza had been the site of violent demonstrations. However, on that Sunday, this huge crowd was telling the country that Jesus Christ is the only one who can bring peace.

Our next Crusade would be held in Santo Domingo, in the Dominican Republic. Those were three weeks of challenging labor.

The Crusade in Santo Domingo at the Olympic Stadium lasted for six days, four of them under torrential rains, although this was supposed to be the dry season. We were so soaked when we arrived at the hotel, that two employees immediately came to meet us holding two enormous dryers they used to dry the ground behind us as we walked.

On the first night we showed up at the stadium under a heavy downpour; but in spite of the inclement weather, there were about 10,000 in attendance, and that was only the beginning. The sky was an unending waterfall, accompanied by the incessant sound of thunder and lightning. One of these lightning bolts hit the stadium and was immediately absorbed by a lightning rod, scorching a few people who were sitting nearby but without serious consequence—thank God.

I had never seen so much rainfall. The torrential rain kept pouring down as if all of the strength of nature had been unleashed to fight against what we were doing. The scene seemed almost macabre, after the power was knocked out by a stroke of lightning and the stadium and the people were occasionally illuminated by the flickering glow of lightning bolts. The silvery light occasionally allowed us glimpses of one another.

But if the weather is raining and stormy, I will continue to preach under the torrential water. Whoever wants to go may leave, but I will remain standing there as long as there is someone who wants to listen, who is attentive to the Word, who is spiritually hungry and needs Christ. I will stay and preach under any weather conditions.

From that literally electrifying moment, I was able to convey my feelings to the people. And the people stayed, and in the days that followed the attendance increased, they sang like madmen, prayed like madmen, and received the madness of the cross with profound sincerity. How moving it was when I made the altar call! In a field that was flooded, with skies unleashed on us, the faces of the people were also wet by tears flowing from their eyes, symbolizing the feeling of their souls.

Once we had finished in the Dominican Republic, I flew straight to the office in Los Angeles. My life was intense, and the rhythm of an agenda so filled with commitments brought us to Spain in May of 1986, to that Spain with its fierce people.

The outstanding event in Madrid was the evangelistic meeting. To understand what happened in its proper perspective, you must remember that in that city of millions there were at that time only about 60 congregations and some 3,000 evangelicals, throughout the whole city and its suburbs. About one million invitations were distributed.

For the first time, Protestants would be using the *Palace of Sports* for a religious function and, to top it off, its use had been secured for free! The cost of renting the site and the sound system alone would have been about 15 or 20 thousand dollars. In that beautiful and comfortable place we had a great attendance, considering the evangelical strength in Spain. We estimated about 2,750 people there, and about 400 of them went forward in response to the invitation, 169 or the very first time.

When we were preparing to leave, the *Evangelical Council of Cataluña* invited us to hold a crusade in Barcelona. They hadn't had anything like that in 15 years, and we went there with the thought that a new day was beginning to dawn for Spain. Two days after returning home, on May 21, I received a telephone call from Argentina with the news that my dear elderly mother had just left to be with the Lord. With a heavy heart, I packed my suitcases and returned to my native country. I stood there in the cemetery with my father, who was already 81 years old. We were truly grieved at our loss, but at the same time greatly strengthened by our God. His servant Esther had left behind a beautiful testament of love.

My schedule of activities was such that, when it came to events of a personal nature, like the death of my mother, there was barely enough time to cherish her memory in my heart and go on, as if nothing had happened. And this was not for lack of feelings. I loved my mother as much as a son can love his mother, and I honor her memory as much as any son can; however, the continuity of the ministry required a quick return to the relentless calendar of evangelistic endeavors.

Later that year, we held a crusade in Ensenada, in Baja California, Mexico. If it wasn't the largest such event, it certainly was one of the most beautiful. Here we saw the marvelous grace of the Lord operating in a very clear way. It became the largest such event in the history of that city.

Each night, we saw in operation the love of the Lord for the unsaved. How could we forget those moving scenes, like that group of teenagers crying, deeply broken at one side of that rustic pulpit? Or those two women, who had been prostitutes, surrendering their lives to Jesus Christ? Or the impact of reading a decision cards that stood out for its dramatic message: "Today I was going to commit suicide, but tonight I have decided that my mind will never again be at the service of Satan; my mind, starting from today, will belong to Jesus Christ."

At the same time, we sponsored some additional activities in the area. My wife Noemi ministered to a group of more than 200 women. I preached at a breakfast meeting for the leadership of the city. There were about 150 people at the meeting held in the *Hotel San Nicolas*. That is where we saw how the Lord had prepared all of these things, so that we could give Him the honor and the glory for all of it.

At this breakfast meeting, two members of the government, the Secretary and the wife of the mayor, surrendered their lives to the Lord. At that time I never imagined how much they would help us to right the wrongs of the devil.

When we arrived in Ensenada, an entire publicity campaign was underway trying to discredit the Crusade. We were bombarded by the Mexican press, who were critical of evangelical Christians, and accused the missionaries of being instruments used by the CIA to change the culture of the country. During the week of the campaign, the newspapers were reporting that the Mexican government had expelled a group of 49 evangelicals from the country, among them 14 missionaries. To make matters worse, throughout the Mexican territory and for a very long time, evangelical Christians have often been confused with Jehovah's Witnesses. The people falsely accuse the Protestant churches of having no respect for patriotic symbols such as the flag and the national anthem.

When the Crusade was about its mid-point, a brother who was involved in politics told us that the government had decided to cancel the event, but because of the friends that we had made at the leadership breakfast, thanks to God, when the representatives of the government arrived with their orders, they were given countering orders that invalidated the cancellation. God had given us the answer to our problem, even before it came to fruition.

In addition, we decided to counter their version of publicity with our own demonstration to the contrary. Linda Pritchett worked with us on a campaign for children to be held simultaneously with ours. We got the idea of buying a thousand little tricolor pennants. We borrowed the national flag from the city hall. We were able to get the marching band from the local police department to play at our event, and invited the authorities to make an appearance at the closing event. With these elements of respect for the country and culture in place, we prepared for the last day of the Crusade.

It was so exciting to witness. There are times when God lets us be the protagonists at these incredibly beautiful events.

We barely had time to savor that episode by the time we arrived in the Old World, in the Netherlands, to participate in the conference called *Amsterdam 1986*. About 10,000 workers for the Lord, representing 174 countries, had gathered there. Later, the United Nations would declare that this event had brought together more countries of the earth than anything else in history, religious or secular, up until that time. That meeting was very momentous! We assisted by leading seminars for the 1,700 Hispanic people who were in attendance. It was an experience rich in communion, fellowship, and evangelistic challenges.

There was an event worthy of another page in The Acts of the Holy Spirit for that year. The Crusade in Colombia, for *Cali's 450th Anniversary,* was one that would give us more unforgettable memories.

The crusade in that third largest Colombian city was held August 29th through September 5th. Cali, in former times, had been the center of an economy that depended on the cattle industry, having the natural grace and generosity of cities built along the shore of big rivers. The Crusade had been scheduled during the time when they were celebrating the 450th anniversary of the city's founding, with ample demonstrations of their folklore, and an overflowing display of joy.

From the first service, the redeeming grace of Christ was abundant, even though we had a lower than expected turnout at the Pan American Soccer Stadium; the attendance was about 10,000 people.

A town councilman, Mr. Claudio Barrero, surrendered his life to Christ, telling me with quavering voice as he was leaving that place: "Mr. Mottesi, for a long time I have avoided this decision, but now it is impossible for me to resist, and I have surrendered my life to Jesus Christ."

It was already midnight. The people in charge of the stadium were shutting off the lights, and yet, at this late hour, large groups of young Christians had stayed to disciple the new converts, and to pray for them and for a revival in their country.

There is no doubt that this crusade in Cali renewed for me the challenge to work harder than before in favor of mass evangelism. There is no task so small that it will not be highly recompensed by our God. Everything that I saw that year here and there was the budding of revival from the Holy Spirit with all of his great manifestations. Serving God is worth it all. Do you also believe that?

CHAPTER 35

EVANGELISTIC EXPLOSION

By the beginning of 1987, the evangelistic work seemed too intense, exhausting, and demanding. The words of Psalm 71:3 became our prayer: "Be my rock of refuge, to which I can always go; give the command to save me, for You are my rock and my fortress."

For several months, the weight of the ministry had become so heavy that humanly speaking we were worn out, but the Lord came to us with this Word that refreshed and renewed our being. We began the year with intense peace and new strength. From the start, our schedule was completely full for the entire year.

ARA Jesucristo, "Now Jesus Christ," was our theme in the Catalan language, written in huge letters. The banner was placed high above the crowd gathered in one of the imposing salons of the Royal Shipyards, a well-known tourist site in Barcelona, Spain.

This World Heritage building, dating to the 13th century, was the shipyard where the *Santa Maria* was built, the ship with which Christopher Columbus would discover America. That place, so full of ancient tradition, was the site of our first crusade sponsored by the Evangelical Council of Catalonia.

I must reiterate that the evangelical population of Spain is very small, about 0.1 percent at that point—in words, the tenth part of one percent! But even though this country is predominantly Catholic, the real religion of the Spaniards is skepticism, which brings many obstacles to faith. In spite of that, we saw 353 people making their very first decision for Christ in that place.

In addition to the crusade meetings, I ministered to local pastors. My wife Noemi also ministered at the Women's Conference to about 350 women. Linda Pritchett held a crusade for children that was attended by 1,920 little ones, among which 70 made a decision for Christ during personal interviews. I need to emphasize the personality of the Spanish citizen. It is extremely difficult to evangelize most Spanish people because of the pride and fierce spirit so pervasive in the culture. Honestly, I went there with fear and trembling.

I knew of the disdainful attitude of the Spaniard toward the Latin American, and moreover, the local pastors tried to convince me not to ask for public conversions and commitments, because the people were not accustomed to that sort of "spiritual exuberance." However, from the very beginning I asked for professions of faith and it was impressive to see dozens of Spaniards coming forward and surrendering their lives to Christ.

Many significant issues happened during my stay in Barcelona. For the first time an evangelist was allowed to be on a live radio program answering phone calls from the public, and we received a lot of favorable publicity from the press. The principal newspapers published news reports, and the EFE, the official news agency of Spain, assigned a reporter to cover our visit. He was a former Catholic priest and very disappointed with the church, but I didn't know this until the last day of the campaign. On the closing Sunday, with the 5,400 people in attendance filling the ancient auditorium so reminiscent of centuries old traditions, the reporter approached me just before I was to go onto the platform and said to me: "Mr. Mottesi, allow me greet you now because after you finish your homily, I am sure that you will be surrounded by many people and it will not be easy for me to shake your hand."

He greeted me affectionately and continued: "I want you to know that I was previously a priest with the Catholic Church. I was completely disillusioned with the church and the faith in Jesus Christ. During this week that I have been near you to fulfill my journalistic assignment, the old faith has begun to shine again in my soul. Our encounter," he went on, "has had a great impact on my life. Thank you very much for your visit to Barcelona."

After Barcelona, the next stop for the ministry was the city of Miami, which represented at the time a strong challenge for our ministry. This place, known as a center of drug trafficking, has one of the highest crime rates in the United States, and many of the Hispanics there are very much under the influence of ancient animist religions.

These things, however, did not stop us from preaching the powerful Gospel from the floating platform of the Miami Marine Stadium on Virginia Key. This stadium features bleachers facing toward the sea. From there, one can see far in the distance the outline of the skyscrapers along the shores of Miami. The platform is an enormous, zigzag shaped canopy that seems to float over the water, while its columns appear to climb over Biscayne Bay.

Those were six nights of arduous proclamation, including the opening night, which was attended by the mayor of the city. The event had an attendance of 22,400 people and 2,200 people registered decisions for Christ. In conjunction with the crusade we held a Leadership Seminar, a Bilingual Breakfast, a children's event with Linda Pritchett, and an event for young people at a local park.

The tone that prevailed during the services was one of praise and adoration. Steve Green accompanied us with his privileged voice, leading us to the very altar of God. A blended choir and local singers assisted in providing an atmosphere of spiritual worship. One night, a young man approached me and showed me a double-bladed knife that he had used to rob and kill. Right then and there, he walked over to the railing and threw the weapon into the sea, surrendering his life to Jesus.

During the two weeks previous to the crusade, the newspapers around the country, including Miami, had been full of very bad news about certain evangelical leaders and their terrible moral failures. Aware that many people were saddened by the news, I directed some comments the media represented there that night:

"I am under the impression that the only news that interests you is something bloody, or that which is full of garbage and scandal. Dear journalists, I want to tell you something: not all of the news is bad. There is also good news. Not everything is dirty. There are things that are pure. Not everything is corrupt. There also are evangelists who are honest, and pastors who serve their communities with integrity."

When I finished saying these last words—words that came out of the my heart with the authority of God—the multitude, as if in unanimous agreement, stood to their feet and broke out into a huge ovation.

Many faces were bathed in their own tears. Others laughed with sincerity. Most engaged in thunderous applause. Something like a wave of rich blessing covered us, imparting an atmosphere of solemn spirituality. God used that moment to pour out his blessing on the Crusade.

On July 11, I set foot on Colombian territory once again, planning to stay in that country until July 28 to hold two crusades, one in Medellin and the other in the capital city, Bogota.

The first event was held in the beautiful place known as the *Park of the Flags*, where 15,000 people made decisions for Christ. The second event was held at the covered Coliseum "*El Campín*" where 10,000 people made decisions for Christ.

Hector Pardo, president of the Colombian Evangelical Alliance, expressed to us his feelings: "After many years of mistrust, this Crusade has brought a beautiful spirit of unity. The pastors of Bogota had lost interest in evangelism, but I believe that this Crusade has prepared us for greater things in the future."

In August, we conducted six pastoral seminars in Puerto Rico, Bolivia, and Guatemala, and it's worth mentioning a comment made about Bolivia. This was one of the two Latin American countries where at the time I had not yet ministered. However, because of our dear Bolivian friends Samuel and Melvy, closely connected to our family and our ministry, we had grown to love that country.

Bolivia, during its 186 years of history as an independent republic, had had 86 administrations. It was the second poorest country in Latin America and one of the main producers of drugs. It was also one of the countries with the lowest percentage of evangelical Christians on the continent.

We held four leadership seminars, in Santa Cruz, Cochabamba, Oruro, and La Paz; of the 1,100 Bolivian leaders who participated, the vast majority was pastors.

The Lord preserved the health of all of the team members despite the intense work schedule. We started each day early in the morning and kept going until very late at night. In two of the cities we ministered, at a height of 12,000 feet above sea level, about 4,000 meters, and it's incredible how that altitude affects the body. While we were traveling from Cochabamba to Oruro at an altitude 15,600 feet (5,200 meters), driving along a solitary road in the high mountains, the axle broke on the automobile that was transporting us, but thanks to God we suffered only a little scare. The Lord was with us!

Tijuana, the fastest growing city in Mexico and the largest center of corruption along the border with the United States—as well as the route most often frequented by persons trying to enter the United States illegally in search of hope—was also the site of a blessed Crusade that year.

CHAPTER 36

ON THE MOUNT OF TRANSFIGURATION

Under the continuous dynamic leading of the Holy Spirit of God, 1988 would have its own stamp forged in heaven. February and March went by in a flash, as I labored in Puerto Rico, Texas, California, Washington D.C., and Florida. It was a time of heavy duty activity.

In May we participated in an historic event, the *Washington for Jesus* rally. Earlier, in 1981, I had had the privilege of preaching at two events sponsored by *America for Jesus*. One of these was at the *Orange Bowl* in Miami, attended by 12,000 Hispanics; the other at the Grand Park in Chicago, in front of 20,000 people. Our friend Dr. John Giménez was continuing to pursue his passion of mobilizing people to intercede in prayer for the nation; and, for that reason, we were now holding the *Washington for Jesus* event, possibly the largest gathering of Christians in the United States. What a privilege and responsibility was given me by the Lord to preach before more than one million people, of all ethnic backgrounds, who had gathered in the capital city of the United States, and also to many millions more who listened to the event broadcast live on television.

The outstanding occurrence during those months was my participation in a pre-crusade seminar in Colombia. I cried like a little boy when 125 young people responded in the affirmative to the radical call to dedicate their lives to the ministry. Three beautiful places on the Colombian coast—Cartagena, Santa Marta, and Barranquilla—were the locations for the leadership seminars we held.

We had additional pastoral seminars and workshops during the second week of April, back in Argentina. Our work was draining. The seminars began at 8 o'clock in the morning and at 11 o'clock at night we were still there telling people goodnight. We were exhausted, but happy to be working to do the will of our King.

I returned to the office to preside at sessions of the executive committee of the Los Angeles Congress 1988, then it was on to Arizona, Washington D.C., and then again to Colombia.

It was a warm night and a light breeze was blowing from the Caribbean Sea. The local bullfighting arena in the city of Cartagena was an impressive sight because of its capacity to hold a lot of people on its bleachers, but even more so because of the arches at the top of the walls that surround the entire Plaza de Toros, which make it even more beautiful.

High on the bleachers, lost in the mass of people, a young girl of beautiful features was criticizing her friend who had invited her to attend the Crusade.

"Why did you have to tell my life's story to the preacher?"

"I have told him nothing," her companion answered, surprised. "I haven't even spoken to him."

"Yes," insisted the young girl, who was a working prostitute, "I am certain that you spoke to him about me, because he is speaking directly to me; he is revealing every detail of my life!"

The prostitute placed her face in her hands, rested her elbows on her knees, and, unable to do anything else, burst into tears. During the entire conclusion of the message she sobbed and sobbed; when we extended the invitation she glimpsed a ray of hope that she could change her life. She stood, wiping away the tears from her face, walked down the stairs toward the very center of the arena, and there she surrendered her heart to Christ.

Two days later, one counselor brought her to us in person. My wife Noemi and I hugged her and prayed for her.

This modern-day Mary Magdalene was one of the 11,236 people who made decisions for Christ during the crusade in Cartagena.

After Cartagena, the next crusades were in Santa Marta, where 5,500 people made decisions for Christ, and in Barranquilla, where we finished with 3,700 people determined once for all to live for the King of Kings and Lord of Lords.

Near the end of May, I spent two days in the intensive care unit of a hospital and then was forced to take another ten days off to rest. Even though I am a very healthy person, excess work and lack of any rest for many months had finally taken its toll on my health.

It was a very beautiful turn of events, a time of reconnecting with my soul and with my Lord. This pause provided the mental, physical, and spiritual preparation needed to return full force to the work of the convention planned in Los Angeles. The two years of intensive administrative effort preparing the Los Angeles event had included continuous traveling throughout Latin America, Canada, the United States, Puerto Rico, and northern Mexico, mainly to motivate the leaders to attend the convention.

The executive committee was slowly taking shape and now included such distinguished persons as Norman Mydske, Daniel De León, and Juan Carlos Miranda, among others. No less important was the executive office, with its army of workers, some full-time employees and many more who were voluntarily serving the Lord. There was also that group of men and women, several professionals among them, who came from Baja California, Mexico, a week before the event was to begin; they slept on mats spread on the floor of classrooms in a church in Santa Ana.

Day and night without resting they prepared the thousand-plus packets of materials that would be distributed to the event participants. How fabulous it was to receive assistance from our friends Dan Nuesch and his wife, and of David Enríquez Navarrete, who traveled from Argentina and Mexico, respectively and specifically, to help our office with the preparations for the Congress.

Yes, it is true; a great miracle of the Lord made it possible for us to organize that weeklong event, held July 25-29, where 6,316 leaders and participants came from some of the farthest corners of our planet, representing 46 countries with Christian work in Spanish. Everyone met under the same roof, that of the *Anaheim Convention Center* in California, near Disneyland.

This *International Congress for the Evangelization of the Latin World: Los Angeles '88*, was a continuation of the Amsterdam events of 1983 and 1986, where the idea was first conceived, enriched, and strengthened by the vision of Billy Graham, who thought it good to sponsor these Congresses *sui generis*, being one-of-a-kind events in the history of world evangelism.

When we first got the idea to hold a Congress of this magnitude, I never imagined its transcendence. It would be the Spanish language version of the Amsterdam '83 and '86 events. Providentially, God granted us favor with the Billy Graham Evangelistic Association, which agreed to co-sponsor this magnificent event. On a certain occasion, Brother Mydske mentioned at a committee meeting that the Billy Graham Association sponsors events or helps others sponsor events, but never places its name alongside that of another organization. "This is the first time that we are doing this," he said.

On Monday the 25th at 8 o'clock in the morning, there was already a line of brothers waiting to register and receive their materials and other pertinent information that would be used throughout the week of activities. We had great expectations!

In my welcome speech, I expressed four emotions that the organization of the Congress had provoked in me: 1) a feeling of gratitude to the Lord firstly, and also to Dr. Billy Graham and his team, and especially Dr. Norman Mydske for his moral, strategic, and spiritual support; 2) a feeling of expectancy about what the Lord would do among so many of his servants who had arrived tired, overworked, but trusting that Daniel 10:9 would become a reality for them; 3) a feeling of regret toward the young people because of the inability of the old guard to understand them in their proper environment, so that they can reach their goals; and, 4) a feeling of solemn consecration to our God, of coming to the fountain, of committing ourselves to his work and renewing our covenant with Him.

Challenged by this perspective of objectives, with fear and trembling as I had never before experienced, I went up on the platform at 7 o'clock that evening for the opening service.

What a night of blessing! It was an event that will always be indelibly recorded in my mind. There would have been over 9,000 people in the audience, but regulations of the city fire department would not allow anyone to stand inside the Convention Center auditorium. The doors were closed after the participants filled the seats. More than 2,000 people were left outside. They had to be content with watching the proceedings on a closed circuit television system, in a huge screen that was installed in an adjacent auditorium.

The cream of the crop of world evangelism was gathered in one place. Flags from so many participating countries framed a precious sight. There were Mexicans who serve the Lord in Tokyo, Japan; evangelists from Africa, and from all over Europe. From Spain alone there were 169 participants, and there were also large delegations from all of Latin America and North America.

The panorama from the platform was amazing. After so many sleepless nights, we finally began to hear the first notes played on the piano by our brother Bill Fasig. The trumpet of Tony Hernandez resounded throughout that large auditorium, which was beginning to feel like a little corner of heaven.

My voice filled with emotion, I declared the opening the Congress:

"The work of this *International Congress for the Evangelization of the Latin World: Los Angeles '88* is officially declared open in the name of the Father … in the name of the Son … and in the name of the Holy Spirit."

The following days, from Tuesday through Friday, we implemented the general program of teaching that included 23 seminars and 139 workshops on a wide variety of themes, from evangelization of children to some practical ways to hold opinion polls, as well as lessons on the many factors crucial to the life of an individual who wants to become a worker approved in the eyes of the Lord of the harvest. Each morning, starting at 8 o'clock on the dot, about 5,000 participants literally devoured the teachings that we shared.

With the schedule always completely packed, we no longer had the luxury of savoring this feast of kings any longer. We had to come down from the Mount of Transfiguration. We could not ignore the cunning of Satan, who never sleeps. We had the very important task of preaching the Good News of the Kingdom. The Holy Spirit of love, and only He, will add those who will be saved and fill the ranks of the children of God. To Him be the honor and glory forever!

CHAPTER 37

WITH ARMS EXTENDED

At the beginning of 1989, I already knew that this year would have a different hue than past years. In early January our Board of Directors had approved something that had been stirring in my heart for quite some time. It was a declaration of faith and a mission statement, an open letter in which we had written down in short and simple words our beliefs and convictions.

This item would influence the entire year. It was a real team effort. The Association did not have, nor could it support, the financial burden of employing a lot of people on a full-time basis. This had been a constant preoccupation for me. I knew that we needed more people on the team but we did not have the money to support them. Nevertheless, in that year God began to build a team with two prongs. One small group was needed in the office; another satellite group would be located in various regions of the world and could respond in times of need with their hearts, their ministries, and their resources.

That is how it was that in Honduras we held an amazing campaign for the Lord. Already in February, the team traveled to this country to carry out the advance work with the leadership. For the first time in the history of our Association, I didn't go with them, and the team brought back magnificent results. In March, when the big campaign was to be held, several associate evangelists would each be in charge of a specific site: Choluteca, La Ceiba, Comayagua, and other towns that had welcomed the team.

Jails, schools, women's groups, government officials, children, young people, professionals, soldiers, refugees, street people, merchants—the team even took care of the people's physical needs while there. Doctors and nurses brought free health care and medicines to the people It was our Project Hope in action. It was a huge success having so many children of God involved in satisfying the needs of so many Honduran people.

The impact was glorious. Governors and mayors were reached, and in all 30,000 Hondurans made professions of faith. And why not, with all of the surrender and devotion displayed by this team that God put together? Also, 53 Salvadorans came to help us and gave their personal testimonies of leading 2,385 people to an encounter with Christ right there on the streets. Obviously, the Holy Spirit would not waste this human willingness to rescue thousands for His glory

I now knew that the Lord was giving me other more hands to extend his Gospel. I continued my work holding numerous campaigns in Philadelphia, Brownsville, in the Plaza de Toros of Reynosa, México, in Puerto Rico, in my native country of Argentina, and, the most outstanding event of the year, in Nicaragua.

Truly, Nicaragua represented another exceptional reminder of the grace of our God. He always has something unexpected for us, and then surprises us with his marvelous power.

While our campaign in 1984 had been very difficult because of the nation's lack of freedom, a few years later the atmosphere in Nicaragua was one of polarization and political turmoil. During September, October, and November, the months during which we had scheduled the leadership seminar and the massive campaign, the country's political season was in full swing in preparation for the nation's elections in February 1990. To be sure, those were to become the most transparent elections in the history of Nicaragua.

The nation's religious spectrum also had changed. In 1979 only 7% of the population was self-described adherents of Protestantism. But by 1989, the percentage of Protestants was a respectable 20%. This clearly demonstrated that politicians could not in any way ignore such a large group of citizens. This time around the Nicaraguan campaign leaders did not have any problem obtaining the necessary permits. The authorities themselves helped to expedite the entire process. They were told that if Alberto Mottesi did not have a visa—not to worry—when he arrived in the country, right there in the airport it would be granted. How things had changed from our first visit!

The seminar was held at the *César Augusto Silva Convention Center*, a comfortable building in the capital city of Nicaragua. And because of the large number of participants, we had to divide the leaders into two shifts: one for the pastors and another for the youth leaders. The first 1,250 pastors began the day at 8 o'clock in the morning and continued until 5:30 in the afternoon. The 1,250 youth leaders arrived at about 3:30 in the afternoon and left at 8:30 in the evening. While the pastors were attending their final plenary service for the day, the youth leaders were arriving and sent directly to attend workshops. It was a seminar with a high level of anointing directed by 16 members of our team.

The inaugural sessions were attended by the president of the Legislative Assembly, René Núñez Téllez, but even more surprising was the closing ceremony.

During a short pause in the activities, when I had escaped to the hotel to rest for a few minutes in between such exhausting sessions, I received a telephone call from a familiar assemblyman, Sixto Ulloa, telling me: "The president wants to greet you. Within an hour he will be going to the Convention Center where he has an office."

I virtually flew to the Convention Center. We felt that not only should we personally greet the president, but we also wanted to seat him at the front of the auditorium. In an instant, the whole program was changed, and on Saturday, September 30, at 2 o'clock in the afternoon, Commander Daniel Ortega made his appearance, escorted by his personal guards, some members of his entourage and innumerable reporters, both Nicaraguans and foreigners. Our radio coverage of the event was through the radio station *Ondas de Luz*, which broadcast our activities live 12 hours daily, and this presidential appearance was no exception.

The emotions of the moment were palpable. The Convention Center was filled to capacity. The flashing lights of cameras toted by reporters were continually streaming video coverage of the signs and sights within. The 2,500 pastors and youth leaders of Nicaragua, all in their respective seats, were witnesses of what God was doing for his glory.

The president of the nation, in military uniform and with circumspect expression on his face, was seated on the platform, in the middle, and on both sides of him, some of our team members and me.

When it came time for me to give the message, before I had time to finish my first sentence, the congregation stood to their feet and shouted praises to the Lord. I spoke to the pastors about the lordship of Christ and halfway through my sermon, while I was fervently involved in my preaching, I heard an imperative voice within me, as clear as day, saying: "Turn around, look directly at the president and preach to him!"

If I had planned this, surely I would have been paralyzed and struck dumb then and there. All media imaginable was there on that platform making it the only center of attention. There were television, radio, and newspaper reporters and thousands of eyewitnesses all present in that auditorium. What I was being asked to do was truly crazy. But I did not hesitate, and immediately took action. Without delaying for a second, without knowing what I would say I turned my back to the large auditorium, and I pointed with my index finger at the person who was the head magistrate of that nation and, speaking directly at him, I said:

"Mr. President, we know, and we are not fooled, that our impoverished and bloodstained big country, our beloved Latin America, needs economic and political solutions. We are not fools, we understand; but with all our hearts we know, with great certainty we know, that the solution will not come from the right or from the left, from the White House or Moscow, nor from Havana. Mr. President," and here I emphasized each word, "the solution will come from returning to God, from serving God, from loving Christ."

The entire auditorium as one voice stood to their feet, deeply moved, and there was an explosion of applause and acclamations that were heard long after my last words.

The president's face flushed with color. His discomfort was visible and he looked like he didn't know what to do. On the one hand, there was his official posture and, on the other hand, there was a man touched in his spirit.

I knew that I had to do something, add a parenthesis to my sermon, and approach him. And so I did. I walked over to him and said, "Mr. President, let me pray for you." He agreed with a slight nod of his head.

Then we closed our eyes and prayed. Commander Ortega looked down without closing his eyes and listened to our prayer. I prayed not only for the president as a leader of the nation. I also prayed for him as a husband, as a father; to summarize, as a person. After the prayer, I returned to my place at the podium and continued with my homily. The conclusion was spiritually exuberating.

CHAPTER 38
THE BEGINNING OF A NEW DECADE

The Congress of Tears in *Amsterdam '83* had indelibly marked our lives and prepared us for vast works that would dignify the power of our God. Certainly, we were never the same again after that worldwide gathering of evangelical Christians.

The renowned Crusade of Nicaragua in 1984, with its momentous concluding night, created a historical landmark in its own right, not only for the country, but also for our own ministry. Once again in Amsterdam, in 1986, we wanted to water the harvest that only God can give, in an international gathering planned for the purpose of capitalizing on what had been accomplished at the previous Congress in 1983. So many languages and races united by one Pentecost!

The same purpose was served with several events, including crusades in El Salvador in 1984 and in Cali, Colombia, coinciding with the 450th anniversary of that city's founding, and in Miami in 1987, in Barcelona the same year, and the Hispanic Congress that was such a huge success in Los Angeles, California.

There was an entire year of preparation. An organizing committee capable of managing all the potentiality they had at their disposal with each seminar and each gathering of pastors. The pre-campaign events were planned with the goal of arriving fully prepared for the campaign in Villahermosa, the provincial capital of Tabasco in Mexico. The publicity and the organization of human resources; from the sisters who swept the Plaza and cooked for the team to the doctor who provided emergency services, the photographers, the cameraman, the musicians, the ushers, the counselors, the secretaries, the technicians in charge of the sound system, those who ran the computers, and transportation, even a choir—they all perfectly fulfilled their commissioned duties. They all made it possible to bring the crusade to a spectacular end.

The ministry has progressively expanded, becoming more and more complex and demanding over the '80s. And then the years of 1990 and 1991 had their own unique structure of unceasing work where we saw in a very concrete way that without the Lord we were nothing. His power and his grace are the only source from which our souls continue to find a reason for ministry.

During the decade of the 1990s my team went ahead of me into Colta, Ecuador, where they held leadership seminars in preparation for our crusade with the Quechua people. Before going to Ecuador, I preached in El Salvador to 10,000 people at a convention themed *Jesus Christ Our Peace*. While I was ministering there, several helicopters flew above the stadium, typifying the cruelest days of the war.

Later, under an old tarp, I spoke to thousands of Quechua people who crowded onto a football field to listen to the message of the cross. At the foot of the Chimborazo, a permanently snow capped peak in the mountains of Ecuador, a region that is home to the Quechua people, one of the poorest, saddest and most marginalized tribe, in all of Latin America, the Master of Galilee arrived with his gift of love.

Later we went to Puerto Rico, and there we met with some servants of God who were highly prepared, both spiritually and intellectually. We saw a panoramic vision of the war torn and impoverished nations of the world that urgently need the Bread of Life.

With renewed strength we returned to the dusty paths of Mexico with a wide range of missionary work in several cities: Parral, Torreon, Ciudad Juarez, Veracruz, Monterrey, and Villahermosa. As always, we visited each site twice, first for the advance preparation for the leadership and later to hold the crusade.

At the end of 1990, we found ourselves involved in two precious events. One of these was a crusade involving several cities in the province of Mendoza, Argentina, which brought 17,550 decisions for Christ. The other event was in Villahermosa, Mexico. It was a combination of ministry to the leaders and public proclamation of the Gospel.

How many were saved at the 1991 crusade in Tabasco? Perhaps in our lifetimes we will never know. Even though we gather statistics, the final numbers are only a poor reflection of an immeasurable reality. Each member of the committee and of the team was caught up in his or her own respective responsibilities. All of them resolutely accomplished their corresponding duties. When the time came they had to make a decision; they had to close the front doors even though there was a multitude of people still arriving. The stadium was completely filled. The fascinating thing was to see more than 30,000 people forming a marvelous kaleidoscope. The sound system was commandeered to inform the people who were still arriving about the gigantic screen that was set up outside the stadium, at one side of the bullring. Not one more soul would fit inside the stadium.

As I watched with eager eyes the behavior of this huge multitude, thoughts came into my mind like a flash of lightning as I relived the high points of some of the great events that God has allowed us to experience.

It was early 1991, and the war in the Persian Gulf brought with it a growing sense of uncertainty and confusion. An unpleasant wave of economic recession around the world had affected more countries than one could possibly imagine. Moral values were at a very low level. At that time, at age 48, after 30 years in the ministry, I had never seen a world so ripe for the harvest as it was at that time. That is why I do not despair. Just the opposite.

During the first week of February we visited Costa Rica, and I still cherish those memories in my heart. From there we went to Guatemala, where I ministered during a weeklong celebration dedicating a new auditorium of the *Christian Fellowship*.

On one of those nights, with my friend, Pastor Jorge Lopez as my companion, we went to the presidential residence where we were to have dinner with the man who was then president of Guatemala, Mr. Jorge Serrano Elias, and his family. Even though I had already met him before he had reached this position, I went to this encounter in formal attire. With open arms, almost shouting, he said to me: "Alberto! Glory to God! How are you?"

He broke with every preconceived notion of maintaining the formal distance between our human positions of power, and we delivered ourselves over to a formidable evening. Out of this experience another project was conceived and born, the *Project 500 or America 500 Years Later.*

Project 500 represents a vision for reaching the unreached, the "sacred cows" of society in each country—the small elite who are the governing class, the rich, the intellectuals. Those who would never go to a church, much less a public crusade, but who are also men and women of flesh and bone who have the same spiritual needs as the poor and the oppressed.

This year, 1991, also included two other important events. My father, José Mottesi, at age 86, died in the arms of my brother, Osvaldo. That was the occasion that gathered all of our families together in one place.

But, when it comes to world evangelism, we cannot slacken the pace. There's no time for pastoral Mondays off or for vacations. The devil does not sleep. Neither should we waste any time without preaching the Good News, so as to snatch lost souls who will be with us forever in Heaven.

In early 1992, after 30 years as an ordained minister, I celebrated the fifteenth anniversary of the Association with my family and ministry team. Halfway through that year we began to work on the largest crusade of our lives, *Project 500 or America 500 Years Later*.

Again, we believed that an effort was needed to reach out to high-level people such as presidents, senators, and representatives. If they would convert to the Lord, we believed that we would see a much faster change in the history of the world. The year of 1992 was important for the entire continent of America. It was the 500th anniversary of Columbus' discovery (or conquest) of America, and celebrations were planned in many places. We wanted to take advantage of that milestone in history using commemorative events to attract civic leaders and elite politicians in each country, so that we could preach to them face to face.

With that in mind, we held 28 gala banquets, which were attended by 18,000 leaders from the realms of politics, government, academia, and business in some of the main cities of the continent. This project marked a before and after point not only in the life of our ministry but also in the Christian history of the Hispanic American world.

Over the years, the effects of Project 500 would go far beyond what we had originally dreamed.

CHAPTER 39

UNDER AUTHORITY

"What abomination are you from?" was the question a little boy asked his classmate at school. The boy was using the wrong terminology, of course. What he was trying to ask was the name of the denomination to which his friend belonged.

Some churches belong to denominations and councils and others are independent. I cannot describe myself with any of these labels. I think that the best way to define our position within the Body of Christ is to say that we are interdependent. No member of the Body of Christ can say to another: "I have no need of you," under any circumstance.

Thanks to God, we have seen an enormous change in this regard within the church in Latin America. There are still a lot of "lone rangers," and even a few "bomb throwers," self-appointed judges of others. They do not seem to know that when they scorn one part of the Body of Christ, they are plunging a knife into the heart of God.

We view our Evangelical Association as one part of a whole, which is the family of God. We also believe that this includes one tremendous responsibility: to be open epistles before the Lord, his people, and also in front of a world that always scrutinizes the servants of Jesus Christ.

One of my concerns from the beginning of the Association was to have transparency in the area of administration. It had been an arduous path to walk. In 1991, I made the decision to step down from the presidency of my Board of Directors. I had been seriously considering this step for quite some time. My board members were surprised at this decision, but the main reason was my desire to have a model administration. I knew that if I left the presidency, I would no longer have complete control of the Association's business, or even of my own family. And that was how I could build the Association into a model of excellence, one that would be completely transparent in its use of monies that were sacred to God. I only accepted to have a voice at the meetings of our Board of Directors, but not a vote.

Once, I asked a man who was close to Billy Graham about the secret of his success. Without a moment's hesitation he answered: "Knowing how to surround himself with faithful and upright men who counsel him and help him in his ministry."

I believe that, in the management of a ministry, there should be a combination of the divine and the human—of the spiritual anointing and the human administration—that consequently results in a solid ministry that serves the Lord and reaches the world.

Now we have a Board of Directors that has the last word in the administration of our ministry. Some of them are English-speaking, but most of them are Latinos. We also have what we call the Council of Department Directors. There have been years when the council met together more than twenty times. I have abided by the counsel and decisions of this group.

The financial records of our ministry are open, and every three months outside professionals come to our organization to examine them. This may be excessive, but we prefer to go overboard in giving an account of ourselves, in being clear, in living under authority, rather than clinging to an independence that only reveals the carnality of the human being and religious infantilism.

The more the ministry grows as the years go by, the more we believe in our interdependence within the Body of Christ. I believe that we have to confront a situation within our evangelical culture in Latin America. There is in many, deep inside the heart, a spirit of domination, a spirit of independence and a hunger for power and recognition.

It is almost incredible how we seek titles and positions with which to embellish our lives. The authority of the ministry does not come from being called apostle, prophet, evangelist, or doctor. These days, there are apostles appearing everywhere who do not have the Biblical credentials of Christian apostleship. It is also possible to obtain doctoral degrees at a very reasonable price, which is one of the biggest shames of the Hispanic church. Without any serious academic training, for only a few dollars, you can easily obtain a doctorate. In reality, the value of the doctorate and its relevance is directly related to the university that bestows it. As Christian leaders, we should feel ashamed of those who are seeking this type of recognition without serious academic study and should feel ashamed of the organizations that are devoted to this business.

Our authority for Christian leadership does not come from the titles one has, or from any type of control or force being exercised on others. Our spiritual authority is directly related to our submission to the Lord and to his visible authorities. Our authority is directly related to our humility. The larger the ministry, the meeker, the more surrendered, the more solicitous of the needs of others, the more open to the advice of others, should the servant of God be.

The greatness of a ministry is not dependent on the charisma but rather on the character of the minister.

From the inception of the Association, the base of our financial support has consisted of our precious donors. Our ministry is a labor of faith, and God has provided women and men to sustain the work. Our greatest achievements became possible through the channel of blessing that God prepared for us to receive the necessary resources.

Once, I thought that God only answered prayers spoken in English. The enormous projects of our English-speaking brothers, their huge budgets ... while we, the Hispanics, were always lacking ten centavos to complete a peso --not even a dollar!

But God has taught me that he is bilingual... that He answers the prayers of any of his children, in any language, and in any place in the world.

We have so much evidence of his support! Like that time when someone I had never seen before, who had never heard me preach, upon learning of our Project 500 Years Later, a series of events commemorating the 500th anniversary of the colonization of America and which would open the door for us to share our Christian vision of the universe with thousands of government, academic, and business leaders, sent us a check for $100,000.

When we began to dream about another project, the International Centers for the School of Evangelists, in our monthly letter to our dear donors I included a note: "With $5,000 we can open a school in any place in the world." One donor, I think someone who gave $20 every month, called us and told us about her experience. After reading the letter, she threw it in the trashcan. Then she heard a voice saying: "Why did you throw the letter away? Go and get it." She was obedient, but when she tried to retrieve the letter, it was already at the bottom of the garbage can. She was only able to retrieve a small fragment of the newsletter; it was the piece containing this phrase: "With $5,000 we can begin a school in any part of the world." Then the Lord said: "Sow the $5,000 and plant a school in Spain." She obeyed and that is how we were able to make those exploratory trips and take the first steps to open a school there. The same thing happened with another donor in connection to a School in Africa.

And when Oscar Merlo, our Dean, was contemplating how to establish an online academic infrastructure, the most economical price he could find to implement the technology was about $75,000. He decided not to tell me anything; he only prayed. Then, an unknown person called from Argentina who had recently completed a similar project for the University of Puerto Rico and the University of the Dominican Republic.

"I heard about what you want to do," the man told Oscar. "The cost of the system would be about $75,000."

"We don't have that kind of money, but let me tell you about our dream," Oscar said in response.

After Oscar's passionate account, there was a silence. Those were seconds that seemed like hours. Finally, this precious person spoke and said: "I will install the system for free."

Is not God the one who provides? Is it not He who sustains His work?

Truly, God speaks Spanish.

In our ministry, we never did anything because we had the money. We did things because God asked us to do them, and the money followed.

When God told his people to walk across the Red Sea, when He told them that the sea would open for them, I imagine the immensity of the sea was imposing, and that when they put their feet in the water it felt cold. But God had spoken. They dared, and the waters parted.

That is how we have always acted. We have believed God's promises, and He has always been faithful.

CHAPTER 40

GREAT CRUSADES OF THE LAST DECADE

When I consider the crusades I've been a part of, many memories come to mind—so many beautiful emotions happening through the years! No book can explain the experiences of hundreds of evangelistic crusades, some small, others huge, but all of them full of the joy of His Presence.

The thoughts and memories of decades of ministry crowd my mind. For example, in 1995 there was the crusade in Santiago, Chile. The beautiful O'Higgins Park, the setting of so many great national celebrations, was filled with a multitude hungry for the God of heaven. The total of more than 7,200 decisions for Christ overwhelmed the capacity of the prayer counselors who were there to assist them.

But there are things that happen at the crusades that we would never, humanly speaking, dare to attempt. However, when the Holy Spirit has full control, powerful things can happen. I remember at that same crusade, having called on criminals fleeing from justice. Seven individuals who were on the run surrendered to Christ. I remember the Friday night when I called on drug traffickers to renounce the profession and place their lives under the authority of God, and a dozen people responded.

I remember another evening when many came forward and placed on the platform knives, firearms, envelopes with drugs, and even amulets that were a symbol of their ties to witchcraft and Satanism. I also recall extraordinary occasions, such as the time when a groom and bride arrived at the last meeting in their wedding clothes. "Our wedding party just ended. We wanted to continue celebrating at the crusade before going on to our honeymoon," they explained.

Perhaps one of the most unusual crusades was the one in Cali, Colombia. I saw Jesus walking along the streets of that city. "You Are Cali" was born in the heart of the government of that city, concerned about the sadness, depression, drug addiction, violence, alcoholism, the enormous number of broken homes and, at that time, a 29 percent unemployment rate. The government, together with private businesses, industries, the Christian people, university rectors, and mass media, among others, launched this movement named "You Are Cali," as an effort to rescue the city. This was in August of 1998, and the Pascual Guerrero Stadium, one of the largest on the continent, was filled to capacity.

During the crusade, we carried out the distribution of free clothing, food, and medicines, among some marginalized neighborhoods. We had a call center with two hundred telephone lines that, for 24 hours a day, answered the needs of the people. More than 5,000 university students had gone door to door, visiting the city's 500 thousand homes once a month for six months, to distribute booklets presenting family values, one for each month. Never had we seen, like we saw in Cali, the secular community turning to the Church and asking for help.

And how exciting to remember the crusade in the Sula Valley in Honduras, in June of 2003! We had to use a huge plot of land in Choloma, a suburb of the industrial city of San Pedro Sula; because past crusades had shown us that the existing stadiums were not large enough to hold the enormous crowds.

The multitude stood on their feet each night, and during one meeting, when I was ready to pray for those who had come forward to accept Christ, I felt a voice telling me: "Don't pray. Someone else is missing. The chief of a gang is missing. He is a criminal and a fugitive from justice. Tell him that today I am giving him one last chance." I repeated these words to the people and they began to pray and the music began to play. Suddenly, there was a movement very far away in the crowd. A little group of people was making their way through the crowd while whispering sounds in the audience were heard, repeating: "The monster, the monster." They were referring to the gang leader who, followed by seven other gangsters, was making a path through the people to give his life to the Lord Jesus.

When the meeting ended, they introduced him to me. He was full of tattoos and chains. His eyes looked swollen from so much alcohol and drugs. But his face was bathed in tears and he said to me: "Do you believe that a God so holy can forgive a criminal such as I?" I hugged him and asked him to forgive the wrongs that society might have done to him. I adopted him as a spiritual son and introduced him to a personal relationship with God.

So many precious things happened during those days. For example, we received an email telling the following story:

"My name is Armando Muñoz. I am a Honduran journalist and I work for the most important newspaper in my country, the daily *La Prensa*, which is edited here in the city of San Pedro Sula.

One morning last June, the managing editor sent me to get some information and cover the event in which you would be preaching to business leaders, mayors, deputies, politicians, and journalists. When I heard you preaching at the Convention Center here in San Pedro Sula, I was impressed by the message that you gave under the anointing of the Holy Spirit., and that Friday morning, I made my best business deal, accepting Jesus Christ as the Lord and Savior of my life.

That Friday night was the first of three days of evangelical messages that you would be presenting in the city of Choloma to over two hundred thousand people who attended. Today, with this email, I want to thank you for having brought me to Jesus Christ.

Thank you! Thank you very much! I want you to know, Dr. Mottesi, that you have in me a brother and a friend, who will never forget you. I have in my possession a recording of the message that you preached, because someday I want to show it with great love to the children that the Lord may give me. Thank you Dr. Mottesi! Thank you!"

I remember the last night of that particular crusade. The atmosphere was saturated with the Presence of God; many people were crying and confessing their sins. At the moment when I prayed for the salvation of the people, declaring the divine grace and the requirements of a Holy God, without anyone touching them, four prostitutes fell to the ground crying, and four gangsters in another part of the field, also crying, fell to the ground and repented of their sins.

That same year there was a crusade in Maracaibo, Venezuela. It was the Celebration of Pentecost 2003 that Pastor José Inciarte, now in the presence of the Lord, held every year. The *Pachenco Romero Stadium* was overflowing. More than 40,000 people attended on the first night, and thousands more were left outside, unable to enter.

I remember a woman who approached me and said: "Twenty-five years ago I surrendered my life to Christ during one of your meetings. Now my four grandsons are all in the ministry." What a joy it is to see the fruits of the Word!

After that first, powerful crusade in Managua, Nicaragua, during 1984, we returned in 1989, and again in December of 2004. On this last occasion, we had a very warm meeting with the president of the country, Enrique Bolaños. We also had a very challenging opportunity to speak at a full session of the National Assembly of the government, where for forty-five minutes I had an opening to expound on the Gospel.

Our associates held one hundred and fifty pre-crusade events, touching almost every city in the country. Among the preachers there were several students from our School of Evangelists. In remote villages the young people confronted the powers of hell, and several witches were converted. During the third and final night, even though the local estimates were larger, we believe that the attendance was about 200,000 people. The approximately fifteen square blocks comprising the *Plaza de la Fe* were completely full of people, who stood there for more than five hours. The response to the invitation to accept Christ far surpassed any estimates and resources.

I also lovingly remember the crusade in El Salvador in December of 2006. It was held outdoors at El Cafetalón, a huge open field. The president of the steering committee, Pastor Mario Vega, said: "Each night, unprecedented numbers of people surrendered their lives to Christ." I remember the testimony of two Christian policemen, who recognized one of the most wanted men in the country. Two months earlier, that man had escaped from the prison in Cojutepeque with twenty-five other dangerous criminals. They saw him kneeling with his face on the ground crying, together with eight other gangsters, surrendering his life to Jesus.

A report from the steering committee estimated that during the three nights of the crusade, we had a cumulative attendance of about 300,000 people.

A key moment of that crusade was the recognition that our ministry gave to Dr. Paul Finkenbinder, known around the world as Hermano Pablo, and his wife Linda. At that time they were both 85 years old, and had been in the ministry for 65 years, many of those years in El Salvador. I remember having spoken of him at that time as "my hero, my role model, my father, and my friend."

How can I summarize so many experiences during those crusades? Perhaps there is something I would like to highlight. Obviously, at our crusades we always had music, praise and worship. How grateful we are to have some of the most well known worship singers working with us at these events, men like Jesús Adrian Romero, Marco Barrientos, Marcos Witt, Grupo Rojo, Danilo Montero, Jaime Murrell, and others. They were all awe inspiring, and their participation was vital. However, what I would like to emphasize is that, even though times have changed, and styles and models of crusades can be modified, I continue to believe, as never before, in the power of the Word of God. Does not Paul himself say that people will be saved by the foolishness of the preaching?

How very dangerous it is to try to orchestrate our lives by the times, and diminish the pre-eminence of the preaching of the Gospel!

I continue to believe in the absolute power of the Word of God. What a wonderful example has evangelist Billy Graham been for me with His frequent expression "The Bible says!" It characterizes an era of preaching that should never end.

I thank God for all of the modern attractions we can use today to enhance the crusades—including videos, music, lights, etc. But, there is nothing more important than opening the Word, sharing the Truth, and calling the people to put their lives under the lordship of Christ. As long as I live I will continue doing this with all my heart.

CHAPTER 41

HAITI 2001

Even though I have preached at hundreds of crusades, I felt that I should dedicate an entire chapter of this book to one very unique event, the one we held in the Republic of Haiti in July of 2001.

Normally, before we organize this type of event, an invitation must be received from a large group of Christian leaders in the region. In the case of Haiti, God had spoken to us very strongly, and I believe this was the only time that our coordinators went and pounded on the doors of the ministers in the area to get things organized.

On two or three occasions, several people without any connection among them had mentioned to us that they received a word of knowledge from God saying essentially that we must go to Haiti. For that reason, our coordinators went there and met with the principal Christian leaders in that nation.

Our team was meeting at the headquarters of one of the Haitian evangelical councils—a meeting that was completely private—when suddenly someone knocked on the door. It was a simple pastor from the interior of the republic. He knew nothing about us, and was unaware of the presence of our team in Haiti. Besides, he had no knowledge of the meeting that was being held there, but he entered the room and said: "I have walked from my village for two days without stopping. The Lord told me to do this, and that when I arrived here I should tell you the following: 'The ambassadors of Christ who are visiting you today, come in the name of the Lord and what they bring is the Divine will.' " Our coordinators told me that all of the leaders present fell to their knees in fear at such a clear manifestation of God regarding this project.

Our associates were in charge of organizing five crusades in inland areas. The conditions were so harsh, that some of our evangelists were not able to bathe for a week, and others returned with infections, and other health problems.

You see, about 200 years ago, the "fathers of the nation" dedicated Haiti to Satan. On August 14, 1991, President Aristides again consecrated Haiti to Satan, and a large number of the members of government at that time practiced witchcraft. On the first night of the crusade, the lights went out in the capital city. The electrical generators that we had installed to overcome such an event didn't work. It poured rain and the truck in which we were traveling with several doctors was involved in a crash on the darkened highway. Certainly, the doctors from Puerto Rico who accompanied me on this occasion played a vital role. Each day they tended to about a thousand patients.

""When we ran out of medicine, I burst into tears," one of the doctors said. "We could only pray for the sick and hope for a miracle." "Several times I felt like I was going to faint," said evangelist Antunez from Honduras, who accompanied us. "The odor of the sick people was frightening."

Another of the evangelists who was there said: "We did not have light or running water where we were staying. The brothers brought a little water for me to bathe, and the water had the smell of death, but God protected us. Many days we only ate a banana and a piece of bread."

Another story that exemplifies the conditions we encountered there was the story of Jean David Larochelle, a young Haitian now serving Christ in Ecuador, and who was our interpreter into the Creole and the French language. He told us that, before his conversion, he used a human skull upside down as a plate for his food. In a long and inspired poem, he writes: "Haiti, my beloved country, how I love you! I have seen you suffer and weep. I have walked through the garbage dumps of your cities. Haiti, history has forgotten you. Haiti, my beloved country, how I love you!

God had been speaking to me about dedicating Haiti to Jesus Christ. On one of the nights, wrapped in the Haitian flag, we did that with all of the passion that we could muster. I remember that we pleaded for the government. We prayed that the president would convert to Jesus Christ and also asked for the children and the youth to do the same. The Presence of God was being felt among the people; many were on their knees, profoundly broken, in the Champ de Mars, an enormous plaza in Port au Prince, the nation's capital city.

A Haitian singer, a Canadian resident and very beloved in Haiti, was in Canada when she felt that God was asking her to go to Haiti. Even though she did not know exactly why, she traveled to the country with her pastor, and then became aware of the crusade. We all understood that God had brought her to be part of this event. She sang at that moment of dedication: "To God be the Glory."

The following day was the final service. People were arriving from all over the country for the conclusion of the crusade. We were about to begin, when a lawyer, a member of the Nazarene Church who was working at the law courts, his cellular phone in hand, told me: "They have just called me from the Presidential Palace to tell me that President Aristides will be sending his most violent strike forces to destroy this meeting." Someone heard this and within a few minutes a lot of people knew what was happening.

Some people said to me: "Let's cancel the event."

Others said: "Make the service very short; preach for only five or ten minutes."

But God was saying: "I brought you here to preach. Preach everything that I have given you."

I am not brave, and I almost could not believe what I was hearing when I heard the recording of my message broadcast live that afternoon on the country's network of radio stations. I had publicly told the president of the country that what he had done, in dedicating Haiti to Satan, was the cause of so much disgrace and misery for his nation. In the message I exhorted him to repent and surrender his life to Jesus Christ.

When the meeting was just getting started, several trucks arrived full of the thugs sent by Aristides. They surrounded the enormous plaza. They were holding heavy chains and liquor bottles in their hands. Many of our people, the elderly and the children, were trembling in fear of what could happen. I remember that I was already preaching with my interpreter at my left, when a pastor boldly approached me and in my right ear said: "Stop preaching or this will be a disaster." Once again, the Voice of God said: "Do not be afraid. Continue preaching."

When we gave the invitation for people to surrender their lives to Christ, hundreds of the violent thugs sent by the president threw their chains and liquor bottles on the ground and knelt, broken, surrendering their lives to Jesus.

How can we not serve the Lord? How glorious it is to preach the Gospel! The Holy Spirit is so powerful! How right was Charles Spurgeon, that great English preacher, when he exhorted his students saying: "If God calls you to preach the Gospel, don't lower yourself to become a king of England."

CHAPTER 42
THE MUSLIM WORLD

Each opportunity to preach the Gospel is a real challenge. Whether we are preaching in front of one hundred people, in a small congregation, or in front of one million viewers, as we have been called on to do at times, or whether in evangelistic crusades where the attendance surpasses 200,000 people, my knees always shake and the feeling of being weak and incompetent is always present. "Not that we are competent in ourselves to claim anything for ourselves," said the Apostle Paul. How glorious that he adds… "Our competence comes from God." (2 Corinthians 3:5)

Even though the truth that we preach is always the same, and the central focus of the message never changes, each of the places where we go has its own unique characteristics that shape the preparation of the message for the people.

When we received the invitation to preach at the first massive evangelistic crusade authorized by the government of Turkey, we felt that God was behind it. We continually receive invitations from many parts of the world, and for many years we had resisted running all over the planet. Our focus had always been on Latin America, and God honored the fact that we concentrated on our own continent, bombarding it with the love of God through radio and television programs, articles and evangelistic crusades. However, this opportunity to go to a Muslim country captured our hearts.

We spent a lot of time reading about Turkey, a country of seventy two million Muslims and only about 3,000 evangelical Christians. We tried to understand something about their culture, what things we should avoid so as not to damage the small Christian presence in that country. We really believe that we should contextualize the message for each situation, but this consideration was never as urgent for me as it was in the case of that nation.

Among the people with whom we were in consultations, exchanging letters, reviewing written materials and holding teleconferences, was Juan Sarmiento, leader of a Christian outreach to the Muslim world. We had made an appointment to speak with him before our trip, to discuss the most recent recommendations. He requested our permission to include Doris Torres in the telephone conference, someone who had been a missionary to Turkey for seven or eight years and was temporarily living in California before returning to the missionary field. The idea sounded terrific to us, and during the conversation we talked about many details, and also prayed. I still remember some of the final words. Doris said: "I believe that the Turkish government is starting to close. There is a trend among the extremists who wish to make their country a more radical Islamic state. Brother Alberto, this is probably a small window of opportunity that has opened. I want to ask you something: Please, preach the Word!"

So we began our work in Turkey in October of 2010, with a closed-door retreat for the forty Latin American missionaries who work there. It was held at a hotel near the city of Ephesus. Also in attendance were several Turkish and Latin American leaders from twelve countries, who were considering serving the Lord in some Muslim country. I preached to them, every time with a broken heart. This small group of workers is a group of Gospel giants.

I met a Turkish evangelist whose family had abandoned him when he became a Christian. I also learned of another Iranian evangelist who, when he converted to Christ, was abandoned by his three children. I felt so clumsy and inadequate by comparison, realizing how the type of Christianity that we experience in the West is often so very superficial and egocentric.

Later, we went to Istanbul for the evangelistic event, a city with twenty million inhabitants and only about a thousand Christians, scattered around in small congregations. Our events were attended by the highest Muslim leader, and also by the ministers of religious affairs for the governments of Turkey and of Spain, the director of human rights from the local government, political leaders, and consuls from the United States, England, Spain, and Holland. We received several greetings including that of the Prime Minister of Turkey. In fact, on the following day all of the newspapers said: "Turkish government recognizes evangelical church."

Pastor Carlos Madrigal, a native of Spain, who was my interpreter there, said: "When we came here twenty five years ago, there were only thirty believers. The meetings were held in houses and Christians were frequently thrown in jail. The churches were built over a lake of blood from the martyrs."

Jon Kregel, a former soccer player from Barcelona who had also played with the Cosmos of New York, gave a powerful testimony. To be sure, he spoke wearing his soccer shirt from Barcelona; the Turks are huge soccer fans. My friend Pedro Eustache, a solo flautist and composer (who has collaborated with music in many Hollywood movies including Mel Gibson's *The Passion of Christ*), and who had joined us on this occasion, was in the middle of a majestic musical interpretation. There were only a few minutes to go before the message would begin and I, seated between two brothers from our team, was struggling spiritually. Speaking to those two men, I asked: "How will the Turks respond to the message of a Latin American speaking through an interpreter? Will they raise their hands as is done in other countries to indicate a decision for Christ? Will they have the courage to walk forward?"

I was really trying to define the last touches of my presentation that would begin in only a few minutes. What should I do, Lord? Suddenly, the words of Doris came like the sound of waterfalls in my ears: "Preach the Word. Preach the Word."

To present Christ as Lord is somewhat offensive to the Muslims. They consider him a prophet but deny that He is King of Kings and Lord of Lords. So, that was my first declaration. It was the main emphasis of my message. We knew that probably there were government spies present at the meeting, but the sense of urgency that filled our hearts was much stronger. We no longer thought about our good public relations with the Turks, or about anything else that circumstantially might affect us. This was, as the missionary said, perhaps the only small window that would ever be opened, and with a passion that I have felt only a few times in my life I preached the lordship of Christ.

I explained very clearly what conversion is. I even asked, as I had always done for many years, that those who were already members of the evangelical churches not come forward. I was more cautious than ever in the invitation, and how exciting it was to see hundreds of Turkish people bathed in tears recognizing Christ as the Lord of their lives.

Yes, preparation for each event is of enormous importance. The message never changes, but each event is a very different experience—presenting the Gospel in Guatemala City, in Paris or to indigenous tribes of the Andes. To customize the message in accordance with the characteristics of the group that we are trying to reach is fundamental. However, there is a point of no return. The time comes when the preacher must throw himself into the hands of the Holy Spirit and must respond to Him, only to Him, to be a faithful herald of the Gospel.

A few weeks after we left Turkey, in December of 2010, we went to Tegucigalpa, Honduras. It was our third crusade in Tegucigalpa. Once again, the National Stadium was not big enough, the multitudes of people overflowed, and the response to the invitation to accept Christ was gigantic. During the series of events there, we welcomed visits from the president of that country as well as the president of the National Congress, the mayor of the capital city, judges of the Supreme Court, and senators of the republic. It was a breath of the Holy Spirit upon this region of the world, so different, so warmly receptive, with such loving Latin American spirit responding to God.

CHAPTER 43
WHEN GOD IS IN CONTROL

There were so many campaigns that began serenely, peacefully, perfectly scheduled and with beautiful results—if only it was always that way, but no, that's not the case. There have been crusades where I would have liked to vanish at the start, rather than having to confront the pervasive manifestations of evil restricting our purposes, an opposition that was furiously Satanic. I remember a crusade in the Dominican Republic, in the middle of a dark night, with a storm pouring down rain and lightning bolts like I had never seen in my life, and having to preach like that, in the dark, soaked to the bones, with the Bible dripping water, and shouting at the top of my lungs.

Back in Nicaragua, I preached on one of the most severe moments of political tension because of their civil war, in a place where the difficulties were exceedingly spectacular. But so were also the victorious results we experienced. Over time, that evangelistic event has become milestone, a historic landmark, not only for the country of Nicaragua, but also in my own ministry.

In Venezuela, the granting of visas to preachers and missionaries had been suspended. However, just hours before our campaign was to begin, with everything already prepared and waiting, at the last minute they "incredibly" granted the necessary permissions.

The hotel where I was staying in Guatemala was set on fire, in an act of terrorism; and in El Salvador, also in a state of full civil war at the time, the guerrillas announced a major offensive during a strike, setting off bombs all over the capital city. Even so, the power of God grew stronger to show us that He is the one who directs the destinies of the nations.

We have witnessed events that were incredibly exciting. There have been joyful and happy times, as well as hours full of anguish. Only one thing is certain: there are no obstacles or contrary forces that can overcome the Kingdom of God.

In this euphoric frame of mind, there have been spontaneous bursts of praise from my heart to Jesus my Lord, exalting Him and glorifying Him. Little by little, sleep overtakes me while a smile appears on my face, the product of a conscious awareness that we are doing the will of God. Alleluia!

What glorious surprises the Lord has for us! We were celebrating an evangelistic campaign in Guayaquil, the port city of Ecuador. The Christian leaders in Quito, its capital city, were able to make arrangements for me to be introduced and speak to a session of the National Assembly there. This is something unique that has been happening to me in several countries of Latin America.

Very early one morning, while it was still dark outside, with about twenty pastors from Guayaquil, I boarded the first flight to the capital city. They welcomed us as if I were a foreign dignitary. Noemi and I were placed in a limousine, and while policemen on motorcycles equipped with loud sirens escorted us through the traffic of that city, I was sitting there almost hunched over in my seat. The people on the streets greeted us as we passed by, perhaps thinking that we were famous personalities from the world of arts or politics.

When we arrived at the government palace, a long-faced pastor was waiting for us.

"Everything is cancelled," he said.

"What happened?" we asked.

The president of the Congress used his veto power and said that an evangelist would not be allowed to speak in a session of the nation's assembly.

"Don't worry," we told him. "Look for a place where our group can gather to pray."

Noemi and I decided to sit down in the little seating area for the public, and from there we could see the development of the Assembly, their discussions, their insults, their votes.

Meanwhile, the devil began to tell me: "How bad this will be for your reputation. People everywhere knew that today you were going to preach to the National Assembly. You will end up looking like a fool."

These are times when an evangelist must decide between concern for his own personal reputation, or radical trust in the God of the heavens who called him, opened, and still opens doors in his Name.

Suddenly, something unusual happened. The president of the Congress said: "I am not feeling well. I feel like I am falling apart and I believe I must to go to the hospital emergency room." Under the circumstances, the vice president took over and assumed direction of the Assembly meeting.

Within five minutes a senator raised his hand and said: "I place on the table the motion to invite the evangelist, Mottesi, to come and give us some words." The Assembly unanimously voted in the affirmative, and within a few minutes this evangelist was standing on the platform in front of the top leaders of the country and proclaiming the Name that is above all names and before whom every knee shall bow and every tongue shall confess that Jesus Christ is the Lord.

When you confidently rest in the assurance that God has called you, He will send supernatural intestinal upheavals upon your enemies, and thwart them.

CHAPTER 44

THE PRESIDENTS OF LATIN AMERICA

It is called San Vito, and it's an Italian neighborhood in the middle of the Central American country of Costa Rica. The crusade there was truly glorious. During that time the pizzeria "Mama Mía" became our center of operations. It was there where we held meetings and made major decisions. Of course, we also ate some of the best pizza in the world there, better than that of Rome, Buenos Aires, or New York.

We were returning to San José, the capital city, in an automobile driven by Sixto Porras, continental director for Focus on the Family, when suddenly I said:

"I would like to speak with President Rodriguez."

"You would have to make an appointment, and it might take some time to get an interview," Sixto answered.

"It's just that I feel like I must speak with him!"

Sixto smiled and said: "It is impossible to speak with a president just because one gets the idea. Besides, out here I don't see any place where we might find a telephone to make the contact."

"Stop! Stop here," I said.

It was a simple country store. Reluctantly, he stopped the car.

In fact, the store did have a telephone that could be rented by persons interested in using it. I said: "Sixto, it's your turn now. Call and contact the president for me."

With a half-incredulous smile on his face, he took the telephone and called the presidential palace. They, of course, made him wait for a long time.

"I told you," Sixto insisted. "It doesn't work like this."

But suddenly the voice of the president's private secretary was heard, announcing that the president was ready to speak with me by telephone.

We spent a long time talking, perhaps close to two hours. Those were moments of sharing the Word, prophesying, praying for him, talking about his dreams. It was really something indescribable.

When we asked the store attendant how much we owed him, his eyes were bulging out of their sockets. He couldn't believe what he'd seen and heard, "No, you don't owe me anything," he said. "Don't pay me anything!"

Before being elected president, on three occasions Rodriguez had attended some of our events held in his country. Of course, he was only a candidate then. But at this time he was the president and some were saying that he probably would not have time for the Christians anymore. But, yes, he did more than answer that call. In July of 1999, his country was planning to honor one of the oldest hospitals in the nation, and he was the one who suggested to the hospital directors: "Invite the evangelist Mottesi to speak as a conference speaker." The event, coordinated by the office of protocol of the presidency, included a choir from the Central University and there were about 400 medical doctors present. Only four or five pastors had arrived, and they became aware of my presence at the meeting only at the last minute. It was not a Christian event. It was an event for the government to honor that institution, and it was the president himself who introduced me as the speaker—yes, these things are truly unforgettable.

Naturally, because the only theme that I know how to speak of is Jesus, that is what I did, presenting Him as the healer of all healers. When I extended the invitation to acknowledge Him as the Lord of life, dozens made a profession of faith.

Another president of the same country, who behaved in a similar friendly way toward me, was Mr. José Maria Figueres. During the two years previous to his election, we had a close relationship. In fact, one day, while holding a great day of prayer in La Sabana, an enormous park near the center of the Costa Rican capital, we announced that President Figueres would be there.

All of the print and broadcast media said that it was false information, that the president—together with the vice president and their respective families—would be far away on Saturday morning enjoying their vacations. A crowd of several thousand people had filled the field in La Sabana. The multitude was praising God with great fervor and the time had come for me to preach. Suddenly, at one end of the field, we heard a huge roar. The presidential helicopter was making a landing there, and then, amid the shouts of the people, the president and his wife, and the vice president and his wife, walked onto the platform and hugged me. "I told you that I would come, and here I am," Figueres said.

We have a passion for sharing the grace of God with the leaders of the nations, and establishing networks of friendship with them is vital.

Of course, speaking of these two former Costa Rican presidents, I remember that when these two men were candidates they were visibly and publicly estranged, to an extent, as some said, that had not ever been seen in that country. During that same time, we were holding one of our outreach breakfast meetings there in San José, and both of them attended. The two men, each one with his entourage, sat at opposite ends of the room we were using.

The atmosphere got a little tense. Suddenly, in middle of the message that I was giving, I strongly felt that I should call the two candidates to the front and urge them to seek reconciliation. So, I asked Figueres and Rodriguez to come forward. At that moment, the atmosphere got much more tense. They stood, one at my left and one at my right, and I said to them: "Before anything else, God. Before any political party, the nation." They shook hands and that historic photograph appeared the following day on the front page of many newspapers.

Over the course of the years, I have had the blessing of being with some very prominent persons. I was able to get an interview with the president of Chile, Eduardo Frei, when I was barely 23 years old. I also met with the president of the senate of Bolivia, who later became the vice president of that republic, and some time later I met Mr. Victor Paz Estensoro, president of Bolivia. During my life I have had the privilege of meeting with more than twenty presidents of various countries.

In one historic encounter that I have already described, I was able to speak to President Daniel Ortega, from the sister Republic of Nicaragua.

Another presidential encounter took place with Mr. Jorge Serrano Elias. Even though I considered myself his friend before his resounding election victory, it was a great pleasure for me to spend about five hours sharing my dreams for Latin America with the new president of Guatemala.

These are just some examples of people who, through their exercise of intense power, find themselves alone. Certainly these men may appear to be surrounded by an army of people who watch out for them. Nevertheless, to walk among the citizenry, they must hide themselves or else, definitely, abstain from doing it. They are a challenge for my ministry. They may be, from my own perspective, among the persons most in need of spiritual support.

We strongly believe that the Church must be an agent of reconciliation. What a shame that in various countries of the continent we have pro-government churches and opposition churches! It is such a great shame! We should never let politics get inside the church. On our church benches, the brethren from the left worship alongside the brethrens from the right, the rich with the poor, the professionals with the illiterate. Christ is the only one who can achieve this, and when the church loses this capacity it ceases to be the church. It doesn't matter whether we sing hymns, or whether we have great and exuberant mystical experiences. If the church is not an element of national unity, it loses its character.

Yes, we want to permeate the politicians with the Gospel. Yes, we want to transform the culture with the values of the culture of the Kingdom of God. We believe in the separation of church and state, but we also believe in the profound relationship between God and the nation.

Over time, we have established relationships with presidents, governors, and mayors. In some cases we have gone to their houses and shared wonderful moments with their families. Obviously, if we were to disclose those conversations we would lose their confidence. But we have discovered an amazing opening in the political and governmental classes toward the Gospel of Jesus Christ.

Once, while sharing these testimonies with a friend, he expressed this thought: "But, those countries are smaller than the area of La Matanza" (a district of Buenos Aires, Argentina, similar to a county or province). Exactly less than a month after that declaration, I was preaching in the Red Room of the Palace of the Pines, standing next to Mr. Carlos Salinas de Gortari, the president of Mexico, one of the largest and most important nations in the world... He shared with me the prickly pears from his own platter and I preached to 700 key leaders of that country.

CHAPTER 45

LATIN AMERICA AND THE EVANGELIZATION OF THE LEADERSHIP

What has happened to us? What have we done wrong? Where did we get on the wrong track? Why, if the Christian church in Latin America has grown so much, is Latin America the way it is? Our reality in Latin America hurts many of us. About 70 percent of our brethren in Latin America live in poverty. In Bolivia, for example, every 24 hours, 250 children die of malnutrition.

Latin America is the most violent region in the world, and a majority of the crimes go unpunished. Corruption continues to be the number one "personality" in political and government circles.

Why such a large breach with our neighbor to the north? In 1820 the gross domestic product of Mexico was four times greater than that of the United States. In 1820 the gross domestic product of Latin America was 12.5 percent greater than the United States. When Harvard University was founded in Boston in 1636, Latin

America already had eight universities that were nearly one hundred years old. But today, none of our universities appears on the list of the 100 best universities in the world.

And there is so much brokenness in families. In Argentina, for example, in 1974 the number of single mothers was about 23 percent. Now that number is more than 50 percent.

Yes, we have seen a lot of statistical growth in Christianity. Without a doubt, our continent can repeat the words of Song of Songs 12:11-12: "See! The winter is past; the rains are over and gone. Flowers appear on the earth; the season of singing has come, the cooing of doves is heard in our land."

There is not the slightest doubt that the spiritual winter has ended. We have no doubt that we are enjoying the springtime, the dawn of a great revival. But why have we not seen a transformation in our culture? It seems that the Church, as the Swiss Christian sociologist Lalive D'Epinay wrote, has been *The Refuge of the Masses*. The disenfranchised find in our congregations dignity, honor, family, strength for living. But we have not had the strength to change our society. We liberated the individual who was demon possessed, but what about the social structures that are full of demons?

If we are going to fulfill the mandate to "go and make disciples of all the nations" (Matthew 28:19), then we must reach the people who lead the nations: The government leaders, the politicians, the academics; those who establish the laws, those who produce the works of art --now so corrupted, those who hold the keys to break into the cultural scene.

Souls by soul, they all are the same; the soul of a carpenter and that of a senator of the republic, the soul of a shoeshine boy and the soul of a judge on the Supreme Court. But in terms of influence, the difference is cosmic.

South Korea went from being one of the poorest countries in the world to being one of the eleven strongest economies on the planet, the third strongest in Southeast Asia. What happened? The Church became disgusted with political corruption. Now, out of the 300 leaders in the nation's parliament,

130 are evangelicals. Out of those 300 leaders, with130 evangelicals plus 70 Roman Catholics, it is not easy for a corrupt law to be approved.

Obviously, there are other elements that are crucial to the transformation of our nations. For example, the role of intercession is vital. In Africa there is a powerful stream of intercession.

In Uganda in 1992, about 33 percent of the population was infected with AIDS. The average lifespan in Uganda was 45 years. So the church began a powerful intercessory movement. Now, ten years later, the percentage of AIDS infected people had fallen from 33 percent to below 10 percent.

But now I want to emphasize this fundamental aspect of transformation: the evangelization of the nation's leaders. The beloved Dr. Bill Bright, founder of Campus Crusade for Christ, said that we cannot consider a country evangelized if we have not reached its leaders.

But despite the bleak moral picture on the continent, I have hope. I believe that this is our time. There was a time when it was England's turn; Germany had its stellar moment. The United States played a vital role. South Korea recently experienced a powerful transformation and other developments. I believe the next territory of revival and transformation will be the Spanish-speaking world.

And for this to happen we will need to discover new missionary frontiers. Not just India, the Islamic nations or the jungles of Brazil's Mato Grosso, but within all our nations, the political arena and the government, the arts, and the academic world are the centers of power where we must excel for Jesus.

We need missionary evangelists whose minds are set on the Kingdom of God and who will endeavor to change these spheres of cultural life.

Evangelism that transforms communities implies the presentation of the message of the lordship of Christ with all of its consequences. This includes the mindset of the Kingdom that comes into the world to govern and transform. It demands a breed of witnesses marked by the Cross, Christians who are dead to themselves, always carrying the towel and the sponge with water, as humble as the Lamb, knowing, without a doubt, that "every knee should bow and every tongue confess that Jesus Christ is Lord."

Is this a job only for the super-talented? Is this an enterprise for the super-anointed? No! It is the work of all.

Someone will probably be thinking, "Me, Brother Alberto?" Yes, you are one of the women, one of the men, who must do your part! It does not matter if you only have a few loaves of bread or a few fishes. If we place what we have in the hands of the doer of miracles, our scarce resources will feed an enormous multitude.

There comes to my mind the testimony of a young man who changed history. William Wilberforce was not a candidate for anything. His father died when he was only nine years old. His health was very fragile and his vision was impaired. Almost every day of his life he had to wear an iron corset because his spine could not support his weight. Perhaps he could have been a candidate for admission to an infirm asylum.

However, when he converted, he felt that the Gospel had to be applied to every sphere of life, and for that reason, the vile institution of slavery that was entrenched at that time in the British Isles could not continue to exist. He decided that the abolition of slavery would be his life's goal.

At 21 years of age, he became the youngest Member of Parliament in the British Isles. Many times he believed that his goal was about to be achieved, but the powers behind the enormous business of slavery would block his intentions. However, he did not waver in his endeavor. There was a majestic and holy determination in the life of William Wilberforce.

It took 40 years of constant struggle, but three days before he went to be with the Lord, slavery was abolished forever in the British Isles.

God does not see us with the same eyes that He uses to evaluate the world. He sees now what you can become in the future, if you decide to work with Him for the salvation of the lost and the transformation of the nations.

CHAPTER 46

A SENSE OF HUMOR

There are some who think that preachers are very serious people and that we never joke around, but they're wrong.

I believe that having a good sense of humor is a vital ingredient for any ministry team. I never thought that the preacher should be long-faced, hypocritical, with arms crossed in the posture of a patron saint, with a gaze fixed on heaven. No. The truth is that we must be able to demonstrate a personality touched by the Spirit, with an attitude that is joyful and radiant, exercising self-control and avoiding excesses, apt to discern current realities, with a maturity forged by the daily experience of living constantly in the Spirit.

There was a series of good jokes that made us laugh until we cried. Several of my brothers could easily be certified in the art of writing jokes, with honors for excellence. Well, even I have placed my little grain of sand, reminding them of some things that were actually experienced, and other things that were fantasies.

I remember one of the Crusades in Villa Hermosa, in the Mexican district of Tabasco. It was the last night and someone had brought a painting of the local jungle to use as a backdrop for the photographs that would be taken of us there. The painting was at least about nine feet wide by six feet high.

Upon the arrival of Danilo Montero, who was working with us at this event, a spirit of mischief came upon me.

"Danilo, look at this painting that was brought as a gift for you," I said. "The brother who left it here said that his daughter painted it and she wants you to have it in your house, or in your office."

"You're kidding me, Alberto," he answered. "That enormous painting can't be for me."

After the conclusion of the service at the Plaza Monumental, Danilo went to eat with the young people, and I with the pastors.

Upon returning to the hotel, that impish mood again came to me. I asked at the reception desk whether Mr. Montero was in his room and I was told that he was not. Then I took a pencil and paper and wrote a note: "Dear brother Danilo Montero: I am the father of the girl who with so lovingly painted the picture. Her desire is for you to have it. Tomorrow we will be leaving early to go to the airport to help you get the picture on the airplane." Then I sent a bellhop to slip the note under the door of Danilo's room.

When Danilo returned to the hotel and read the note, his keyboardist, who was with him, said that Danilo's face clouded over as he sat down on the bed and said: "Then this wasn't one of Alberto's jokes. What am I going to do with this monster of a painting?"

The next morning as the time approached for the airplane to leave, Danilo still had not appeared. When he finally arrived, looking all around, he asked: "Where are they?"

"Where are who?" we asked him.

"The people of the painting!"

We could not hold back any longer and broke out laughing.

"What is this, a servant of God making these jokes?"

Yes, we lived at a very high speed and with great responsibilities, but we never lacked for moments of laughter, of jokes that leave one smiling for a very long time.

Danilo Montero did eventually take his own good-natured "revenge." It was during the Crusade in Cancun, Mexico. After an event is ended, there are always some details that require attention. Often there is a farewell planned by the organizing committee, usually a late night dinner. Whenever possible, we take the first flight out, even if we only get two hours of sleep. When the flight is not leaving until the following afternoon, naturally our desire is to get a little rest, but the schedule is always exhausting.

One early morning, when it was still dark, upon arriving to our hotel room, Noemi and I found a note: "Dear Pastor Mottesi: I was converted at one of your crusades. I was a nun. I followed your advice and formed a family. Now I have 17 children." At this point, I said: "How wild! She took that part about motherhood seriously!"

"Tomorrow at 7 a.m." the letter continued, "I will be there at the hotel with my entire family to greet you." The letter was signed: "The ex-nun, Sister Tibursia."

"Dear God!" I exclaimed. "She ruined our slight chance of rest!"

After getting ready to welcome "the sister" and waiting long and in vain for her arrival, we finally gave up and went to breakfast, where we were welcomed by the laughter of Danilo and his entire band.

What fun have we had, and good humor is so healthy! There is a very good reason why *Readers Digest* magazine has a section of humorous stories called: "Laughter: The Best Medicine."

I have another anecdote. It was an embarrassing moment. In Monterrey, Mexico, I boarded an American Airlines plane and sat in the front row, in the aisle seat. As you might imagine, I have flown millions of miles with American Airlines. The frequent flyer program often gives me free access to first class seating.

The cabin was full when suddenly, an airline executive boarded the airplane and said to me in a loud voice: "Mr. Mottesi, today you are passenger number 60 and American Airlines is celebrating its 60th anniversary. Smile. You have won this prize."

She immediately proceeded to place in my hands a big bottle of wine while someone snapped a photograph. The people behind me were applauding. Then the woman left, leaving me holding the wine bottle as a gift.

While the flight was in progress and I was leafing through a copy of the American Airlines magazine, a voice inside began saying to me: "They will publish that photograph. Can you imagine? Thousands of people will see the evangelist holding his bottle of wine." A chill ran through my body.

For 15 days I thought about this dilemma until finally I decided to call American Airlines and ask.

"I hope that a Christian employee answers my call," I told myself. I knew that there were two Christian women who worked on the Executive Platinum Desk. I even think that one of them converted under our ministry.

When I explained what had happened, Blanca Sepulveda broke out laughing. "Give me the date and the flight number," she said. She left me on hold for ten or fifteen minutes. "Problem solved!" she exclaimed. "The photograph was erased from the archives." Only then did I breathe a sigh of relief.

These are some of those comical, embarrassing experiences that later become a source of enjoyment and delight in our memories.

CHAPTER 47

SHE

It was love at first sight. When we exchanged glances for the first time, hers reached deep into my soul. Since that first encounter at the parks of Ezeiza, in Buenos Aires, between courtship and marriage, more than 50 years have gone by. It is a lifetime!

It makes me sad to see how couples wither away. Not only are there divorces and heartbreak everywhere, but there are even marriages that remain unbroken only as a formality. They lost their shine, their light was quenched, the battery that charged their love ran out, and so they live together under the same roof without enjoying the symphony of love.

For us, after more than 50 years together, these are the best days of our lives. We are better friends than ever before. We talk more than ever. We feel that the harmony of our relationship is reaching its highest note.

One afternoon I realized that I had some extra time at my disposal. I decided to spend it organizing my suitcases. I selected the suit I would wear later that day. I noticed that one of the inside pockets had a bulge. I put my hand in the pocket and realized immediately that it was a very pleasant surprise from my wife.

Actually, by this time I should not have been surprised, because Noemi, with every trip that I make, always manages to pack away some handwritten note, some lines in which she tells me what is on her heart, and of her love for me. Yes, there was the usual text but she'd also had the idea of putting a red rose in the middle of the letter. I was moved by this gesture. I carefully read her words, almost as if I was hearing the unmistakable timbre of her voice. "Dear Alberto: Our love is and must continue to be like this rose. A perfect rose! I love you very much and I will be praying for you every day. Take care. The one who loves you, Noemi."

I remained in ecstasy for a few seconds. I put the rose to my lips and kissed its petals, almost as if I were kissing the woman God had given me, the one who has become the perfect woman for my life. With every day that passes, our love grows stronger. So many years of marriage have provided plenty of opportunities to confirm the foundation on which our home is built: our precious Savior and Lord, who has been our guardian and sustainer.

From the beginning, our love always included the Church, God and the ministry. In reality, second only to the Lord, Noemi has been an extraordinary help to me.

Noemi loves the Lord and His work very much. I remember that when she was pregnant with our second son, despite her discomfort- and pushing our eldest born around in his stroller, she went out to the streets of Buenos Aires to distribute brochures and flyers for the ministry. She is still a key piece in the ministry of the Association.

It has not been easy, to be sure. A calling like mine implies a huge burden of suffering for the family. The constant absences from home, if they are not cushioned by a strong understanding and trust in the protection of God, can degenerate into overwhelming anxiety and burning issues for all of the members in the home.

Thanks to God, Noemi has been an admirable woman. She has known how, with intelligence and wisdom from on high, to maintain good family relationships, something that cannot be measured by quantity, but only by quality.

On several occasions, returning from a long trip in the wee hours of the morning, I have approached the beds of my children and, placing my hands on their little heads, prayed to the Lord for them with deep emotion.

I do not remember when or where, but Noemi was in the midst of preaching when I entered and sat down on one of the back rows. I was much moved listening to her words, when suddenly I heard the voice of God asking: "Alberto, do you believe that Noemi has a ministry?

"Of course, Lord. Without her I would not be able to do the work; she really is my ideal helpmate."

"You do not understand me, Alberto. I did not ask if she helps you in your ministry. I asked if you recognize that she also has a ministry."

That's when I understood.

I realized that not only did she help me a great deal, not only did we work together as a team, but also that in her was a ministry given by God. In my spirit I released her to serve the Lord.

During these recent years God has placed her in large auditoriums, and has even given her the responsibility of having to minister to pastors. We began to realize that many of our attitudes in the church do not come from the Scriptures but rather from our patriarchal male-dominated culture. We believe that there is an enormous potential among millions of Latin American women that, if released, could produce a spiritual revolution throughout the continent.

Noemi coordinates what we call in our ministry, "Let's Save the Family." This area of our Evangelistic Association represents the hands of the Lord Jesus. Hands that caress, hands that heal, hands that restore.

"Let's Save the Family" trains Christians to launch local projects, such as the Centers of Family Restoration, to help their communities. We also sponsor Centers to Rescue the Family, where pastoral and professional volunteers provide around-the-clock (24 hours a day, seven days a week) assistance to broken families.

There are so many testimonies about the triumphs of the Gospel! For example, the case of the drunken man who was walking in front of our Center in Baja California, Mexico. When he saw the sign for the Center to Rescue the Family he decided to go inside. Those in charge of the place ministered to him until his drunkenness began to dissipate, and then they led him into an experience of salvation with Christ. When he was lucid, the man confessed that he had planned to kill his wife and his mother-in-law. He asked them to wait for him to return with the two women. On that day, he brought his entire family to the Center, found salvation, and began the process of healing his wounds and restoring relationships.

Noemi also plays a vital role in our office. Hundreds of letters arrive, sharing a gamut of life tragedies, and she answers each one of these in a personal way.

Sometimes, people ask us how she manages, with so much work, to answer personal letters. But for us, both for her and for me, the ministry is not only about pulpits, stadiums, or television studios. The ministry has to do with people, with lives that are suffering and in pain, with human beings who are hungry for mercy. This is the ministry of "Let's Save the Family" managed by Noemi: a balm of mercy for those wounded by the world.

CHAPTER 48

MY CHILDREN AND MY GRANDCHILDREN

They really are exceptional people. Both of them hate lies. They are honest men. Despite the success they have achieved as professionals, their character is still one of meekness and respect for others.

Marcelo, who was born in 1965, and Martin, who was born in 1970 –you can figure their ages, are our precious sons. I have a deep admiration for both of them. They have taught me many lessons.

Marcelo is an attorney and Martin has a master's degree in business administration (MBA). Marcelo is a partner with one of the largest law firms on Wall Street and Martin is president of a manufacturing firm on a national level. The two maintain intense professional activities, are very involved at their churches, and still fervently support our ministry.

Even though they are now grown men with bristly beards, how sweet it feels when they embrace me, kiss me and say: "Father, I love you very much!" I feel like they are not only my sons, but also my friends. My best friends. Their help and counsel has been a real treasure for us. Their wives are also like our daughters. Lisa, wife of Marcelo, and Lela, wife of Martin, are both exceptional human beings. Their faces are full of light and their hearts overflow with generosity.

Marcelo met Lisa in high school and they later attended the same university, Biola in Southern California. When Marcelo went to study for his doctorate from Georgetown University, near Washington D.C., Lisa went to work at a hospital in Thailand serving Cambodian refugees, and their separation was very difficult.

"Father," Marcelo told me, "my feelings are not clear. I need to know with certainty that Lisa is 'the one.' "

"Well," I responded, "the best way to find out is to go and discover the truth."

Making use of the ever helpful credit card, I added: "You have a ticket to Thailand purchased. Go and discover."

From that precious union were born three marvelous grandchildren: Gabriela, Nicolas, and Daniel, who are already in early adolescence. They live in New Jersey and even though the physical separation from them is painful, they often visit us or we them. I admire Lisa for her extraordinary vocation of serving others; and I enjoy helping my grandchildren with their extracurricular activities.

Nicolas is a great basketball player and the best of his age in his baseball league in New Jersey. Even though I don't understand very much about the sport of basketball, I am a fan of my grandson. Daniel is an exceptional soccer player, just like "Lionel Messi." I also enjoy sitting down and listening to Gabriela, with her heavenly smile and kindness, play the piano, and also Danny, our brilliant Danny, and the blasting trumpet of Nicolas that sounds so sweet to the ears of my heart.

I have so many experiences with our grandchildren! I remember the day when we were walking through a forest and it began to rain. The weather was very cold. Nicolas, who would have been about seven or eight years old, in his innocence declared, "*Nono*, take my coat to keep warm." I believe his coat barely would have covered one of my arms or legs.

When they hug us, what tenderness and sweet emotions do our grandchildren evoke in us!

When Martin and Lela met, they immediately fell in love. She has a European background, and came from a rural setting. She's the best cook I have ever known in my life—what amazing suppers she prepares! Their daughters, Isabella and Sofia, are the youngest members of our family. Their smiles and love are celestial.

The week before I wrote this chapter, I had just returned, on a Sunday afternoon, from an evangelistic tour of six days visiting four cities in Mexico. I had preached for six nights and also five mornings, traveling to and from venues in the afternoons and evenings. More than 10,000 professions of faith! When I came home I was tired. My entire body was aching with exhaustion. My two granddaughters were with Noemi at the airport, waiting for my arrival. When we pulled in the driveway, ready for dinner, they announced: "Today we are having a fashion show and here is your ticket." So it was that after eating, we made ourselves comfortable and the girls raided Noemi's closet and used her dresses and hats to make a "fashion show" for their grandparents.

I could hardly keep my eyes open, but how we enjoyed that family time. When Martin drove over to collect them and return to their house, how sweet were the shouts of the granddaughters, saying: "I love you! I love you!"

Our five grandchildren call us "*Nono*" and "*Nona*." They adopted the Argentine custom so influenced by the Italian culture. They call the parents of our daughters-in-law "grandfather" and "grandmother" but we are the *nonos*, and all five of them love to read good books, just like their grandpa. They devour books every day.

Today, I wrote this chapter after leaving the *General Santander* stadium where we held a glorious crusade. In just one night we had over 3,000 professions of faith. In the automobile they were using to transport us, we were listening to one of the beautiful songs of Jesús Adrian Romero and it reminded me of my five grandchildren. The lyrics said: "I have two excuses in my mind to cut short my day and go home. They are a pair of magical princesses. They have learned that I am weak and with only a smile they can get anything, they have become the owners of my heart and they brighten my existence whenever I think of them [and I of my five grandchildren]. They are like a spring garden dressed each day with beauty and splendor; they are like carrier pigeons that the Lord sent from heaven to speak to me of his love."

Yes, love for the grandchildren is something very different, very special, very captivating. And their existence has allowed me to see my own children in a different light. Something that amazes me about our beloved sons is the depth of their dedication to their wives and children. Their children maintain a very full schedule of sports, community and extracurricular activities, but there they are, my two sons, despite their own responsibilities, supporting their offspring. Also, early in the morning they take their children to the different schools and at night they always end the day with Bible stories and prayer.

I believe that our descendants have the stamp of Noemi. This is her achievement. She always taught them about priorities: first, God; second, the family; and third, the ministry. If the family is not well, then something will sound out of tune in the ministry. On the other hand, if the family is well, then this becomes one of the strengths of our ministry.

The Lord has been good to us. While I was traveling, He rewarded Noemi's dedication to the family. I don't know how much longer we will live, but I candidly confess that I would like to be here long enough to see all of our grandchildren with their own homes established—Christian homes, having families with Biblical values. How I long to see descendants who will continue loving God with all their hearts.

CHAPTER 49

MY TEAM

"Hear! Hear! The Word of God!" fervently announced the boy. The megaphone was helping him broadcast his invitation to many neighbors who, in most cases, out of curiosity approached to see and hear this daring young man.

That was the start of Emilio Meza Jr.'s career. The towns and communities of his beloved El Salvador were his first pulpits. Emilio would board the public bus and ask the driver: "Could you turn down the music for just a few minutes?" That was enough. His style caught people's attention, taking into account that the country was in a state of war. "What would you do if you knew that there was a bomb on the bus?" he would say.

On one occasion, his pastor asked him to ride with him, to attend the national convention of their denomination in the capital city. That very Saturday was his eighteenth birthday.

"Pastor, could I have permission not to attend the convention today?"

"Do you have something else to do, Emilio?" his pastor asked.

"It's just that today is my eighteenth birthday. I want to win eighteen lives for Christ."

So, with his pastor's permission, he went out to the streets to preach and did not stop until he had gathered eighteen souls for the Lord.

Now he is the liaison with our field coordinators and the manager of our Radio Department.

Another passionate soul is José Luis Saenz. He was born in Toluca, Mexico, and like many Hispanics he felt the attraction of California, where he met Christ.

One day, while listening to the regional Christian radio station, he heard an announcement about our School of Evangelists and felt like it was for him. He studied, graduated, and got so attached to us that he ended up working as part of our team.

Now he is our Director of Television. He is very creative, a true innovator. He has a great ability to surround himself with volunteers and coworkers who are all dreamers, just like him.

On one occasion, one of the groups from our school that works in prisons invited him to go with them and teach. He is also a good preacher.

"However, you cannot go inside wearing those pants," he was told. He thought it was a joke, but when they were going through the prison's security systems with their musical instruments and sound equipment, the guards stopped him.

"You cannot go inside."

"Why?"

"Because your pants are the same color as those of the prisoners."

"But I have to preach there."

"I am sorry. You cannot go inside."

In his determination, he ran to a bus station in front of the prison, and in middle of all of those people shouted loudly in English and Spanish: "I need to trade my pants with someone so that I can get into the prison and preach."

Who knows what they might have thought of him. "Another mad man," someone might have thought, and no one moved.

Only one fisherman said: "I will help you." And, right there in the bathroom of the bus station, José Luis traded his fine pants laden with the scent of the cologne he liked to wear, for the stinky pants of the fisherman who smelled like his work, of catfish and sea creatures. He ran back to the prison and within a few minutes was preaching the Gospel.

Oscar Merlo is another revolutionary for Christ. His life was marked by a pious grandmother whose guidance brought him into a close relationship with the Holy Spirit. During the last forty-five years of her life, the grandmother prayed daily between four and six o'clock in the morning on her calloused knees.

This "mark" was what, after moving to California, brought him every Friday night to the Full Gospel Prayer Mountain, the Mountain of Prayer established in Hemet by Dr. Paul Yonggi Cho. There, he ardently sought God in nights of communion with Him.

When he was eight years old he "preached" for the first time at a public park in San Pedro Sula, the industrial city of his beloved Honduras. At the age of nineteen, at a youth meeting he was invited to read aloud "A Letter from Jesus to the Young People" and he was given two minutes. Suddenly, he lost track of time. After ten minutes, the pastor who was to preach approached him and said: "Continue, don't stop." After twenty minutes, one hundred young people were broken and kneeling at the front, surrendering their lives to Christ.

Oscar became a pastor, president of the youth of his denomination, executive at a corporation, and now he is the Dean of our dear School of Evangelists.

As he finishes his doctorate at Fuller Seminary, we believe that his academic preparation, combined with his deep spiritual dimension, will mark thousands of the young people who will be attending our School now and in the future.

The person with the most years working in our offices is Lili Santos. We have employees of several nationalities. Lili is from Ecuador, and she helps Noemi and me with many facets of the office work. It matters not whether it is a Saturday or Sunday,

day or night, she is always willing and able to resolve situations. Sometimes, when we have missed a connecting flight, she is already on the computer making other arrangements. Even in the middle of stressful and tense situations that often arise, her voice remains serene. She is extremely detailed and outspoken. A couple of years ago she was battling cancer, but even in the midst of her struggle she continued to keep track of everything.

There are so many people to whom we owe gratitude for their faithfulness.

My dear brother in the faith, Paul Finkenbinder, often said to me: "Some will be with you forever. Others will temporarily pass through your life and ministry. Give thanks to God for all them, and keep going."

From among the field coordinators, the one who has spent the longest time on the team is David Enríquez. We call him the *Chaparrito de Oro* (Golden Shorty). He is a Mexican from the *capirucha*, a colloquial term for the capital city. He was an engineer, but a passion for serving the Lord flowed through his veins. And even though he has organized crusades in several countries, he is lovingly chained to his beloved Mexico.

When we were planning the Presidential Breakfast in his country, the elderly leaders there said: "It cannot be done." But that is the wrong thing to tell our ministry. He took the challenge. And not only did he succeed. We had our event in the Red Room of the Palace of the Pines, the headquarters of the Mexican government. It was the first time that something like this had happened there. The man who was president at the time was in attendance, along with seven hundred key leaders of that country—proving that faith truly moves mountains!

Orlando Estevez has organized gigantic crusades. This Honduran businessman who represents us in Central America was the architect of the Evangelistic Celebrations in the Valle del Sula in his own country, and in San Salvador, the capital city of El Salvador.

And Dr. Eduardo Gomez is the gentleman on the team. We believe that even when he bathes, he gets in the shower still wearing his suit and tie. This distinguished Colombian, with whom we have been united in friendship for more than thirty years, organizes the events with governments in Latin America. Once, after traveling all night and all morning from Bogotá and arriving in Córdoba, Argentina, in the afternoon, although obviously in need of rest, he was willing to wait another five or six hours before sleeping, because he saw the country's vice president at a meeting and did not want to miss the opportunity to reach him. He waited patiently to speak to the vice president. Dr. Eduardo is a statesman in the Kingdom of God.

They are many, my companions and my friends, one of the most remarkable strengths of our ministry, and I am greatly indebted to them. I love them with all my heart.

CHAPTER 50
THE PASTORS OF MY BELOVED LATIN
AMERICA

Pastors are a gift of God to the Body of Christ. They come in all varieties—some are very formal and academic, while others are more spontaneous and wild. But I do not have the slightest doubt that all of the Hispanic pastors have hearts full of passion.

The Hispanic pastor is a dreamer. He is always behaving like a mountain climber. In the heart of every Hispanic pastor is a "sender" of missionaries, an evangelist to the masses, a mass communicator, someone who does works of mercy.

You can see them preaching a powerful message to their small congregations, or driving the vans to pick up the elderly for a Sunday service, and certainly you will find them in the aisles of the hospitals—and it's because every Hispanic pastor has the heart of a father.

I find it amazing that the Holy Spirit has opened such a large door with the pastoral guild. Through Divine grace, we have access to and friendship with pastors who represent a wide spectrum of different doctrinal positions and worship expressions, from one extreme to another, within the family of God. It's just that for us, unity with our fellow "militia" members does not depend on believing everything exactly the same, in terms of every single point of doctrine, nor on having the same systematic theology, or on worshiping in exactly the same physical posture. Our strong unity comes instead from the Presence of Jesus Christ in our lives.

It doesn't matter what the name of your church may be. Frankly, it doesn't matter all that much whether you worship with an organized ritual, or whether your meetings are so rowdy that benches end up broken. If I see that you are a man or a woman of faith, who deeply loves God, if your eyes penetrate the firmament awaiting the Second Coming of Christ, if your lips pronounce with devotion the Name that is above every other name, you are my brother, my sister, my fellow warrior in the Kingdom of God.

During the decades of our ministry, dozens of times each year we preach to groups of pastors. Sometimes there are only a few dozen from some council, and sometimes there are 20,000 of them gathered together, as was the case in Colombia. What an honor it is for me, but also what an enormous responsibility!

Pastors tend to be very critical of other preachers. They are like the chef who goes to eat at someone else's restaurant, and from the first moment he is analyzing the taste of food prepared by someone other than himself. But, at the same time, pastors are also very needy people. We pastors go through life giving the Bread of Life to others, but who takes care of us? Who prays for us? Who prays for our children? Who helps us overcome our own burdens?

For this reason, when I preach to pastors, I believe it is a vital opportunity to minister to those who minister to many thousands more. Ministering to the personal life of a servant of God is like ministering to the hundreds or thousands of people they minister to as pastors.

Sometimes I am asked, what do I preach to preachers about? There are fundamental values that function as a spine in a servant of God: his character, his integrity, his family, and his commitment to the Kingdom of God. I love to open Bible passages such as the 24th chapter of the Gospel of Luke. It's a very captivating account of a time when Jesus was already raised from the dead and appeared in the midst of his disciples. For them this moment was an occasion to celebrate.

It seems to me that among the disciples there might have been a few Hispanics, because immediately they thought of holding a party with a great feast. Already they were hearing musical strains! There is an extraordinary shine on the faces of the disciples. While the table was prepared, speaking amongst themselves they were probably saying: "I told you so! The Master promised to return and here He is with us."

However, Christ confounds them with the words that He shares with them next. The first thing that stands out for me is in verse 39: "Look at my hands and my feet. It is I myself! Touch me and see; a ghost does not have flesh and bones, as you see I have."

What Christ is telling them is: "Men, you will not achieve anything alone. This is not about fishing from the sea. This is not about selling insurance or painting walls. This is about eternity and the Kingdom of my Father. I have to be real in your life. Look at my hands and my feet. Death could not stop me, and the tomb could not conquer."

He wants to be real in our minds.

He wants to be perfectly real, increasingly real. In this day and age, our minds are being bombarded as never before in history. There is an enormous wave of perversion flooding our minds, but he wants to be real in our minds.

He wants to be real in our families.

It is there, at the heart of the family, where we reveal the quality of our Christian character. If I want to know about you, I will not ask someone who sees you on Sunday at church. I will ask your wife, your husband, your children, those who know in your daily routines and know how you react when confronted with the crises and challenges of life.

He wants to be real also in our congregational life.

So many churches are as cold as a cemetery! Even some churches that make a lot of noise are actually very cold. They have left the living God outside the church.

Three years ago I went to preach at the 100th Anniversary of the Revival in Korea. I could only stay two and a half days, and I did not attend a church service there. Our event was at the Coliseum of Seoul.

My interpreter wanted me to meet the pastor of the church that sent him as a missionary to Peru. That is why, very early in the morning we met with this venerable elder. Three times a week he needs dialysis. However, no one could prevent him from being in his pulpit at 5 o'clock every morning teaching the Word.

I realized that this church was about 20 years old and had 60,000 members. I asked him:

"What is the key to your success?"

"Very easy," he answered. "It is just that here—" he was referring to the church building, "each morning, without exception, no matter what the weather is like that day, there are 10,000 members of the church seeking the face of the Lord."

May He be real in our congregations!

I also like verses 45 through 48 very much: "Then He opened their minds so they could understand the Scriptures. He told them, 'this is what is written: The Christ will suffer and rise from the dead on the third day, and repentance and forgiveness of sins will be preached in his name to all nations, beginning at Jerusalem. You are witnesses of these things.' "

He wants to open our eyes.

Obviously, the Scripture passage says: "… So they could understand the Scriptures." But in looking at this chapter in its context, there are other obvious things as well.

For example: "May we open our eyes to discover ourselves."

I believe that it is sinful to overvalue oneself. Pride of any type is offensive to God. The interesting thing for me is that the prideful are often not aware of their pride. But also it is sinful not to understand the role that we must carry out. While I existed only in my grandmother's dreams, God was already placing deposits of glory in my account for the Kingdom of God. While I was in my mother's womb, God was already placing deposits of anointing in my personal account.

You are not a small thing: You are a co-heir with Christ. Everything that the Father gives to the Son, He also gives to you. You are an ambassador in the Name of Christ. You are king and priest. You need to understand your transcendental role in the Kingdom of God.

He wants to open our eyes so that we can discover true Christian leadership.

Some of my colleagues act like they want to be Hollywood stars. A couple of years ago, the two biggest newspapers in Southern California, the *Los Angeles Times* and the *Orange County Register*, published a one-and-a-half page article about Pastor Rick Warren. He is the author of the book, *A Purpose-Driven Life*, a book that after the Bible, in any language and in any literary category, is possibly the best-selling Christian book in all of history, and the articles spoke in a dignified way about this Christian ministry. It was mentioned that each week Pastor Warren ministers to more than 70,000 people. My wife and I were moved as we read the newspaper that morning.

That very afternoon, Noemi and I were going to a birthday party for the granddaughter of one of our closest friends, a Bolivian family that attends Brother Warren's church. Among those in attendance was the worship director of that church. When he greeted us, the first thing that came out of my mouth was, "What a tremendous article about the pastor in the newspaper."

The young man said very seriously: "Rick did not like it."

"Why?" I asked him.

"It's just that the article presented him as some kind of super-pastor and when I arrived early this morning at the church office, I found him lying face down on the floor, asking God to forgive him if he had robbed some of His glory."

We need to rediscover the character of true Christian ministry, which is not that of a haughty boss, or one who acts with arrogant conceit, but rather one who puts on an apron, picks up the sponge soaked in water, and is ready and willing to wash the feet of others.

He wants us to discover the power of intercession.

"If my people, who are called by my name, will humble themselves and pray and seek my face and turn from their wicked ways," the Good Book says. *My people!* He is not talking about prostitutes or drug traffickers. *My people!* Then, "I will hear from heaven and will forgive their sin and will heal their land" (2 Chronicles 7:14).

I know that we pray. But much of our praying is like sending request letters to the Lord, saying: "Remember that I am your son. I need you to resolve this problem. What would happen to your church if I were not a part of it? Answer me soon. I will send you another letter next week. Amen."

And God says: "What is happening to my daughter, to my son? They say that I am their maximum authority, their owner, but when I want to talk to them, they run away. They seem to have a spirit of rocketing to the moon."

We need to rediscover the importance of our time of intimacy with God, which is like a relationship between father and child. We should be children who don't come to the Father only to ask for something, but who also sit down with him to have a good time of fellowship.

When a church reaches a certain level of intercession, God puts it at the helm of history. The course of history is not in the hands of politicians or in the hands of the large international companies. History is in the hands of the children of God.

There is such power, hidden still for many, in intercession. "The weapons we fight with are not the weapons of the world. On the contrary, they have divine power to demolish strongholds" (2 Corinthians 10:4).

The party continues with even greater amazement for the disciples. Perhaps they thought this would be a good time for joyful leisure, but Jesus continues to share some things that make them stop and think. First He says: "Alone you can do nothing; I have to be a reality in your lives." Secondly, He treats them as near-sighted when He tells them to open their eyes. There is a third word that I am certain they are not able to fully comprehend: "I am going to send you what my Father has promised; but stay in the city until you have been clothed with power from on high" (Luke 24:49).

He wants to give us the authority of the Kingdom of heaven.

The text was badly translated. The original does not say, "Have been clothed with power," but rather, "*you will be* clothed with authority." Authority is much more than power. Authority is a level of power that—when exercised outside the church—has the ability to produce change in the Name of Jesus. Authority is leaving the defense and going to play for the offense.

Not long ago I imagined a scene in the office of God, the Father, in the Kingdom of the heavens. I saw that he opened the windows and looked toward the earth and said: "What is happening to this world that we have created? Human beings continue to rebel and the cities are full of sin. Immorality is noticeable everywhere. What can we do?"

Then I saw that Christ raised his hand and said: "Father, do you want me to return and die on the cross again?"

"No," said God, "the cross was once and forever."

The next thing I saw were twenty angels who raised their hands and said: "Send us! Don't continue trusting in those lazy Christians on earth. Didn't you realize that most of them are only warming the church benches on Sunday mornings?"

"No," said God, "my plan is not about sending angels."

Suddenly, I saw that he turned to look at the earth and turned toward the Hispanic Americans and said: "Look, look at these Hispanics. They are a little disorganized and very romantic, but they have a heart for me. I will use these Spanish-speaking people, these pastors and these Christians, to represent me and invade the earth with my Glory."

CHAPTER 51

TO THE CHURCH AND THE YOUNG PEOPLE

These are some of my convictions, and I feel they are vital for the Hispanic Church in the world, so I want to engrave them on your heart.

These things may also be part of other cultures, but in ours it is a shameful sin. To gossip, to criticize, and even to demonize other brothers who may behave differently than us. This is a sickly practice.

I knew of an evangelist who, because he had gone and preached to a group that was not liked by the director of a certain publication, was listed as an apostate.

I am reminded of the story narrated in Matthew 12:22-37, when Jesus heals someone who is demon-possessed, blind and mute. The Pharisees said that this was the work of Beelzebub, prince of the demons. The Scripture passage clearly teaches that it is a sin, a blasphemy against the Holy Spirit, to give the devil any credit for works that are of God. Be careful, brothers, when you criticize or judge! It is truly a dangerous activity.

I sincerely agree with the meaning of Dr. A.W. Tozer, the late Christian Missionary Alliance leader, when he said:

"There is a glorious unity of the saints, a mystic brotherhood of the farsighted, who have long been straining their eyes to catch a glimpse of the King in His beauty in the land that is very far off. With great joy and deep humility I claim membership in that brotherhood."

This is the oldest and the largest church in the world, the fellowship of those wounded because of the cross, of those in love with God. As the years go by I am less and less concerned about a person's denominational affiliation. If someone has his eyes set on heavenly things, if he nods his head and whispers the always blessed Name of Jesus, then this person is my brother, no matter what his label may be. He is my brother, whether he understands this or not. If by some disgrace he has been taught to believe that his church is the only one and that I am destined for perdition because I do not belong to his church, even so I will continue to regard him as a member of the family of God, if I find in his life the marks of the Cross and in his eyes a look revealing that he is a man of faith.

Dietrich Bonhoeffer, a martyr of the Nazi holocaust, called superficial evangelism "the gospel of cheap grace." It is a gospel without the cross, without repentance, without compromise. Our Gospel is, the Bible says, the Gospel of the Kingdom of God, the Gospel of the Lordship of Christ, of the Government of God.

When I hear a special emphasis placed on "my salvation, my miracles, my prosperity," it seems to me that a message of ego-centrism is being shared with us. The Bible is very clear: "For from Him and through Him and to Him are all things. To Him be the glory forever!" (Romans 11:36)

It is not only about blessings, which are many and glorious. It is also about his demands. "If anyone would come after me, he must deny himself and take up his cross daily and follow me" (Luke 9:23). The Cross, you see, is a symbol of obedience.

We try to appease the world by lowering the Kingdom requirements, but we have no authority to do so. Our entire relationship with God is based on His grace, His unmerited favor, obviously. However, if this is not accompanied by an unconditional surrender it becomes a "monologue" of love. Christian life should be a "dialogue" of tenderness.

This sort of *chieftain-style leadership* is a classic element of our culture. But the Church is not ours. None of us died for it on the Cross. The people of the Church do not belong to us. Leadership that functions as if it were the owner of the flock should be aborted. It has already done too much wickedness.

We are not the owners. The servants of the Lord are simply that: servants. We will not find our role model in Hollywood. It is in Jesus Christ. He became flesh. He lived among men. The original literally says: "He pitched his tent among men."

We must return to *servant leadership,* wearing the apron and carrying the water-soaked sponge to wash the feet of our brothers. Please, no more super-heroes in the ministry, only servants anchored to the Cross and willing to give up everything for Him.

But I am neither a pessimist, nor a prophet of doom. Not only do I have concerns, but I also have convictions. For example, I believe this is the time for the Hispanics. The next revival will be heard in Spanish and will bear the flavor of plantains and hot chili on its heart.

At one time it was England's turn, and from there missionaries were sent around the world. Germany experienced its peak moments as well. The United States and Canada had stellar years, more recently South Korea.

But I believe the next revival will be called "the Spanish-speaking people."

I spend a lot of time asking young people for forgiveness. Forgiveness, for the dirty world in which they were born. When you arrived, drugs were already here. Political corruption also was here. Adultery was part of the scenery.

I ask forgiveness also for a Christianity that is full of carnality and favoritism. When you arrived at church, the denominations and the councils were already present. Religious pride was already present. But you young people will change the Church and transform the world in the Name of Jesus.

We are passing the torch. Take it without fear and do not bend the knee to any temporal power or idolatry disguised as piety. Kneel only before the King of Kings and Lord of Lords.

The Church has relinquished its rights even though it has no divine authorization to do so. We have entrenched ourselves within the church. The Hispanic Church is so lovely, so tender, so healing, but also so out of touch with reality.

We have yielded our rights in, for example, the fine arts. The Church was the one that produced the fine arts or greatly influenced them. However, we ended up turning our backs on all of them. When we removed ourselves from that sphere, taking away the salt, the preserving element, the arts became debased. We should not complain about so much perversion. We are also to blame for it.

We have abandoned politics. We tended to say: "Be careful about politics! They're dirty." God put man in the garden so that he would manage it for Him. The man failed God. Later, God raised up his Church. With his death and resurrection He invested it with the power and authority of the Kingdom and yet, we also fell short. God did not conceive of the Church as a lovely "religious club" gathering on Sundays to scream and shout for joy. God conceived it so that as His representatives we might bring every sphere of life under the Lordship of Christ.

The arts, politics, the legal system, the media, educators, the scientific world, the business world, *everything belongs to God.* "The earth is the LORD's, and everything in it, the world, and all who live in it" (Psalm 24:1). "For God so loved the world ..." (John 3:16).

It is time to wake up and act decisively. Let's send our young people to the best universities (and support them). They will do what the adults never did.

I hear music. It is a majestic symphony. It is an army of young people who are marching. They are authentic revolutionaries. The true revolutionaries are not in the jungles of Colombia or

Peru; they are not hidden in the depths of Chiapas. The true revolutionaries are warming a bench at church waiting for us to legalize the passion they have to win the world for Christ and transform its communities.

We should recognize their calling, deliver the torch, and send them out to do the work, the greatest work, the most glorious work commissioned to human beings: "Go and make disciples of all nations, baptizing them in the name of the Father and of the Son and of the Holy Spirit, and teaching them to obey everything I have commanded you. And surely I am with you always, to the very end of the age" (Matthew 28:19-20).

"And He died for all, that those who live should no longer live for themselves but for Him who died for them and was raised again" (2 Corinthians 5:15).

CHAPTER 52
PROPHECIES AND MIRACLES

I really don't know how it started. Some call it prophecy. I am aware of the abusive things that have been done with this Biblical gift and the fear of it in some sectors of the Body of Christ. However, it is there in the Word, and it is supported by the testimony of millions of people who have been blessed through this gift.

But I am not talking about someone who raises his voice and says to another: "God is telling you ..." Frankly, I do not believe that God speaks to his children in a melodramatic tone. I believe that God speaks to his children in a natural way, as a father to his children. Yes, many times He uses someone to communicate something to another, and He does this with clarity, with love and always to bless.

In our case, without thinking or planning it, many times we have been used to deliver words to churches, pastors and even to nations. I remember in particular Pastor Osvaldo Carnival who on several occasions invited us to minister at his church in Buenos Aires, Argentina, and we always found some excuse not to accept. We didn't know how to tell him that we rarely traveled to Latin America to visit only one church; that we only traveled for large events. However, on one occasion He told us: "It's just that years ago you gave us a prophetic word and it has been completely fulfilled. I want you to come and see the fulfillment."

On the opening night of the Leadership Congress there were 5,000 present. When I was introduced, they presented that prophetic word that I had given so many years earlier. What a great joy! And that is how it has been in dozens of cases. Over and over again they tell us: "What you said was fulfilled."

Generally speaking, from the pulpit at crusades the Lord has also led us to give words to nations. I do not remember what city it was or which event or on what day I gave a word to Colombia, but I know that it was only a few years ago that I said: "Precious Colombia, your oil wells will multiply, your oil resources will grow ..." But Colombia had never been a big producer of petroleum. Its neighbor Venezuela, yes; but ... Colombia?

Recently, the president of the Savings and Housing Fund and the Minister of Mining of that country confirmed to me that Colombia's petroleum production rate has increased from 700,000 barrels daily to more than one million barrels daily. They have recently discovered oil deposits so large that they are not prepared for the exploitation of this resource. For the following year they were expecting to produce about 1.5 million barrels daily and within ten years the oil production could be gigantic, catapulting the national economy to a better place.

As it turns out, recent earthquakes in the Western hemisphere shifted the land and the oil deposits buried under the Colombian substrata became accessible.

To me, words of prophecy are the words of faith, of encouragement, words that signal the way. Always, next to a king there was a prophet who spoke to him or to his nation in the Name of the God of heaven.

And miracles also happen. Obviously, I am not a typical healing evangelist. Some call me "the evangelist of the Word"; others call me "the evangelist of Grace." Many have referred to me as "the evangelist of the Lordship of Christ." It is worth mentioning that our ministry has not emphasized the gift of healing; however, the glorious thing is that miracles have often occurred.

There are dozens and dozens of people who have told us about radical changes in their physical health at some of our meetings. From that time when a woman blind from birth in Managua, Nicaragua, who in 1984, during our first Crusade there, was miraculously healed by God while we were praying the prayer of salvation with those who were making a profession of faith, to the Consul of Venezuela in Cucuta, Colombia, who told us at the conclusion of our Crusade there in April of 2011, that for many years he had been suffering from intense pain in his spinal column and that during one of the meetings of our evangelistic event he was completely healed. On very many occasions I have seen the miraculous hand of God intervening in our times of brokenness!

We also have experienced miracles in our personal and family life. Near the end of September 1998, an ultrasound exam of our pregnant daughter-in-law indicated that our second grandson would be born with enlarged kidneys and with tumors. "He might live for a week. If he lives any longer than that, he will have a lot of problems." That is what the doctor had told our son Marcelo and his wife. Later on, he confirmed the diagnostic.

A few days before the birth, Marcelo took his wife to a kidney specialist for one last analysis and to request that the specialist would be present at the child's birth to immediately administer treatment. "Doctor," he had asked, "is there any possibility that our son will be born without problems?"

"None," the doctor had said. In fact, that same month he had treated eleven similar cases and all of those eleven children had died. "There is no possibility that this child will be normal at birth," said the neonatal kidney specialist.

Of course, we were deeply distressed.

We offered to give the Lord anything He might want in exchange for the health of our grandson. Three or four close intercessors began to bombard the Kingdom of heaven with intercessory prayer. Our prayer was: "Lord, we are ready to accept Your will. You know that we love You, and that we will continue to love You regardless of what may happen. Our relationship with You does not depend on whether You may or may not do something for us. But if You offer us the option of asking, of crying out to You and hope for healing, then we choose this grace. We surrender our grandchild into Your hands. He is for You and for your Glory."

On Monday, November 30, at 10:47 p.m., our precious second grandson was born. The following day, our son and his wife were prepared for another ultrasound exam of the newborn child. When the child was brought out of the room where his mother remained, and our son went in for the news, the four grandparents held hands in the corridor of the hospital, surrounded the baby's crib and pleaded for his complete healing.

A few minutes later Marcelo and Lisa, with shining faces, returned to the part of the hospital where we were waiting for them. "He is normal. The baby does not have anything."

The doctor simply said: "I am surprised. This is a different child. I don't have any way to explain this."

Nicolas Jose, our miracle grandson, is proof that we should never give up. God continues to do miracles!

CHAPTER 53

OUR WINDOW ON THE WORLD

What an amazing opportunity we have today as Christians! I remember when I was a child, in my country, listening alone to a radio program by the Seventh Day Adventists, called "The Voice of Hope." Even though we understood that there was a small difference with them regarding the emphasis of keeping the Sabbath, how wonderful it was to listen on the radio to Biblical readings and hymns filled with heavenly beauty. Later, there was a daily radio broadcast of about five minutes in length directed by one of the oldest preachers of the Biblical faith in my country, Mr. Angel Bonati. Those daily five minutes were like bread of heaven and fresh water for a summer afternoon.

How different things are today! Hundreds of Christian radio and television channels announce the blessed Name of the Lord. From large networks to small broadcast stations administered by local churches, Christians are filling the airwaves over Latin America with the Good News of the Gospel.

But are we doing any good?

When we began the daily radio program that is now heard in almost every city, town, and village on the American continent, we prepared carefully for it. . We studied many other programs and everything, from the name of the program, the signature tune, and the introductory remarks, was examined, taking into account the nature of our market and how to best capture the listeners' attention and not lose the audience. We learned much from Hermano Pablo, whose program "A Message to the Con science" established a new way of doing radio evangelism. Of course, our two programs are among the most widely distributed radio programs in the Spanish-speaking world.

"A Moment with Alberto Mottesi" tries to paint a picture in the listener's mind. This was the strategy of Jesus. He did not begin with deep theology and generally never departed from the Scriptures. He began by referencing things that are part of our ordinary lives and then applying His Truth to the life of the individual.

When I teach about the efficient use of media in our School of Evangelists I often say that the message never changes, it cannot change. However, we should be willing to change the format or the method with which we share the Gospel.

"Would you dare to prove what you are teaching us?" one of our graduates said to me.

"What are you referring to?" I asked him.

"I would like to propose a model for a television program to see whether you would like to do it."

While the radio program has been produced consistently by that time for almost thirty-five years, for television we had only sporadically produced some projects, a few series of 16 or 50 programs, but never on a regular, continuous basis. By this time there were so many Christian television programs, featuring good preachers presenting a Sunday sermon and evangelists filming their crusades that I didn't want to be just another one doing the same thing. I felt that we were not hitting the target by competing with the type of programming that was already available for broadcast on television channels. It seemed to me that it was mostly Christians who watched these programs and not even all Christians watched them.

When Jose Luis Saenz shared with me his proposed model for a new program, I felt that it could be an important evangelistic weapon. *Café Libre* is a comedy show that is set in a cafeteria where humorous things happen, after which I arrive on the scene. There I am not a pastor, doctor, reverend or evangelist. I am only Mr. Alberto who is having some coffee while chatting with the owner of the cafeteria. The counter of the cafeteria becomes my pulpit and in a very simple way we share evangelistically the Word of the Lord.

This program became one of the most watched shows on Christian television. We received hundreds of letters, and I remember one from a woman, I believe from Venezuela, who said: "Every afternoon when *Café Libre* is on the air I sit down with all of my children to watch the program. There is always a valuable teaching for us on *Café Libre*."

But, what about the elite thinkers of Latin America? What about those who are not interested in our religious musings about life couched in humor? What about those who are opinion leaders and want to feed on something a little more intellectual?

We began to recognize that the projects we had done aimed at influencing opinion leaders had established a network of relationships that we could now use to make a difference. That is how another television program, "New Latin America," was born. This program is dedicated to convey r the ethics of the Gospel. We interviewed specialists in every area, including politics, the arts, government, law, family, and so on, and discussed what God says about these things. The goal of this program is to help change the culture.

We are responsible not only for the salvation of individuals but also for the character of our nations. Has the Bible not said: "Go and make disciples of all nations"? This has to do with bringing the culture of the Kingdom of God to our communities.

The casual and conversational tone of the *Café Libre* program appeals to a general audience, while the *New Latin America* program has a much smaller audience but a great potential to produce big changes.

For example, we were hosting a gala banquet to reach leaders in the Mexican state of Tabasco, that country's largest oil-producing state. That night we had a thousand key leaders present, including the governor of the state and his entire cabinet, senators, several mayors, leaders from all of the political parties, academics, and businessmen.

When the governor came forward to speak briefly, his first words were: "Mr. Alberto, I watch your program every Sunday night on television." What a privilege to be able to touch the lives of those who have the potential of transforming our nations!

As of the writing of this book we are starting production of a third evangelistic television program called *Hupomone*, an entertainment show to awaken hunger for the Word of God. But we are certain that other projects and new ideas will arise. We are praying that throughout the Body of Christ there will appear scriptwriters, producers, and artists who will create programming that can compete with the best secular programming. We have the best product, something that Hollywood cannot offer. We only have to learn the new methods and formats necessary to make communication understandable to the ears and the eyes of the 21st century.

CHAPTER 54

SCHOOL OF EVANGELISTS

I believe that the School of Evangelists will be our most important legacy. I do not have the slightest doubt that it was birthed in the heart of God.

Perhaps we are wrong to call it the School of Evangelists, because in the minds of some people this name evokes a narrow definition of the classic traveling evangelist. That is not the case. Obviously, we do want many to become evangelists like myself, but the focus of the school is on developing leaders at every level with an evangelistic passion: businessmen, salesmen, teachers, painters, professionals, politicians, communicators, sportsmen—every Christian who is on fire to win the lost for Christ. There are already some denominations sending their candidates for ministry and their working pastors to our school for advanced preparation.

The project began many years ago. In fact, I have in my archives a rough draft of the first school proposal for the Carmel Project, prepared by my friend, Dr. Marcel Pontón. He was an academic with a great love for souls, who taught at Fuller Seminary and at the University of Southern California, and now teaches at our school. When he first gave us these foundational ideas for the Carmel Project, the time was not yet right. Later, the Lord brought him back to our minds.

The need became urgent for a school that would emphasize a ministry now almost extinct in the Body of Christ. So we began a very arduous process. We formed a committee of advisors recruited from several of the most important Christian universities, and we made some very clear decisions. We decided that our school should offer a combination of highly academic teaching and evangelistic fire. For that reason, six of the professors who teach at our school have Ph.D.'s, which in the United States means their doctorates were earned in the classroom and are not token gifts. The mixture of serious academics and fervent evangelists allows us to offer one of the best faculties in the world. In reality, the level of the faculty is what gives character to an institution.

It goes almost without saying that to have Dr. Eduardo Font as president for the first decade was a gift of God. His experience as a founder and professor at several well known educational institutions gave our school a solid foundation.

On September 24, 2002, we began classes. The opening ceremony was very warm. Among those in attendance were several of the most prominent Christian leaders.

The School of Evangelists was "Dedicated to the Glory of God and in tribute to Hermano Pablo (Dr. Paul Finkenbinder), mentor and role model for this ministry," according to the bronze plaque unveiled that day.

Of course, as I mentioned, what adds stature to a school is its faculty, not a building. But we needed a building. The Evangelistic Association was renting offices that were not large enough, and our committee had advised us not to rent a church building. "Have your own personality," they insisted.

We had a president, professors, and a starting date and yet we still did not have a location. In my heart, I thought that at the last moment perhaps some pastor friend would open the doors to his church building.

I was praying when I heard the Voice: "Go to the building at Westminster Avenue and Harbor Boulevard."

"That one was sold," I replied.

It was a building that I had looked at three years earlier but did not pursue because the price was far out of our reach.

During the search we had seen some eighty buildings. Whenever we saw one we liked, a committee comprised of an architect and two engineers would inspect it and give us their opinion. We had made offers on two buildings but—thank God—the owners had rejected them.

"Go to the building at Westminster and Harbor," the Voice insisted.

"Lord," I said, "in California all of the buildings are selling very rapidly. That one is no longer available." (It might seem that I knew more than God.)

But the voice insisted a third time.

When I arrived at that intersection I saw a "For Sale" sign on the building.

"Certainly," I thought, "someone has already purchased the building and it is being resold."

When I entered it, I could not believe what I discovered. It had never sold. While I was walking down the hallways I heard the Voice: "I saved it for you until today. After today I will not save it anymore."

I was shaken. I ran to the office, and we sent an offer via fax. A few minutes later we got a call from the real estate salesman who was in charge of the building.

"How strange," he said. "I have not had any offer on this property for several months and in the last few minutes I have received two."

"Which one is better?" we asked.

"You know that I should not be saying this, but your offer is a little bit better."

So many brothers generously invested in this project! We have several years to pay it off, but the down payment was very large. Our friends overwhelmed us with love.

At the front entrance we have what we call the Founders Hall, with the names of the hundreds of people who planted a seed in our ministry and made a difference. To date we already have had three glorious graduation ceremonies. Dozens of graduates are planting churches, holding crusades, producing radio and television programs, and directing ministries of their own. They are our treasure. Many of them were not brought to Christ by our ministry, but we did help to establish them in ministry

But, what about those who cannot come to our school in Santa Ana, California? My brother Osvaldo, a career academic, always told me: "Traditional theological education is a luxury. The education must be taken to where the people are."

One day I was thinking about my retirement. After 50 years in the ministry, I thought: "It is time for me to take a vacation in Cancun." And, what a surprise! The Voice told me: "I want you to establish over the next ten years 400 extensions of the School of Evangelists."

"What? This is a joke!"

"No, it is not a joke. If you establish 400 extensions of the School of Evangelists, I promise to unleash through these a tsunami of evangelism and revival," the Voice continued to say.

And that was the beginning of the Extension Centers that we are planting all over the world.

Oscar Merlo, a young pastor involved at that time in the business world, was our first target. Eduardo Font and I, when discussing the school's future direction, decided to think and pray about the candidate. We did not mention Oscar. But when we met together, we discovered that we both had his name on our hearts. It was, however, a matter of economics. He was earning a large salary as an executive at a large multinational business. But could the draw of the world be stronger than our God?

Indeed, he came to work with us full time, adjusting himself to our lower level of economic resources. On the day that he began to work at our offices his former employers called to offer him a juicy contract. "You do just not understand," he told them. "God called me, and that is what makes the difference."

He has two university degrees and now, while tending to the responsibility of managing the local school and its extensions, he is also studying at Fuller Seminary for his doctorate. We want to offer the best that we can to the new generations in the name of Jesus.

CHAPTER 55

NEW LATIN AMERICA

It is a very beautiful experience. I had accomplished it as a boy and now I was asking Noemi to repeat the experience with me during South America's autumn months.

Driving across the Andes, on a highway that crosses those majestic mountains, is an indescribable experience; something that takes away your breath, contemplating the greatness of the Lord's Creation.

We had finished preaching at a youth event held annually in Córdoba, Argentina, and we were traveling toward Mendoza. From there, we would make the Andes' crossing on a bus. Seated on the front row of the second floor of that bus, rounding the curves of the narrow highway, practically hanging over the edge of the abyss, is an experience that I can assure you is never forgotten.

When we arrived in Santiago, the capital city of Chile, we had enough time to make a short tour of the city before boarding the evening flight returning to the United States. We never mix ministry trips with tourism, but the time remaining before our flight departure offered us an opportunity to include this little excursion.

The city tour included the Palacio de la Moneda, which is the presidential office. It was there, when I was just twenty-three years old, that I first met with a president, at that time Eduardo Frei Sr. Now, I was there as a tourist. There were many others in our group, including quite a few Asian people taking photographs as we entered the Patio of the Cannons. This area was decorated with enormous photographs of then-President Bachelet as well as those of other past presidents.

Without knowing why, I left Noemi alone, standing in front of one of those photographs and walked to the center of the Patio, exclaiming: "What do I have to do with this?" I turned around to see if someone had heard me. They would think I was crazy if they heard me talking to myself that way.

Then suddenly I heard that Voice, the same one I had been hearing since I was eleven years old. And the Voice sweetly said to me: "Go." And when He said, "Go," I knew that He was referring to the famous faces that I had just seen in those photographs. "Go and tell them that I love them. Go to those on the right and to those on the left. Go and tell them that I love them and their countries." I burst into tears because of the emotion. At that moment "New Latin America" was born.

Why, if the Gospel and the Church have grown so much in Latin America, do we still have so much corruption, so much violence, so much deceit and evil? It is because we have focused only on evangelizing the common people. The evangelical church became what the Swiss sociologist Christian Lalive has called The Refuge of the Masses. The Church was established as a place of refuge, a family, a hospital, and a counselor for the masses of less privileged people on the continent.

Soul for soul, all are the same, that of a carpenter and that of a senator of the republic, that of a professional and that of a shoeshine boy. But in terms of influence, the life of a leader is of supreme importance.

If we want to see a New Latin America with justice, with real democracy, with respect for the most vulnerable peoples, with better distribution of wealth, we need to win for Christ those who govern, those who establish the laws, those who influence culture through the arts, the opinion leaders. For that reason, New Latin America is an attempt to reach the segment of the population that to a great degree can determine the future of our nations.

Not long after the experience in Santiago, Chile, one midnight after preaching, I was having dinner at a little Dominican restaurant called *Nuevo Paraíso* (New Paradise), located in the Condado area of San Juan, Puerto Rico. Among the many Christians who were there with us was an old friend, a co-worker in many ministry undertakings. I shared with Eduardo Gomez, a leader of the Colombian church, my experience at the Palacio de la Moneda, and together we dreamed about what has now become a reality, the New Latin America project that has in its sights about 100 thousand key leaders throughout Latin America.

We chose to launch the project in Bogotá, Colombia, with an event held September 18, 2007. About 960 outstanding leaders gathered at the Hotel Tequendama. Starting the previous day, the entire area was filled with national security guards posted by the government. All indications were that, with so many security guards present, the president was planning to attend.

At 7 o'clock in the morning there were senators of the republic, judges from the Supreme Court, governors of several states, mayors, members of the diplomatic corps, and other religious leaders at our event. The ambiance was very elegant and everything was very well prepared for the arrival of the nation's President Álvaro Uribe.

At the main table, looking out at everyone else, were Pastor Héctor Pardo, who presided over the Organizing Committee, with Pastor Eduardo Gomez, the coordinator of our project, two presidents, former President Ernesto Samper at my right and current President Álvaro Uribe seated at my left.

After singing the verses of the national anthem I went forward to give my speech. Normally I always preach first and then the highest authority present gives a response. The result is that when the authority speaks, if he was touched by the Word and by the Holy Spirit, he has already been disarmed and does not speak as a politician, but as someone who has just been impacted by the Word of the Lord.

It was not a surprise that, when he went forward to give his response, Uribe said: "I have here a prepared speech, but I am going to set it aside. I feel that I should speak to you from my heart." He recalled, during his presentation, our first encounter many years earlier when he had been the governor of the province of Antioquia.

After my speech, in which I had given an analysis of the corruption prevalent in our Latin American culture and extended a call to a life of integrity and relationship with God, the people gave me a standing ovation.

While I was returning to my seat, Samper at my right and Uribe at my left stood to greet me, but I could not hear their words. Amid all of the hubbub and commotion in the room again I heard that Sweet Voice: "I prepared you for this." It was difficult for me to contain my emotions. I could not be seen crying in between two presidents, but I had a big knot in my throat. God was putting his stamp of approval on this area of our ministry that was touching the lives of thousands of Latin American leaders.

CHAPTER 56

GOLDEN MOMENTS

Those were not just crusades. Those were special days. Sometimes the events were held in countries that could have used their own preachers, but I was given the honor of being invited to expound the Word to them. And there have been so many of those golden moments throughout the years! For example, the two mass gatherings called America for Jesus, that were held at the Mall in Washington D.C.

The first meeting lasted for twelve hours and featured a dozen or so preachers. There were only two Hispanic preachers and at the time when I was scheduled to preach, the police report indicated there were more than a million people present. Other estimates went as high as 1.2 million people.

On both occasions these gatherings were held at critical moments, at times when the nation was going through a difficult electoral process and facing the kind of historical crossroads to which only the Church of Jesus Christ has a clear answer.

I also remember the Praise to Jesus offered in Mexico City. "Evangelicals will be hosting a religious celebration of unprecedented size in Mexico at the Azteca Stadium," was how the *Diario*

Reforma, one of the main newspapers in that country, described the event in an extensive article that also included large photographs of the occasion.

The event occurred on October 14, 1999, and lasted for seven hours. For the first time in history, the Azteca, one of the largest stadiums on the continent, was filled with a multitude of people praising God and proclaiming his Word. The meeting was broadcast around the world via satellite by the television network Televisa. In Latin America, the Enlace network also broadcast part of this historic event.

People began arriving at the stadium at 8 o'clock in the morning and by 2 o'clock in the afternoon the stadium was full, with more thousands of people outside trying to get in. Each one of those 100,000 people in attendance received a copy of the *America Nueva* (New America) newspaper, an edition especially prepared for the occasion. I was called on to deliver the evangelistic message, at the end of which several thousand people expressed their decision to surrender their lives to Christ.

What an honor it was for me to be a part in the lives of our dear nations of Hispanic America!

In Mexico, also, on two occasions I ministered in the *Marcha de Gloria* (Glory March). This parade involves about a million people walking through the center of the capital city and culminates with a large gathering lasting an entire afternoon and all night long and concluding the following morning, on the Saturday before Easter Sunday. The city's main plaza El Zocalo is filled from corner to corner with about half a million people. I was asked to preach there in 2003 and again in 2007. Dr. Quiroa, the Guatemalan organizer of the event in 2003, said: "The main plaza is not large enough. The evangelistic call was impressive, and no less than 50,000 people publicly confessed Jesus Christ."

Yes, our hearts have been very united with Mexico in recent years. And not only with Mexico, but also with the other countries that have opened their arms with so much love.

What can I say about Spain?

An elderly Spanish pastor said: "All of my life I have dreamed of a day like this."

"God visited Spain on June 10, the 'Day of Jesus,'" was the message in an email sent to us a few days later by the organizing committee.

That was in July of 2000. For about four hours, about 300 pastors along with 80 official representatives of their denominations and movements, met together in an historic encounter. The denominations and movements signed a pact of repentance and unity. There were public petitions of forgiveness. The leaders bonded with hugs and everyone participated in the Lord's Supper. What an honor it was for me that at that meeting, held behind closed doors because we did not want reporters present. I was given the honor of presenting the Word and presiding over the Lord's Supper!

Later that afternoon, there was an evangelistic gathering. The police could not believe what was happening. They had insisted that the attendance at the final meeting in La Puerta del Sol, at the country's 0 kilometer mark, would not exceed 10,000 people. However, the international news agencies EFE, *Antena Tres TV*, the *El Mundo* newspaper, and other mass media outlets that were covering the event said that between 20,000 and 25,000 people gathered to praise Jesus.

After I finished my message exalting the complete lordship of Jesus Christ, in the midst of a jubilant atmosphere, shouts were heard: "Spain, this is your hour." "The springtime of the Spirit has come to our nation."

A written report by Christian leaders of Spain declared: "The evangelical church in Spain has experienced the most glorious day in its 130 years of history." Precious Spain, so fiercely resistant to the Gospel, even to you has come your great day of revival.

In South America I remember the large gathering of 70,000 young Peruvians gathered in Lima, the capital city. In a wintery climate, under a constant drizzle, the crowds of people remained standing for more than five hours. That was in 2002, at an event championing family values. How significant that the gathering was held on the main street called "El Paseo de los Héroes" (Avenue of the Heroes) in front of the Palacio de Justicia (Palace of Justice)!

And what about the Súper Clásico held in December 2005 in Buenos Aires? The River Plate stadium, the largest in Argentina, was not large enough. About 100,000 young people filled the last inch, every corner of that place. How precious that Pastor Dante Gebel invited us to be honored guests, along with other evangelists. Dante was announcing the event as the last of the Súper Clásico events that he would organize. Poor Dante! When it was my turn to speak I said that the Súper Clásico was not over, that there would be future events, and the people broke out into wild shouts of happiness. Dante did not know at the time that he was giving me an opportunity to share the Word at a very crucial moment in our career. That meeting and what Dante had done guided by the Holy Spirit was like a divine seal on everything that would come afterward. And the Súper Clásico event was repeated in September 2011. One night on that occasion, Dante asked me to give a word to the government, and another word to the youth the following day. That evening there were 70,000 young people vibrating in the love of Jesus at the one and only stadium of La Plata!

Global conferences have been of great transcendence in my journey. For example, at the Lausanne Congress of 1974, the World Vision ministry presented a film about six ministries that were making an impact in different regions of the world. We were one of those six ministries! That Congress produced the Lausanne Covenant, a document that literally influenced lives throughout the Body of Christ on a global scale. Then there was the Pattaya Consultation held in Thailand in 1980. Pattaya means a place of shelter for the troops. There I met my great friend Paul Landrey, who would become an extraordinary advisor to us. I owe a great deal to Paul for all of the inspiration and encouragement with which he has impelled our ministry.

What can I say about those three events, the International Conference for Itinerant Evangelists, sponsored by the evangelist

Billy Graham in Amsterdam, Holland. The first event had an attendance of about 3,000 people and the second and third events each drew about 10,000 people. What a privilege it was for me that at all three events I was asked to expound on the message of the evangelist! I spent so many hours and days in preparation, pouring out my soul in his Presence to find the appropriate bread for those heralds of the Gospel.

Then there is COICOM, the Confederation of Ibero-American Communicators of Christian Mass Media, which is held each year in a different city of the American continent. I have only missed two of those events, and at the other eighteen or nineteen events that I did attend, I have always been given the honor of preaching to the Christian communicators of Latin America. What a great responsibility it is! I am always filled with fear and trembling when I go there to speak to those key leaders of the Christian world.

There are so many other golden moments I could recall, like the night when Biola University, one of the largest Christian universities in the world, granted me an honorary doctorate. Or at the convention of the National Religious Broadcasters, when we were given a "Golden Microphone"—in 50 years it was only the second time this award had been given to a Hispanic ministry. We also received the Esperanza Spirit Award at the National Hispanic Prayer Breakfast in Washington D.C., and which included a warm encounter with the president of the United States. There have been many other things as well that are exclusively gifts from the Lord.

How good is our God! We have experienced truly golden moments! These are precious pearls that, when we remember them, as if they were a bouquet of roses, we place at the feet of our beloved Savior and Lord, in honor of Him and only for Him.

CHAPTER 57

A MESSAGE TO GIVE

I confess that my knees still tremble. Whether I am preaching before 100,000 people or in front of a congregation of fifty brothers, I experience the fear and trembling of my youth. It is such a great responsibility! It is not about giving words, doctrines, or theological convictions. It has to do with bringing God to the people. It means bringing something from heaven down to the mire of the world. It means to touch a sick man who is cancerous with sin, with a medicine that heals. It means to bring hope to the one who does not have any.

I see the preacher of the Gospel as a herald. He does not have his own message. He is only a bearer of a word from the King who has sent him. He has the authority of the King and is a representative of the kingdom. However, he does his work with great humility. With his life and his words he indicates to his listeners that he is radically prostrate, submitted, controlled by the incomparable Majesty of the One who has commissioned him.

In the process toward the pulpit there are stages that cannot be avoided. On various occasions I have been asked: "How much time did it take you to prepare this message?" My answer is always the same: "It took me my entire life."

It requires the development of a Biblical mind. It requires internalizing the foundational truths of the Kingdom of God. It means allowing the Word to become incarnate within oneself.

The process also includes understanding the audience that we want to reach. I am one preacher in the pulpit at a crusade and another very different one at the microphone of a radio production or on the set of a television studio, and another completely different preacher at a church. Nor will I be the same when speaking to politicians, governors, and academics. The message does not change, but the method of transmission must change. I must be coherent to the ears of my listeners.

Thus, the time of preparation will always include a deep relationship with the Word, an understanding of the "market" that I will be trying to reach and something fundamental—without question, unavoidable, non-negotiable—which is my personal preparation. The vessel must be clean.

The true preacher of the Gospel develops a deep sense of his own uselessness. "For these things, who is sufficient?" the Apostle Paul asked himself. And immediately he added: "But our sufficiency comes from God" (2 Corinthians 3:5 NKJV). There is a real sense of our human fragility and, Glory to God, the complete sufficiency of the Lord.

Something interesting always occurs to me. When I have done the Bible work, studied the characteristics of the people that we are going to reach, prayed, and prepared the message, still there is often the feeling: "I wish they will ask someone else! I wish someone will say, 'Our plans have changed, and we asked so-and-so to preach.'" The responsibility of speaking in his Name is so serious!

And in the moments before I walk to the pulpit, there are still elements that may play an important role, especially if it is a large public event or crusade; for example, the news of the day. The evangelist is a prophet. He stands there to speak to a nation in the Name of God. It is assumed that a servant of

God Almighty will say something more profound about war and peace, about ecological disasters, about the dramas of daily life than the commentator on a television screen.

The Holy Spirit will take preeminence before and during the exposition of the message. The Glory of the Holy God will manifest itself in abundance, and the Word will have its effect. I always aim for the message to have a central idea, a high note of hope, a clear presentation of the Lordship of Christ, and a high dosage of divine mercy—what Christ is and what Christ does.

Ah! There is also a fundamental element: the Invitation.

An invitation to what? I do not have the slightest doubt that it must be an invitation to radical, unconditional surrender to the Lordship of God over us. Anything less is only religion. Complete surrender is the Gospel of the Kingdom of God, the only message that has been entrusted to us.

The message of the Cross.

An old friend, now gone to be with the Lord, Carmelo Terranova, pastor of the Cathedral of Hope in Puerto Rico, one day said to me: "For several years now, without your knowing it, we have been doing a study of your messages and we discovered something: at some point in your messages Isaiah 53 will always appear."

"Surely He took up our infirmities and carried our sorrows … But He was pierced for our transgressions, He was crushed for our iniquities; the punishment that brought us peace was upon Him, and by his wounds we are healed … and the LORD has laid on Him the iniquity of us all … He was oppressed and afflicted, yet He did not open his mouth; He was led like a lamb to the slaughter, and as a sheep before her shearers is silent, so He did not open his mouth."

Yes, I am passionate about the Cross, and yet the blessed truth it represents is often forgotten in many pulpits. The marvelous Cross of Christ is central to the Gospel. That is where the course of history was changed. The world was never the same again. A terrified hell understood its defeat. The Cross and the Resurrection are what give a vital meaning to our faith. What certainty of victory! What a glorious conviction of forgiveness, mercy, redemption, and victory there is for us, the children of God!

A couple of days ago, before writing this chapter, something interesting happened to me. I was waiting for the valet to bring my automobile parked at the St. Joseph's Hospital of Orange in California, when a man approached me and without saying anything and gave me a hug that shook my whole body. "You don't know me," he told me. "I am one of the millions influenced by your ministry. I follow your work closely and I want to thank you for your ministry."

I simply responded: "It is the Lord, my brother. Only the Lord."

"Yes," he said, "it is the Lord, but He works through his prophets. Thanks for your faithfulness!"

He left me thinking. I received the testimony like a bouquet of roses that I placed at the feet of my beloved Savior.

I remembered that great verse: "But the righteous will live by his faith" (Habakkuk 2:4). Someone interpreted it this way: "The righteous will live by his faithfulness." My faith should lead me into a life of faithfulness.

Faithfulness to what? Faithfulness to God, to his beloved Son and to the blessed Holy Spirit, faithfulness to the Bible, faithfulness to my family, my friends, the Church. and even faithfulness to the lost, because they are hoping for something better from the servants of God. Faithfulness to the holy message that has been entrusted to us.

Again those words resound in my soul:

"Heaven and earth will pass away but my words will not pass away" (Luke 21:33).

EPILOGUE
TO SERVE MY LORD

The amazing purposes of God have brought us to this moment. We are very grateful to Him.

Obviously, it has not been easy. But the Lord never promised the absence of difficulties and suffering. We have had many and perhaps we will have more, and we are not complaining, because in these things God glorifies Himself. Sharing these stories and making people aware of what the Lord has done with our lives is only for the purpose of exalting the goodness and mercy that God has manifested toward me and my family, in using this vessel of clay, miserable, filled with limitations and traumas; and to tell others that, if the Spirit of God thought it good to raise up this unworthy instrument, it could well be that He may use any other life that is willing and completely surrendered in love to Him.

May this book serve to lift the faltering courage of many of my colleagues in the ministry.

May it inject passion in the young people, motivating them to live out a radical commitment.

May it provide a vision of great works, knowing that the builder is God, the Almighty.

May it produce in the next generation of Christians, great dreams for the glory of our God.

May it promote the spiritual fire that consumes the soul with a desire to reach those who do not know the Gospel.

May it awaken the conscience of those who are greedy for human power and who only seek their own personal interest.

May it touch lives that have never experienced the love of God.

May undefeatable armies be raised up to promote the powerful advance of the Kingdom.

The final chapters of my life have yet to be written. Possibly someone else will write them, assuming that there may be something important, something worthy of mention and that gives glory only to our marvelous Savior. If that is not the case, I hope only to be faithful until the very end.

I wish to mention one last thing.

On several occasions I have asked myself: "Alberto, if you knew you were going to die now, what would you ask for?" I never have to meditate very long on the answer. My heart is in my calling, which has been and is, the passion that day by day continues to consume me, as my number one priority, serving in the Kingdom of God. When I cease to exist on this earth, I want my children to place on my tombstone a plaque engraved with the following words: "He lived, he loved, and he passionately served his Lord."

We would like to hear from you.
Please send your comments about this book
to the address below.
Thank you very much.

Vida@zondervan.com
www.editorialvida.com